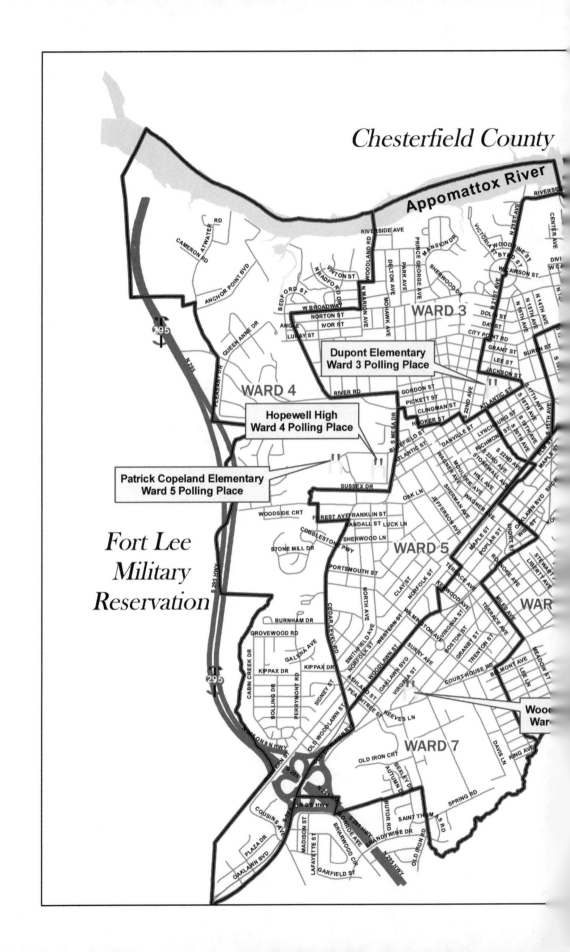

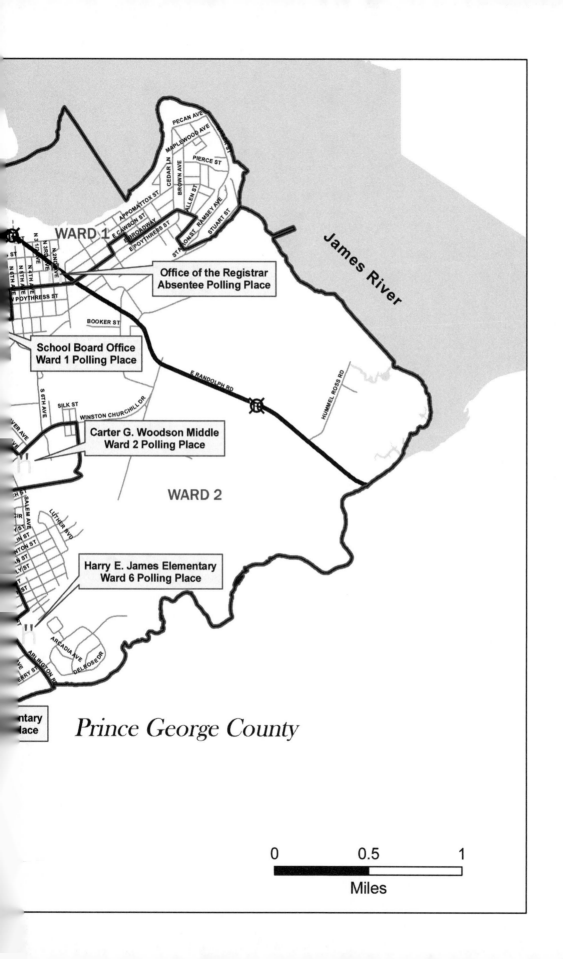

WARD 1

Office of the Registrar
Absentee Polling Place

School Board Office
Ward 1 Polling Place

Carter G. Woodson Middle
Ward 2 Polling Place

WARD 2

Harry E. James Elementary
Ward 6 Polling Place

Prince George County

James River

PECAN AVE
MAPLEWOOD AVE
PIERCE ST
CEDAR LN
BROWN AVE
ALLEN ST
APPOMATTOX ST
E CAWSON ST
E BROADWAY
E POYTHRESS ST
RAMSEY AVE
STUART ST
STATION ST

N 3RD AVE
N 2ND AVE
N 4TH AVE
N 5TH AVE
W POYTHRESS ST

BOOKER ST

S 6TH AVE
SILK ST
WINSTON CHURCHILL DR

E RANDOLPH RD
HUMMEL ROSS RD

SALEM AVE
LUTHER BLVD

ARCADIA AVE
DELROSE DR
ARLINGTON RD

ntary
lace

0   0.5   1
Miles

Making the American Dream Work

A Cultural History of African Americans in Hopewell, Virginia

Lauranett L. Lee

an imprint of Morgan James Publishing, LLC

Making the American Dream Work

A Cultural History of African Americans in Hopewell, Virginia

Lauranett L. Lee

ISBN: 978-1-60037-466-1
Library of Congress Control Number: 2008929954

Published by:

SPS Press Publishing
An Imprint of Morgan James Publishing, LLC

DBA SPS Professionals, Inc.
2013 Cunningham Drive #321
Hampton, VA 23666
Phone 757 265-8714
www.spspresspublishing.com

COVER: *In 1989 local citizen Jay Bohannon created a mural honoring the working people of Hopewell. As visitors enter the Municipal Building the mural serves as a greeting on the wall facing the front doors.*

Table of Contents

List of Illustrations

Section II

Section I

W"We hold these truths to be self-evident, that all men are created equal, that they are endowed by their Creator with certain unalienable Rights, that among these are Life, Liberty and the pursuit of Happiness."[1]

When Dr. Martin Luther King Jr. referred to the Declaration of Independence during the mid-twentieth-century civil rights movement, he stated, "Never before in the history of the world has a sociopolitical document expressed in such profound, eloquent and unequivocal language the dignity and the worth of human personality. The American dream reminds us that every man is an heir of the legacy of dignity and worth."[2]

Central to the American Dream is opportunity and the principles of liberty and freedom as well as education, gainful employment, and home ownership. It is associated with the Protestant work ethic whereby many believe that prosperity can be achieved through hard work and determination. The American Dream originates from a "turning away" from traditional "old world" European political and social practices. Early on, Europeans in colonial America realized the possibility of creating a new society based on freedom and wealth. Hopewell's seemingly mythic founding is rooted in America's infant years. Located at the intersection of the Appomattox and James Rivers and initially part of Prince George County, twenty miles south of Richmond, Hopewell is well placed to realize "a greatest hope ever begun in our territories" as one of its founding fathers, Sir Thomas Dale, proclaimed.

Prior to English settlement Algonquian Indians occupied both sides of the James; their central location was where Flowerdew Hundred is located in Prince George County. The Appamattuck Indians lived along the Appomattox River. Between 1607 and 1625 nearly 7,000 settlers arrived in Virginia but only 1,000 survived. The Virginia Company of London sent the first group of settlers, essentially entrepreneurs, to what they called the "New World" in 1607. George Percy reflected on the event in his 1625 memoir. On the eighth day of May they "Landed in the Countrey of the Apamatica" where they initially met resistance. This was their first exploration up the James River to its intersection with the Appomattox. Its occupants were Indians of the Powhatan chiefdom. By 1607, Wahunsonacock, the paramount chief called Powhatan by the English, commanded between 9,000 and 13,000 people from thirty tribes consisting of two hundred towns. The territory of the Algonquian-speaking chiefdom stretched from what is now Washington, D.C., to North Carolina. England had designated this expanse "Virginia." Percy and his crew negotiated with the paramount chief, claiming, "Wee made signs of peace" and eventually they "let us land in quietness." Thereafter English settlements were founded between 1607 and 1613 along both banks of the James River. Of the river Percy declared, "This River [James] which wee have discovered is one of the famousest Rivers that ever was found by any Christian." Percy later served as president of the colony, stoically surviving the "Starving Time," the winter of 1609–10, when only 60 out of 500 colonists survived and greeted the spring.[3]

In the fall of 1611 one of the early governors of the colony, Sir Thomas Dale, first established the village of Henrico on the north side of the James at the Appamatuck Indian town. Months later, in January of 1612, Dale occupied the area Percy had visited, and named the Appomattox Indian village "the new Bermudas." The name was soon changed to Bermuda Hundred. By 1613 he established "Bermuda Cittie" to distinguish it from Bermuda Hundred, which was located on the opposite side of the Appomattox River.[4] Six years later the name had changed again and was then called "Charles Cittie." Subsequent name changes include Charles Hundred and Charles City Point.

As deputy governor and marshal of Virginia, Dale established the first system of private land tenure in English America. "Sir Thomas Dale hath allotted every man three Acres of cleare ground, in the nature of Farmes."[5] By 1617 the first servants had completed their indentures and established their own estates. That same year a third charter went into effect. Settlers acquired ownership of the land, ending "common holdings," and four "corporacouns" were established, each with a proposed capital city. Prince George County was part of one of the four "corporacouns." Bermuda City, then renamed Charles City, was chosen as the site for the chief city of the Charles City Corporation, which lay on both sides of the James. In 1619 when Virginia's colonial legislature, the House of Burgesses, met for the first time, participating burgesses came from Flowerdew Hundred, Charles City Plantation, Ward's Plantation, and Martin's Brandon.

That same year black indentured servants arrived. Initially, Virginia's black population grew slowly. By 1623 at least twenty-three people of African descent were in Virginia, at least eleven of which were living at Flowerdew Hundred.[6] As late as the middle of the century barely three hundred could be counted.

In 1661 the House of Burgesses ruled that black servants would retain a servant status for the remainder of their lives. A year later, the House of Burgesses further codified slavery when it legislated that children born in the colony would be held in bond or free according to the condition of the mother.

After the Royal African Company was chartered in 1672 the slave trade accelerated and by the end of the century Africans were being brought in at the rate of more than one thousand per year. Planters began to rely on an enslaved work force rather than indentured servants. Virginia became not merely a society with slaves but a slave society in which slaves existed at every level, from agricultural laborer to the liveried servant. Co-existing with black and white indentured servants and landholding free people, enslaved people's long path to freedom was continually challenged. And hard won.

During the eighteenth century the black population increased dramatically. In 1708 in Virginia there were approximately twelve thousand blacks and eighteen thousand whites. In 1750 there were 101,452 blacks and 129,581 whites. And six years later, 120,156 blacks and 173,316 whites. In many communities blacks outnumbered whites, causing concern among whites, both gentry and the middling class.[7]

On June 13, 1774, the Rhode Island General Assembly passed an act for the nonimportation of slaves, making it the first American colony to do so. Four years later, Virginia legislators declared that "hereafter, no slaves shall be imported into the Commonwealth by sea or land." Yet, not until 1807 did Congress ban the importation of slaves from abroad; the ban went into effect on January 1, 1808.

During the Revolutionary era the rhetoric of liberty gave impetus to the emancipation of slaves, and in 1782 Virginia repealed its longstanding ban on private manumissions. The following year the state passed a law granting freedom to all slaves "who served in the late war," thereby further increasing the free black population, which co-existed uneasily on the fringes of a society that espoused freedom. Archival material such as a 1782 manumission paper for fifty-five-year-old Sarah of Surry County states that her offspring as well should be allowed to "enjoy their full freedom." Another fragment from the past tells us that thirty-year-old Arrena Pickett received her certificate of freedom on November 12, 1824, as "one of the Negroes emancipated by the last will and testament of General George Washington," who owned property in New Kent County.

Opposition to the Atlantic slave trade also increased after the Revolution. In 1787 Rhode Island led the way among northern colonies, followed by Massachusetts, Connecticut, and Pennsylvania in 1788. Economic change in the upper South had also promoted opposition to the slave trade.

By 1790 Virginia had already taken the lead in the black population, which it held during the entire slave period. At that time the center of black population was twenty miles west-southwest of Petersburg, in Dinwiddie County, Virginia. Of the 304,000 blacks in Virginia, 292,627 were enslaved; the remaining 12,866 were classified as free blacks. The free black population began to grow and by 1810 the

Upper South, which included Delaware, Maryland, Virginia, District of Columbia, Kentucky, Missouri, North Carolina, and Tennessee, had a free black population of 94,085, compared to a northern free black population of 78,181.[8]

Whites were particularly concerned about the growing class of free blacks. Although the talk of liberty had fueled the antislavery movement, most white Americans did not want to live with blacks, either enslaved or free. As the free black population increased, Virginia began to take measures to check its growth. Free blacks were required to register with the county clerk. In 1793 Virginia barred free blacks from entering the state.

With the official closing of the trans-Atlantic slave trade in 1808, the domestic slave trade became more profitable. By 1815, about the time of the movement of the slave population into the cotton kingdom, the domestic slave trade had become a major economic enterprise. Large numbers of Virginia slaves were sold to the labor-hungry plantations of the Cotton South, from Carolina to Texas, and enslaved families were separated. Although Virginia continued to have the largest population of enslaved African Americans in the country, the rate of growth was greater in North Carolina, South Carolina, and Georgia. Approximately 55 percent of the slaves in the South cultivated cotton, another 10 percent labored in the tobacco fields, and another 10 percent produced sugar, rice, or hemp. The majority, who worked in the fields from sunup to sundown, lived on large plantations. Fifteen percent of enslaved people worked as domestic servants. The remaining 10 percent worked in trades and industries.

Some of America's founding fathers supported the American Colonization Society, established in 1816. Its state and local chapters encouraged the relocation of educated and industrious blacks to Africa where they would guide the colony to prosperity. By 1821 the society had founded a colony in West Africa known as Liberia. Nearly half of the immigrants to Liberia came from Virginia and many of them had lived in or near Petersburg. One of them, Joseph Jenkins Roberts of that city, became the first governor of Liberia and later its president.

In the aftermath of various slave uprisings (such as the Gabriel Prosser conspiracy in Richmond [1800] and the Denmark Vesey conspiracy in South Carolina [1822]), life for the enslaved and free blacks in Virginia became even more restrictive. Tensions rose. And they reached a fever pitch after August 22, 1831, when Nat Turner rebelled against slavery and led a massacre of whites in Southampton County. After Turner was captured and hanged, the chasm between white and black, free and enslaved, became insurmountable. And blacks—slave and free—suffered restricted mobility and endured an ever-tightening lack of freedom.

1831. Chapter XXXIX. All meetings of free Negroes or mulattoes at any school house, church, meeting house or other place for teaching them reading or writing, either in the day or the night shall be considered an unlawful assembly. Warrants shall direct any sworn officer to enter and disperse such Negroes and inflict corporal punishment on the offenders at the discretion of the justice, not exceeding twenty lashes. Any white person assembling to instruct free Negroes to read or write shall be fined not over $50.00, also be imprisoned not exceeding two months.

It is further enacted that if any white person for pay shall assemble with any slaves for the purpose of teaching them to read or write, he shall for each offense be fined, at the discretion of the justice, $10.00–$100.00.

1834. Chapter 68. A free Negro shall not migrate into this Commonwealth from any state in this Union, or from any foreign country, under penalty of thirty-nine lashes on his bare back at the public whipping post. Returning after removal is to be punished according to the act of 1819. Special fines and penalties are set for masters of vessels who bring in any free Negroes. An exception is made for travelers who have any free Negroes in their employment.

In 1835 the right of assembly was taken away from almost all free blacks in the South.

1848. Chapter X. Section 29. Any person entitled to the possession of a slave who shall permit such slave to go at large, trade as a free man or hire himself out, shall be fined $20.00 to $50.00, and such slave may be sold for the use of the Commonwealth.

1848. Chapter X. Section 30. Permitting a slave of unsound mind, aged or infirm to go at large without adequate support shall be punished by a fine of $20.00 to $50.00.

1848. Criminal Code. Chapter 120; Chapter XXI, Section 5. No person shall be capable to be of a jury for the trial of a felony unless he be a freeholder over the age of twenty-one years and possessed of a visible estate of the value of $300.00 at least.

By 1850 enslaved people were seeking any and every means of escape. In 1850 Henry Brown, whose family had been broken up by sale, shipped himself in a box from Richmond to Philadelphia. Upon his arrival he was met by members of the Philadelphia Anti-Slavery Society, a group associated with the Underground Railroad. Thereafter he was known as Henry "Box" Brown.

> **1853.** Chapter 55. The sum of $30,000 is appropriated for five years for the removal of free Negroes from the Commonwealth. The Colonization Board of Virginia is given power to act under this law. The annual tax of one dollar is levied on every male free Negro of twenty-one years and under fifty-five years, and collected as other taxes on free Negroes are collected. The fund arising from this source shall be applied to the removal of free Negroes.

In the decades before the Civil War, slaves became increasingly valuable as workers in Virginia's growing industries, such as Tredegar Ironworks. From Carolina to Texas, slave owners increasingly began taking out life insurance policies on enslaved workers, particularly men. White Richmonders, who successfully petitioned the state legislature in 1854 to challenge prohibitive Virginia and city of Richmond taxes, argued that there was a "growing demand for insurance on the lives of slaves." Documents such as an 1858 American Life Insurance and Trust Company policy illuminate the value placed on a skilled enslaved person.[9]

As the nation moved toward a civil war, blacks and whites, northerners and southerners, families and individuals grappled with possible death and destruction. During the Civil War, the nation dissolved, yet slavery persisted. At war's end, African Americans, who had also fought valiantly to free themselves, faced another war and they sought equality.

> **1860**. Chapter 54. If any free Negro commit an offense punishable by confinement in the penitentiary, he may at the discretion of the court, in lieu of such confinement, be sold into absolute slavery.

> **1861.** Ordinance No. 84. In July it is ordained that all able-bodied male free Negroes, between eighteen and fifty, shall be enrolled. They shall be selected as laborers, having reference to their condition and circumstances, and be entitled to such compensation, rations, quarters, and medical attendance as may be allowed other labor in the public service. Negroes who fail to obey when requisitioned shall be subject to the penalties provided for persons drafted from the militia who fail to obey.

By the beginning of the Reconstruction era laws regarding education became more democratic.

1867–1870. Constitution of Virginia. Article VIII, Section 3. The General Assembly shall provide in its first session under this constitution a uniform system of public free schools, and for its gradual, equal, and full introduction in all counties of the state by 1876, or as much earlier as practical.

Historians such as June Purcell Guild and Philip Schwarz have researched and published on Virginia's laws and statutes. Their research enables us to know the evolution regarding the formation of race relations and societal inequities.

The promise of financial security and constitutional freedom appealed to untold numbers of immigrants who came to America. Emma Lazarus penned the epic words now etched on the pedestal of the Statue of Liberty: "Give me your tired, your poor, your huddled masses yearning to breathe free, the wretched refuse of your teeming shore. Send these, the homeless, tempest tost to me, I lift my lamp beside the golden door." Immigrants found a haven where opportunity awaited. One immigrant "sickened at last of poverty, bigotry and kings" held on to the hope that "there was always America."

Dime-store novels, such as those written by Horatio Alger Jr., idealized the American Dream during the mid-to-late nineteenth century. Intelligence and hard work were central to success. By the beginning of the twentieth century men such as Andrew Carnegie and John D. Rockefeller exemplified the image of successful capitalists.

Russians, Italians, Poles, Greeks, Jews, and other groups of people were lured to America in hope of a better life. The majority of immigrants gravitated to large industrial cities like New York, Chicago, Philadelphia, and Detroit. Smaller towns, such as Hopewell, also received their fair share. In fact, Hopewell became known as "a wonder city," a place where the American Dream had great potential.

They tell a tale that's weird and strange, when the town was new,
A country laddie was homesick, sad he was and blue;
A smiling stranger said to him, "Hope you are real well."
And thus was named the city now where thirty thousand dwell."
Powder Town Rag[10]

During the spring of 1912 engineers from the E. I. du Pont de Nemours and Company inspected Hopewell Farms in Prince George County as a proposed site for a dynamite plant. They purchased approximately 2,000 acres and named it Hopewell in reference to the ship *Hopewell*, which had brought the Eppes family to the area. Construction began on May 17, 1912, and was completed by July 1914. The Wilmington, Delaware, company built a dynamite factory and then converted to the manufacture of guncotton during World War I. In 1916 Hopewell was incorporated as a city. During World War I, Hopewell became the hub of an extensive munitions industry. Following the war, DuPont relocated elsewhere.[11] In 1923 City Point was annexed to Hopewell. Additional annexations from Prince George County in 1952 and 1969 further enlarged Hopewell to 11.3 square miles. Hopewell, located at the intersection of the Appomattox River on the north and the James River on the east, was, indeed, positioned to yield the "greatest hope ever."[12]

Yet, for some, the American Dream remained merely a dream. Hopewell, like many other localities, practiced racial discrimination. Segregation was a way of life. Inequality existed in various forms: employment opportunities, residential options, educational facilities, and public accommodations. It was as if, Martin Luther King Jr. said, "America has given the Negro people a bad check, a check which has come back marked 'insufficient funds.' "[13] A national civil rights movement forced America to examine its race relations policies and practices. African Americans pushed and prodded until the American Dream became a shared reality. Hopewell's African American history tells us how one community continued to make America live up to its ideals. Their pursuit of equality through education, home ownership, access to public accommodations, and the right to vote and participate in a full and equal life is evidence of how the people of Hopewell continue to make the American Dream work. This is their story.

Listening to the voices of Hopewell's citizens is a reminder of the American Dream. Their memories speak of times long gone yet very near. Times spent with family and friends in schools, churches, communities, home, and on their jobs were remembered with wistful smiles and knowing eyes. This study pays particular attention to African American life and culture in Hopewell, Virginia, by way of historic sites and oral interviews. These primary sources enliven the past, enabling us to explore, and we hope to understand, historical moments as a continuum.

Life in Hopewell is much like life anywhere. People are born into a family, a community, a historical era, and they make their way in the world. What is unique about Hopewell is the way in which people of different cultural backgrounds live side-by-side in an eleven-square-mile city. At one time at least twenty-three languages were spoken in Hopewell. Numerous factories provided jobs and economic opportunity for thousands who came from as far away as Eastern Europe. Approximately 38 percent of its residents—a population of 22,354—compose part of its multicultural population. Among other cities of a similar size Hopewell rates in the top 16 percent regarding racial diversity. In education, its schools are fully accredited. Home ownership figures prominently; 56 percent of the housing is owner-occupied. Hopewell symbolizes the American Dream. From its very beginnings, opportunity awaited.

Making the American Dream Work: A Cultural History of African Americans in Hopewell, Virginia examines the individual and collective actions of African Americans to push America closer to the ideals of the founding fathers. They strove to break from the Old World where hierarchy ruled. Yet, in their pursuit of liberty and justice they grappled with the institution of slavery as well as persistent racism and discrimination. From the arrival of Africans to America's shores in 1619 to Hopewell's founding in 1916, residents have persistently endeavored to create a place that exemplifies all that America has come to mean. In their history one can see the evolution of the American Dream.

The city of Hopewell exemplifies an experiment in possibilities.[14] Its ever-changing landscape has endured the ravages of wars and industrialization. One of its strengths is its elasticity; the ability to adjust to change enables its citizens to pursue the American Dream. Eight historic sites chronicle a history that spans the centuries. Kippax, Weston Manor, Appomattox Manor, the City Point Historic District, City Point National Cemetery, the Beacon Theatre, the Downtown Hopewell Historic District, and the Hopewell Municipal Building enable us to understand the city's evolution.

Ten oral histories, commissioned by the Hopewell City Council, were conducted by the author during the summer of 2005. The council graciously allowed me creative control. I came to know the heart of Hopewell as I met people in churches and at public functions. When I asked and sometimes cajoled them to let me interview them, I had the pleasure and honor of interviewing ten residents of Hopewell who opened their homes and shared their memories and stories. I wanted to talk with folks across a wide spectrum of life who could present different perspectives of Hopewell. Of the ten interviews, two of them were family couples. Renee Patrice Gilliam and her mother, the late Mrs. Joy Gilliam, were two of my first interviewees. I had not planned to interview Mrs. Gilliam but she had so much to share that it could not stay shut up in her bones. I am grateful for the time we shared and very thankful for her memories. She passed away on February 10, 2007. Patrice's interview explores the pain of being on the frontline of the desegregation process. Her mother's comments illuminate the experience of a teacher as well as a parent during the desegregation process.

The other family couple I interviewed was the Reverend Curtis Harris and his wife, Mrs. Ruth Harris. This was the first time Mrs. Harris had been interviewed. Although her husband is a public figure, she has steadfastly remained a private person, tending to the domestic sphere. Her involvement in creating a better life took many forms, both in and outside the home. Their son, Kenneth Harris, was also interviewed. As the son of a civil rights activist and as a preacher's kid, Kenneth Harris allows us to see what it was like for a child to be intimately involved in the national movement for civil rights.

Three of the interviewees were ministers: one female, Barbara Crosby, and two males, Curtis Harris and Rudolph Dunbar. Both Crosby and Harris were natives of Virginia; Dunbar was born in Alabama. His observations allow us to see Hopewell from the perspective of someone who came from the deeper south, whereas Crosby's and Harris's interviews illuminate a perspective of Hopewell from the span of a lifetime. Harris was the first African American mayor of Hopewell, has been a longtime civil rights activist, and still pastors a church. Crosby pastors New Hope Christian Center, which offers opportunity to the homeless and others seemingly disfranchised from mainstream society. She's also an entrepreneur, offering nursing care to the homebound. Her interview illuminates the saying, "it takes a village to raise a child"; home, school, and church figured prominently in Crosby's formative years when she came of age during the tumultuous sixties.

Although this project focuses on African American history, in order to appreciate another perspective I interviewed two white people. Jeanie Langford's knowledge of Hopewell's history provided a backdrop for understanding where Hopewell has been. As a librarian at the Appomattox Regional Library System, she was the first person I interviewed. Her family came to Hopewell when she was three years old. She grew up in Hopewell and noted the changing race relations during her teenage years. James Willcox came to Hopewell to work as an engineer for Hercules. Originally from Darlington, South Carolina, he came to Hopewell during the turbulent 1960s. He remembers an encounter between civil rights activists and Ku Klux Klan members on the steps of the Municipal Building. Photographs and newspaper accounts further document the occasion.

Three women, all who claim to be retired, are still very much active. Juanita Chambers worked as an educator and administrator in the school system for many years. She currently sits on boards and committees that advance the city of Hopewell. Maza Wilson worked at Fort Lee until she retired and then she became commissioner of recreation. Her involvement in the recreational life of Hopewell's young people is well remembered by those with whom she has come in contact. When Florine Martin, who has volunteered in a variety of capacities, sought a volunteer opportunity for her daughter, she found that segregation still occurred. She fixed it.

Excerpts from several other interviews, which were conducted in 2005 by students in Dr. Tomoko Hamada's anthropology class at the College of William and Mary, are included in this narrative. They are also part of a larger body of work that first began in 2001 under Dr. Hamada's supervision, entitled: "In their Own Words: Hopewell Citizens Talk about their History." I thank Meghan Townes, Kathryn Swanson, Rachel Estavan, Melissa Anderson, Christine Moe, Stephanie George, Kevin Williams, Nick Lembo, and Ben Skolnik. In addition, the Center for Archaeological Research at the College of William and Mary conducted research in Hopewell and enabled researchers to investigate three properties.

Aware of an unexplored area of the city's history, council members, led by the Reverend Curtis Harris, sought to redress the omission of Hopewell's African American history. In 2002 the city council commissioned Dr. Edgar Toppin to conduct an oral history project and write a history of African Americans in Hopewell. I had planned to assist him. Doc inspired me to study history after I heard him give a lecture in 1990. He taught history from the people's perspective, paying attention to everyday working people as well as the leaders and well-known personalities. He recognized the value in all people and believed their history should be sought out and studied for the betterment of future generations. For me, Doc's interpretation of history illuminates the persistent pursuit of the American Dream. He passed away on December 8, 2004. This book is dedicated to my mentor, Dr. Edgar Toppin.

Life of the Enslaved

Members from various African cultures adapted their crafts, culinary skills, agriculture, religious practices, storytelling, and facility with language to create a new culture, an African American culture. Records such as deeds and inventories, census records, land and personal property tax records, and wills provide opportunities to learn more about disenfranchised people within the domestic sphere.

Religion

Although the majority of enslaved people came from Angola, many came from other areas of the African continent as well. Because of contact with Islamic traders, some Africans had Muslim religious training. Others were Christians. King Ezana of Ethiopia was converted to Christianity in A.D. 333, making Ethiopia the world's oldest continuously Christian nation. Despite the harsh circumstances of their lives, enslaved people in the colonies were able to maintain a sense of hope for deliverance, which was bolstered by their religious faith. Biblical verses, such as those found in Chapter 25 of Leviticus, formed a channel of resistance for enslaved people. Here they found justification to dream of a day when God would cause "the trumpet of the jubilee to sound" and when God's command that "ye shall not oppress one another" would be heeded by their masters.

Control and management

Slaveholders maintained control through the use of the whip. Public whippings became the most commonly used form of punishment. Several instruments were used to administer whippings; the most common were the rawhide whip, the leather strap, the cowhide paddle, and the buckskin cracker whip. These and other instruments were usually directed at the uncovered back of the slave, who was immobilized during the whipping by being tied to a whipping post, a tree, stumps in the ground, or some other objects, or by being placed either in stocks or pillory. Discipline, deference, deterrence, and degradation ruled the plantation.

Resistance

The average age for runaway slaves throughout the South remained consistent. In Virginia, the average age was twenty-seven. To run away and remain at large for an extended period of time required agility, ingenuity, and bravery. The runaway had to move about with extreme care because any white citizen in most slave states had the legal right to stop any person of African descent and demand to see his pass.

Gender

Thomas Jefferson considered "a woman who brings a child every two years as more profitable than the best man of the farm." Many planters felt this way because in addition to their reproductive capabilities, enslaved women also worked in the fields. Slaveholders who had enough slaves for work gangs organized them according to gender. Women fenced, planted, and picked cotton; dug potatoes; and did almost everything else common to mid-nineteenth-century agricultural production. While plowing became more prevalent over time, particularly on cotton plantations, hoe agriculture remained central to the lives of almost all field hands. Since skilled opportunities were more available to enslaved men than to women, and since plantation labor was characterized by an extremely high labor force participation rate, women, and to some extent children, often composed the majority of a plantation's field hands.

Planters' wives

Plantation mistresses played a prominent role in the management and oversight of the daily lives of plantation workers. As mistress of the plantation, which was essentially a business, the female head of the household supervised the spinning, weaving, cleaning, cooking, and entertaining, as well as the care for the well-being of the slaves. They supplied goods and services at an unprecedented rate, not only for their white family, but also for the increasing number of their enslaved charges. When the slave population increased, the burden of household management for plantation mistresses also increased. They were expected to provide for their slaves in four significant areas: food, shelter, clothing, and medical care. Although the quality of care varied from plantation to plantation and the degree to which each mistress provided for slave families depended upon slave contributions as well, planters increasingly relied upon their wives to oversee the important domestic world of slave care. For example, when her slaves were ill, Julia Tyler of Sherwood Forest treated their chills and fevers with quinine laced with a jigger of whiskey.

Tyler defended the institution of slavery in an 1853 letter published first in the *New York Herald*, followed by the *Southern Literary Messenger* and the *Richmond Enquirer*. Her letter was a rebuttal to an open letter from English women who urged southern ladies to end the institution of slavery. Mrs. Tyler admitted that the slave system was fraught with political disadvantages. Essentially, though, she believed America's domestic problem could not compare to that of the depressed white laborers of London. She wrote that the Negro "live[d] sumptuously" and enjoyed warm clothing, with plenty to eat. In addition to working for the master, most enslaved people tended their own gardens. The produce from these gardens supplemented the meager rations doled out by their owners.

Clothing

Slave clothing was usually made on individual plantations. For this purpose, slave owners in the nineteenth century imported coarse, low-grade materials advertised as "Negro cloth." The testimony of former slaves details the discomfort they endured when breaking in the scratchy new garments. Many of them compared the rough cloth to constant needle pricks. In contrast to the crude clothing of field hands, personal servants and attendants were dressed in fine clothing. Since the dress of personal servants reflected both the wealth and status of the owner, it was imperative for great planters such as the Eppes, the Bollings, and the Gilliams to adorn their personal attendants and house servants with finery befitting their station.

Adornment

Despite the hardships of slavery, people took every opportunity to express their individuality. Discarded clothing from the owner's family was the chief source of ornate slave clothing. Runaway slave advertisements describe such wear as boots or shoes with buckles, fur hats, and choice pieces of clothing. Bark, indigo, red clay, sumac, and walnut hulls or leaves were among the items slaves used for dyeing fabrics. They made starch from wheat bran and crafted buttons from dried gourds and rams' and cows' horns. Small cowry shells, which had traveled with many of them from Africa, were also used to fashion necklaces or to braid into one's hair.

Talents

Slave musicians found themselves entertaining frequently in the mansion homes at dances, parties, and informal gatherings. Musicians, like other skilled workers, often earned extra cash for their owners when planters hired them out to other planters. To stage the lavish balls held throughout the South, slaves served as attendants, musicians, cooks, and entertainers. Sometimes, enslaved people were allowed to keep the extra money they made.

Recreation

Dances were the most popular recreational pursuits engaged in by members of the slave quarter during social gatherings. Slave narratives contain occasional references to European-style dances such as minuets and schottisches. However, most of the dances resembled African dances in terms of method and style. They were performed from a flexed, fluid body position as opposed to the stiffly erect postures of

European dances. Enslaved people placed emphasis upon satire, improvisation, and freedom of individual expression, often imitating such animals as the buzzard, eagle, crow, or rabbit.

In the evenings after the work was done, enslaved people would gather outside the cabins and listen to elders tell stories or remember their former lives or recollections of their ancestors. A rich oral heritage stemming from African roots gave rise to a unique African American culture.[15]

Kippax Plantation

*I*n January 2006 the Archaeological Conservancy, a national nonprofit organization, signed an option to purchase the Kippax Plantation Archaeological Site. Kippax was one of the first settlements in colonial Virginia identified as a hub of cultural interaction and economic trade between the Quiyoughcohannock Indians, Africans, and Europeans. The conservancy is dedicated to acquiring and preserving archaeological sites throughout the country. In 2005 the organization received a matching grant of $205,000 from the Virginia Land Conservation Fund. In order to acquire all of the 9.27-acre parcel an equal amount must be raised.[16] A former professor at the College of William and Mary, Donald W. Linebaugh, has studied the site extensively. Excavations on the slave quarters, beginning in 1988, illuminate the lives of those who physically worked the land.[17]

Kippax Plantation was nestled between Bermuda Hundred and Fort Henry (Petersburg), two important trade centers. The closest major body of water is the Lower Appomattox, which empties at the confluence of the Appomattox and James Rivers in the southern section of Hopewell. Young immigrants, sixteen-year-old Robert and his brother Drury Bolling, settled here and traded with Appamattuck Indians, bought and sold enslaved Africans, and created a new way of life from what they and their contemporaries had known in England. Within a short amount of time Robert Bolling became a merchant and landowner of the planter class. In 1675 the property, then called Farmingdale (also Farmindell), became home for merchant and trader Robert Bolling and his first wife, the former Jane Rolfe.

When Robert Bolling died in 1709, his son, Drury (from Bolling's second marriage, to Anne Stith in 1681), inherited the property and lived there until 1726, when he died. His probate inventory opens a window into the Bollings' lifestyle: imported bed linen for four bedsteads, ceramics, furnishings, and books were some of the items listed among his possessions.[18]

Drury Bolling's daughter, Frances, married Theodorick Bland, an elite planter who owned Cawson's. The married couple lived at Kippax for nearly ten years. It was during this time the plantation called Farmingdale (and alternately Farmindell) became known as Kippax; its name derived from the name of the Bland family seat in the village of Kippax, England. Their son, Theodorick Jr., joined the military in 1776 and was commissioned a captain in the Virginia Light Dragoons. In 1785, tax records show that

Theodorick Bland Jr. paid taxes on "himself, as well as 18 blacks, 16 young blacks of undisclosed ages, 10 horses, 26 cattle, and a wheeled vehicle." Between 1786 and 1790 his holdings had increased and he was credited with "20 to 30 slaves, eight to 11 horses/asses/mules, 20 cattle, and a four wheeled vehicle."[19]

The property remained in the Bland family until approximately 1829 when it was deeded to Joshua Poythress. Joshua Poythress's household included his wife, Jane; two females between the ages of 10 and 20; and seven slaves: a boy and girl under the age of 10, four men between the ages of 24 and 36, and a man between the ages of 36 and 55.

From 1867 until about 1895 the property lay fallow. New owners then built a two-story farmhouse. Since 1917 the property belonged to the Heretick family. Twenty-four-year-old Stephen Heretick Jr. had emigrated from Austria-Hungary to Pennsylvania in 1900. Three years later he married Mary Mikuska. One of her family members encouraged the couple to relocate to City Point, where a Czech/Slovak community began to develop and grow. Two of their eleven offspring resided on the current 9.78-acre parcel until their deaths in 2004 and 2005.

In 1981 the College of William and Mary conducted archaeological fieldwork. They excavated artifact assemblage from the 1730–40 decade suggesting the change in households from the Bolling to the Bland families. By 1988 excavations north of the plantation house uncovered the slave quarters. We can better understand the living conditions of enslaved people from archaeological findings that indicate habitation from the very late seventeenth to early eighteenth century. A variety of features were uncovered within the 10x10 units such as a brick-lined root cellar, three smaller cellars, and a small brick hearth. In addition, numerous nonstructural postholes as well as a large ashpit leave their marks on the landscape. Among the colonoware ceramics and Staffordshire slipware were beads used for trade and adornment as well as tobacco pipes and a wine bottle dating from 1690 to 1710.[20]

Artifacts from the Archaic (ca. 8000 B.C. to 1000 B.C.) period to late Woodland (1000 B.C. to A.D. 1000) period have been recovered from the Kippax plantation Archeological Site. Its location near the intersection of the Appomattox and James rivers makes this site central to early trade relations. The significance of the site extends over a period of 200 years and enables researchers to study the evolution of slavery.

Courtesy of Virginia Department of Historic Resources

Appomattox Manor

On June 30, 2007, citizens and friends of Hopewell gathered at Appomattox Manor, a National Park Service (NPS) site, to commemorate the 142nd anniversary of freedom for African Americans. Rebecca Rose, executive director of the Washington Cultural Foundation, along with NPS staff, organized the event to draw attention to a significant moment in America's history.

Courtesy of Virginia Department of Historic Resources

We are able to know something about the lives of enslaved and freed people in City Point through the diaries written by Dr. Richard Eppes, a planter who documented his management of Appomattox Manor from 1851 until 1896.[21] Arriving in 1635 on the ship *Hopewell*, his ancestor Francis Eppes had patented land near Charles City Point and named a part of his tract Hopewell Farm. "Captain Francis Eppes is granted 1,700 acres of land in the County of Charles City, lying East upon Bayly's Creek. Due 50 acres for his personal adventure and 1,650 acres for the transportation of his three sons and thirty slaves." In 1702 Prince George County was partitioned from Charles City County.[22]

His land advantageously situated on a bluff in City Point, Richard Eppes could stand at the rear of the manor and visually command the Appomattox and James Rivers as well as two of his other holdings, Eppes Island Plantation and Bermuda Hundred. Appomattox Manor served as Eppes's seat of plantation control. The Eppes family also owned Hopewell Plantation. An original plantation guide in the archives of the Virginia Historical Society provides insight into the management of plantations.[23]

Presiding over his land and slaves with precision, Eppes believed his agricultural work merited attention because "I am engaged probably more extensively than any man in the State in improving my land." Eppes recorded his daily transactions as well as "every important event occurring on my estates," where corn and wheat were the mainstays. As a gentleman farmer and fiscally conscious businessman, he managed his plantations by system and order. Like George Washington and other planters of his status, Eppes maintained strict discipline over his enslaved workers. He inventoried supplies and equipment, budgeted for rations, meted out corporal punishment, and bought and sold people and land as needed. When he considered additional land purchases, Eppes wrote, "My object in buying is to have surface for my surplus hands as I shall be overstocked in 8 or 10 years." The quest for wealth, as evidenced by a plantation society, could only be maintained by a massive labor force. "This is one of the evils attendant on slavery and there is no choice left ergo large farms a natural consequence where slavery exist."[24] In 1860 Eppes owned 127 slaves; 61 of them were male. Children were also included in the inventory.

Slave children were always present on plantations. In the big house, children performed domestic tasks such as housecleaning and kitchen work. They also worked as livery hands. Frequently, they were companions to the master's children. Slave children who carried the master's children's books to and from school learned by listening outside the schoolroom. When planter's children wished to "play school," they literally had a captive class in the plantation's enslaved children. Slaves sometimes traded their skills or possessions to whites for education or books. Laws against teaching slaves to read and write, laws punishing slaves who wrote passes, and the testimony of ex-slave interviews and fugitive slave narratives all suggest that some slave literacy training continued until emancipation.

Rag dolls were the most common nineteenth-century black dolls. Slaves and other American girls usually had handmade dolls. The earliest homemade black dolls were crude, and few have survived. They were usually made from pieces of leftover cloth and dressed in calico, muslin, or feed bag cloth. Cornhusk and nut-head dolls were also prevalent in rural areas. Representations of themselves were infrequent but where possible parents would try to instill a sense of self-worth in their children.

Two of the extant dependencies at Appomattox Manor include the kitchen and laundry house. Oftentimes, the fireplace from which meals were cooked would become smoky, so kitchens were usually separate from the main domicile. Sometimes kitchens caught fire; as a separate structure, it had least potential to cause damage to the main house. Likewise, the laundry room was separate from the main domicile. Scholarly work

Courtesy of Virginia Department of Historic Resources

on the drawings and photographs from the Historic American Buildings Survey as well as plantation paintings help us better understand the topography of plantation life.[25]

Eliza Caldwell, also known as Sarah, was an enslaved laundress at Appomattox Manor. The labor-intensive work was usually handled by enslaved women who laundered the clothing and bed, bath, and table linen of their owners. They spent long hours bending over scrub boards, lifting wet clothing, wringing, and hanging as well as ironing.

In 1858, Eppes' diary noted the attempted escape of Eliza's (Sarah's) husband, James, in Petersburg. He and two others were captured aboard a schooner. In 1863 Eppes noted the absence of three of his slaves. He believed the Yankees had encouraged them to leave.

On May 19, 1862, a skirmish between Georgia infantrymen and Union naval officers and seamen occurred at City Point. Union officers and seamen had gone ashore to give medical care at the request of local residents. Approaching the village with white flags flying above several houses, the Union men came under fire and three seamen were killed. The navy gunboats responded with a brief bombardment that caused some damage to Appomattox Manor and Weston Manor a little distance west.

No further action occurred until May 1864, when the Army of the James headed upriver under Union Major General Benjamin F. Butler's command.[26] Butler's first goal was to occupy City Point as a staging area. From there, Butler could attack Richmond and chase Confederate General Robert E. Lee's army while Union General George G. Meade's Army of the Potomac attacked from the north. The plan of commanding General Ulysses S. Grant was to trap Lee's army and end the war. However, his plan failed and the Confederate army became entrenched at Petersburg. For the next year, City Point served as a massive military installation as the Union army laid siege to Petersburg.[27]

Numerous contemporary illustrations depict the scale of military activity at City Point, where supplies of weapons, ammunition, and provisions for the army arrived daily by steamships, sailing vessels, and barges. By 1865 the military hospital originally built to accommodate six thousand patients was housing as many as ten thousand sick and wounded. An abattoir, for butchering livestock, as well as a bakery was also part of the Union's facilities.[28]

After the Civil War, Eppes relied on a workforce no longer enslaved but free. He reduced his landholdings and concentrated his efforts on the Eppes Island plantation, renting portions of the remainder of his property to middling farmers or tenants.[29]

The Reconstruction era held many possibilities and pitfalls. Newly freed men and women sought employment opportunities where they could. In addition to presiding over their own homes, some black women chose to take in laundry rather than work within the domestic space of their former owners.

Eliza Caldwell's work as a laundress may have been an occupation she continued as an entrepreneur after slavery ended. Though backbreaking, the labor afforded her an opportunity to work from her own home. Others may have worked as domestics, doing "day's work," that is,

Courtesy of Virginia Historical Society

ABOVE: *Artist Joseph Becker recorded commerce at the City Point fish market.* Frank Leslie's Illustrated Newspaper, *March 18, 1865*

RIGHT: *City Point from the James River, about 1864.*

Courtesy of Library of Congress

leaving their places of employment to return to their own homes. Others "lived on the lot," that is, staying in the home of their employers, only going home on their day off, usually Wednesday and every other Sunday. After the Civil War, the majority of black women continued to contribute to the economy through domestic service. From oral histories and paintings we are better able to examine regional differences, the conditions, and the daily experiences under which domestic workers toiled. In addition, detailed records from the Eppes papers allow a better understanding of the transition from slave labor to wage labor. Eppes continued to document the labor output at Appomattox Manor even as he endeavored to compensate the formerly enslaved workers.[30]

Courtesy of Virginia Historical Society

From left to right: The names of the first two women are unknown. The remaining two women are Patty George and Liddie Jones Cook. All lived at Appomattox Manor.

Weston Manor

1776. Virginia Bill of Rights passed June 12. I. All men are by nature equally free and independent and have certain inherent rights, namely, the enjoyment of life and liberty, with the means of acquiring and possessing property, and pursuing and obtaining happiness and safety.

*W*eston Manor sits tucked away near a grove of trees on the western edge of Hopewell. The Virginia Georgian plantation home of the Gilliam family, at Weston Lane and Twenty-first Avenue, is one of the few plantation homes left on the lower Appomattox River. The land was originally patented in 1637 by John Baker and remained in the Baker family until 1668. By 1723 John Hooley owned the property. In 1787 the property was acquired by William Gilliam, who a year later paid taxes on 273 acres. His marriage to Christian Eppes on April 3, 1789, solidified alliances within the planter class. The newlyweds began construction on their home immediately. No dependencies exist now, but at one point the plantation contained a kitchen, barn, and overseer's house. Although the working plantation was agricultural in nature, not enough is known about the specific products grown there. Research, however, is ongoing. We do know that the water was very important to the livelihood of this planter. Ferrymen such as Paul and Tom were experienced and highly valued. Both enslaved men were mentioned in Gilliam's will. An inventory of the enslaved workers identifies forty-three people owned

Weston Manor.

Courtesy of Virginia Department of Historic Resources

by William Gilliam and his son, John. It is likely, however, that the Gilliams owned more chattel property because of the size of the plantation as well as other holdings nearby.

In the latter part of the war, Northern officers occupied Weston when City Point harbor was being used to supply troops engaged in the siege of Petersburg. By 1869, Phillip Dolin, a New Yorker of Irish descent, bought Weston Manor. After the DuPont development of nearby Hopewell in the early twentieth century, much of the Manor's acreage was sold. By 1971 Weston Manor was listed on the Virginia Landmarks Register; a year later it was listed on the National Register of Historic Places. Since 1972 the Manor has been owned by the Historic Hopewell Foundation Incorporated.

Patrice Gilliam and her mother, the late Joy Gilliam, recalled some of their family history when they were interviewed on June 21, 2005. They tell the other side of a family history rarely heard. Among the African American population there were black Gilliams who had a "great deal of white blood; they were free Negroes. They were never slaves." Phil Schwarz's research on the Gilliam family in his book, *Migrants against Slavery*, supports this oral history.[31] George T. Gilliam was the son of a free black woman named Silvia Turnbull and Reuben Meriwether Gilliam, a white man. George was light enough to pass for white.

Photographs and archaeological evidence provide further clues about the free black population and in particular the free black Gilliams. Some family members chose to stay in Virginia, despite its repressive laws and dissipating race relations. As slaveholders themselves, they amassed wealth and became members of a small, elite group of similarly situated free blacks. Others, however, chose to migrate to free states in the North and West. In time many of them "crossed over," becoming "white" in fact and in deed.

Courtesy of Virginia Department of Historic Resources

Looking at the Appomattox River from Weston is a gentle reminder of the passage of time. As landscapes change, so too does the appreciation for working-class history. The Historic Hopewell Foundation plans to reconstruct two of the dependencies—the kitchen and laundry room—that flanked the manor home. Researchers from the College of William and Mary conducted archeological digs that have provided important clues to our understanding and interpretation of the built environment and its relationship to the natural setting.

City Point National Cemetery

Protected within a double wrought-iron gate and surrounded by a fieldstone wall are interments of at least 5,156 soldiers and sailors from the Civil War. The majority are of Union soldiers; 118 are of Confederates.

In 1863 and 1864, war visited Prince George County. Largely swampy areas on the eastern edge of Prince George County saw thousands of black Union soldiers. From June 1864 until April 1865 City Point became the "busiest place in Dixie." Grant built up one of the largest supply depots of the Civil War and his army received the best food, clothing, and ammunition in the field.

An army of blacks heeded the words of Frederick Douglass, who encouraged them to "take up arms in behalf of your country." On May 22, 1863, the United States Colored Troops (USCT) was established by the government. By the time the

Soldiers' graves near general hospital, City Point

Courtesy of Library of Congress

war ended, nearly 200,000 black soldiers had served in the USCT. They fought in more than 400 engagements and 39 major battles with losses totaling 36,847. One of those battles, the Battle of the Crater, was fought in nearby Petersburg, Virginia, in July 1864. The Federal attack columns, including nine regiments of USCT, formed a perimeter around the Crater. Unable to advance due to poor leadership and confusion, the Union troops were driven out of the Crater by Confederate counterattacks. General Grant called the Battle of the Crater "the saddest affair I have witnessed in the war" because some of the Confederates slaughtered black troops after they had surrendered.

A large army general hospital at City Point, where John Randolph Hospital now stands, accommodated the sick and wounded. Many of the combatants of the 1864–65 siege of Petersburg were interred near the hospital.

The burial ground near the hospital became part of the national cemetery. City Point National Cemetery, established in July 1866, contains six burial sections on 6.6 acres. It was one of twenty-one national cemeteries established that year. The army hired thousands of former slaves into the United States Burial Corps to bury the dead.

After the war ended, the cemetery expanded. During an excavation in 1955, the remains of seventeen unknown soldiers of the Civil War were discovered. Union and Confederate buttons were found in some of the graves. Re-interment in the City Point National Cemetery took place, followed by additional re-interments in 1959 and again in 1982. The cemetery officially closed for interments on July 26, 1971.

Research into the identities of those who gave their lives for freedom is a ripe area for future exploration.[32]

Courtesy of Virginia Department of Historic Resources

The City Point Historic District

In April 2007 I awoke to news that a tree had been taken down in City Point. Ordinarily this would have been of little consequence except that this tree was on a national historic site. The National Park Service, which maintains the site, removed a sycamore tree that had begun to lean perilously close to the cabin where Grant had been headquartered at Appomattox Manor. A dying magnolia tree that had been hit by lightning was also taken down. As landscapes change, we become cognizant of the ways in which historic preservation addresses change over time.

The City Point Historic District, located at the very tip of a peninsula, is home to several important sites spanning three centuries. Among the more well-known buildings are Appomattox Manor, the Civil War Catholic Chapel, and St. John's Episcopal Church, where escaping enslaved people found shelter in the basement in 1864. The boundaries include the James River to the east and Appomattox River to the north and west. A steep, wooded ravine partially defines the southern border and also separates the historic district from early-twentieth-century residential development.[33] Most of the buildings date from the nineteenth century in the roughly seven blocks, although a variety of housing types co-exist, including early-to-mid-twentieth-century buildings. The highest concentration of antebellum structures is located on Prince Henry Street, one of the earliest settlement locations within the district. Most of the styles are Greek Revival and Federal examples. Headquarters Camp Equipage was located at City Point House. The Belch House is said to have served as a military hospital. St. John's Rectory, a two-story frame house, was built about 1848; during the war, Union troops inhabited the

Courtesy of Virginia Department of Historic Resources

Civil War Catholic Chapel

building. The Christopher Proctor House, built in an early Federal style about 1800, preserves much of its original character including east and west porches and a frame smokehouse. During the Civil War, workers laid paving on the hill leading to the wharf on Pecan Street, where heavy foot traffic occurred.

One of the oldest streets in City Point is Water Street. At least seven wharves were situated east of this street in the first half of the nineteenth century. In 1836 the City Point Railroad Company was chartered, connecting City Point with Petersburg. Two years later the line opened, making it the oldest section of the Norfolk and Western Railroad system. Although its demise occurred soon after, a second attempt was made in 1855 and included the construction of a wharf and a brick depot. The City Point Railroad Company operated until the early to mid twentieth century. During the Civil

Wharf below City Point, on bank of the James River.

From June 1864 until April 1865 City Point became General U. S. Grant's supply base during the siege of Petersburg, making it one of three of the world's busiest ports. The United States Colored Troops, black civilians, and escaped slaves worked for the Union army as cooks, laborers, teamsters, nurses, and laundresses.

Courtesy of Library of Congress

Above: *USCT soldier guards 12-pounder Napoleons, at City Point.*

War, City Point was an ideal location for General Grant to establish military headquarters as warehouses in this area supplied the Union army. From June 1864 to April 1865, Grant was headquartered at Appomattox Manor, transforming the area with the arrival of thousands of soldiers. Wooden warehouses sat next to small, temporary shelters. Depots, tents, and additional wharves also dotted the landscape.

In August 1864, Union General Benjamin Butler ordered a canal cut through a neck of land at a bend in the James River in nearby Chesterfield County to shorten the route to Richmond. Fifty men were killed from enemy fire during construction, which was mostly done by the United States Colored Troops. The completed canal was never used during the war.

Courtesy of Library of Congress

USCT pickets, near Dutch Gap canal, November 1864

On May 5, 1864, under the command of General Edward W. Hinks, City Point had been captured by African American soldiers. Under General Hinks's command they had faced unanticipated resistance on June 15, 1864, from Confederate troops at Baylor's Farm (where the Hopewell Visitor's Center is now located at 4100 Oaklawn Boulevard). After retreating and then advancing again, the Union soldiers, many of them members of the United States Colored Troops regiments, eventually broke through the Confederate lines. It is estimated that at least 350 lost their lives.[34]

On January 31, 1865, Vice President Alexander H. Stephens led a Confederate Peace Commission to City Point with the intention of negotiating a compromise with Grant. Only three months later, on March 27, when President Lincoln and members of his cabinet met with General Grant to strategize at Appomattox Manor, they learned that Petersburg had fallen.

After the Civil War, the population decreased considerably, returning the site to its small-village character. Then with the arrival of DuPont Company followed closely by World War I, City Point endured staggering population growth. The guncotton/

E. L. Henry captured the majestic beauty of wartime City Point,
from the pilothouse of a transport on the James River, in November 1864.

When Lieutenant General Ulysses Grant arrived on June 15, 1864, a tent east of Appomattox Manor became his headquarter. Here, too, was the location of the advance supply depot of the Union forces. At least 280 buildings, eight wharves with warehouses covering eight acres, twenty-two miles of railroad tracks, Class I (rations) to support 125,000 men and 65,000 animals, an extensive repair shop, and seven hospitals enabled General Grant to wage a siege lasting nine and a half months and stretching across thirty-seven miles. City Point depot provided unparalleled support. By April 2, 1865, Union forces had captured Petersburg, the Confederacy's supply center. After the war ended on April 9, 1865, until the end of that summer City Point resupplied the Union armies as they returned north.

munitions plant opened on October 27, 1914, attracting more than 35,000 workers. As during the Civil War, temporary housing dotted the landscape. However, plant operations ceased with the end of the war in November 1918[35] and out-migration returned the area to a small residential community. It is this elastic nature to adjust to change that has enabled the city of Hopewell to endure.

Downtown Hopewell Historic District

Near the famous Appomattox,
On Virginia's fertile soil,
Stands a thriving little city,
With a welcome here for all.
And the town is full of hustlers
You can bet that is no jest
They are men of brain and muscle,
For the fire proved the test.
When the town was laid in ashes
They proved they had the vim
Quickly arose a city
Out of mortar, brick and tim.
And the knockers are scratching
The place they wear their hats.
For Hopewell is a city that will stay upon the map.[36]

Situated fifty feet above sea level just south of the Appomattox River, the city of Hopewell represents the evolution of an early-twentieth-century boomtown into a modern city. The historic district includes fifty-two properties; two of those buildings are the nationally recognized Hopewell Municipal Building and the Beacon Theatre.[37] After a 1915 fire that burned the majority of properties in the Hopewell's downtown area, a rebuilding frenzy took place that lasted from 1916 until 1930. Numerous commercial buildings including the D. L. Edler Bank, Larkin's Hotel, and Butterworth's Furniture spared Hopewell's residents from a trip to Richmond or Petersburg.

One building marked the change from segregated to integrated education in the mid-twentieth century. Situated at 205 Appomattox Street, the recently demolished Patrick Copeland School was named for the Reverend Patrick Copeland.

In 1621 the Reverend Copeland, chaplain of the ship *Royal James*, had solicited from the "gentlemen and marriners" aboard the ship funds for a free school at Charles City Plantation, to be called the East India School. The school was intended to provide a free education for indentured servants. On November 21, 1621, the Virginia Company of London gifted 1,000 acres for the school. However, in the spring of 1622, Opechancanough, a major chief of the Pamunkey nation and closely related to Chief Powhatan, led an attack on the settler population who had encroached on their lands. At least one-third of the English population was killed and plans for the school were scuttled.[38]

Only one block north of the main commercial area, at the upper end of the Downtown Hopewell Historic District, stood Patrick Copeland Elementary School. Built in 1939, the school represented the quest to provide a free public education and thereby create a learned citizenry. Although the building was demolished between December 5 and 9, 2006, it is a part of Hopewell's history that lives on through its students. During its time, thousands of students received an education. A detailed physical description of the Patrick Copeland School from the National Register of Historic Places enables us to envision its aesthetic presence on the cultural landscape. The description has been included in its entirety because it contextualizes our understanding of the now-invisible educational institution as a significant site in the desegregation era.

> This Art Deco, two-story brick school is divided into three main sections with a stone band running along the roofline as well as the base line. The stretcher-bond center section is seven bays wide with a projecting middle bay within which the three-door entrance and transoms are recessed. The recession is framed with a soldier brick course. This bay also has a stone entablature, stone dentil bands, and an octagonal clock insert. Separating each bay are decorative vertical soldier brick bands. The double-hung 3/3 windows are in groups of threes across the façade. These window sets have rowlock brick lintels and stone sills. The projecting western section has two large bays made up of 5-course American-bond brickwork and two rows of louvered windows. The projecting eastern section has stretcher-bond brickwork, only three double-hung 3/3 windows, two fixed 3-light windows, and a double door with transom. There are small stone panels between the first- and second-floor window sets spaced across the central and western sections of the building. A projecting one-story, one-bay brick unit with a single window covers the connection of the eastern and central sections.[39]

When interviewed, Patrice Gilliam, a former student at Patrick Copeland, remembered her first day of being on the front lines of the desegregation efforts. "I knew that I was going to be going to Patrick Copeland in September [1963], and it was under court order." Her grandmother, Mary Bowman Gilliam, said that "she didn't think she'd ever live to see black children go to a white school, and she didn't believe it."

Grandma called Yellow Cab, and I thought she was going to work. Usually she would walk to work, or she might catch the bus up here and go wherever, but she called the Yellow Cab. And it was about a quarter of 8:00, and when we drove up in front of Patrick Copeland and got out, there's a building right across the street from Patrick Copeland. It used to be a dance ... here of late it was a dance studio, but it used to be Appomattox Cleaner, and Grandma was standing in the doorway of Appomattox Cleaner dressed with an umbrella to get ... keep the morning sun off of her because she wanted to see us walk into Patrick Copeland.

Patrice Gilliam later learned that "federal marshals were there the day that we went into the school, but I didn't know them. I didn't know who they were. You didn't see them walking around in the school. I don't know if they were outside. I don't know, but we had that protection."

Courtesy of Carmela Hamm

Her younger brother, Reuben, also was on the front lines of desegregation. Patrice and Reuben, already close, became closer as they learned to look out for each other as best they could. The racial climate was such that they had to be mindful of their own and each other's safety. Their mother, the late Joy Gilliam, recalled that the only way we would know that something was going on with him, she'd [Patrice] would come home and tell us.

Now, she passed by his classroom one day, and the teacher had put him off in a row all by himself. She had pulled him aside from all of the other children and had him sitting over by himself. ... Of course the next day I had business at school, and I had business in the principal's office with the teacher.

As time progressed the racial climate evolved. Patrice remembers that when she decided to run for Miss Hopewell High School, her sponsor was Butterworth's Furniture Company. "Mom and Dad and my Aunt Octavia, and my Aunt Julia" had all purchased from Butterworth's. "My picture was on a poster that sat in his storefront window." Though she didn't win ("I started out as number 27 and I ended as number 27"), the experience opened the way for successors. As her mother said proudly, "she broke the ice for everybody else." In the late 1960s the possibilities, especially for high school graduates, seemed endless. The civil rights movement had created change on every level. Patrice said of her senior year,

"We ended it with the Age of Aquarius and we danced to the Fifth Dimension's "Age of Aquarius" and in my last will and testament ... I left my seat at Hopewell High School, and the right for every black child in the city of Hopewell to have an opportunity to attend the public school of his or her choice in the city of Hopewell, and the right to run for whatever office or whatever superlative that he or she felt they were worthy of.[40]"

Courtesy of Virginia Department of Historic Resources

By the 1960s like many downtown areas across the nation, the city of Hopewell had undergone changes. Consumers were willing to travel greater distances to spend their discretionary income. Revitalization plans have sparked new interest in preserving the character of downtown districts.

The Beacon Theatre

Courtesy of Virginia Department of Historic Resources

On February 17–18, 2007, the historic Beacon presented "Colorful Voices: A Celebration of Black History," the first such public event held on the premises. Some of the longtime African American residents remember when they were relegated to the balcony. As Juanita Chambers recalled growing up in Hopewell, she shared her feelings about the Beacon Theatre. "Momma said her children couldn't go to the Beacon Theater but other children did go. They could go, you know, and buy the ticket and go … oh, shoot, momma called it the peanut gallery." Now, as a civic leader in the community and a member of the school board, Chambers says she attended a retreat at the Beacon. "I had to let the baggage go, and go on and contribute and do what I had to do about the Beacon Theatre."

Designated as one of America's treasures by the Save America's Treasures foundation, the Beacon Theatre has come a long way.[41] Located at the corner of East Cawson and North Main Streets, the newly rehabilitated vaudeville and movie theater now holds a variety of events. It was founded by M. T. Broyhill, C. B. Swain, and John Cunningham, original partners in the Hopewell Amusement Corporation. In 1928, when the theater opened, it was during the height of the vaudeville period and was one of nineteen such theaters built; it was equipped with a $10,000 organ and a six-piece orchestra. Originally named the Broadway Theatre and Pythian Lodge Building, it cost $150,000 and seated 981 patrons. The three-story, mid-sized building also housed the *Hopewell News*, storefront offices, apartments, and a meeting hall for the Knights of Pythias fraternal order. During the 1930s races were segregated. Photographs from the era show an annual community event as well as the early inculcation of separatism. Six hundred children attended the "colored" Christmas party sponsored by Tubize Corporation; the white children celebrated their Christmas party at the Broadway Theatre as well, though on a separate day.[42] From 1930 until 1950 the Beacon Theatre held live performances and movies, though it operated under Jim Crow, that is, segregated practices. Chambers and her siblings were among a growing number of African Americans who traveled from Hopewell to Petersburg to attend a movie theater rather than sit in the "peanut gallery" at the Beacon.

> They did a wonderful job with the Petersburg situation. When you buy a ticket, a round-trip ticket, go to Petersburg and come back, you got a movie ticket on certain days, especially on the weekend. So we wanted to go the movie … they had three movies in Petersburg … the Barney Theater, the Gem Theater and Ildehaur, I guess that's what it was. And you could go to either of these movies with this ticket that you would get with your regular ticket going to Petersburg. And I remember it used to be 35 cents. But 35 cents was difficult to get but we could go to Petersburg and come back, and we went on Sunday. You know, sometimes after we go to church, if you get up and go to Sunday school, go to church, you might get permission to go to the movie.

Courtesy of Carmela Hamm

The Broadway was auctioned off in 1932 when the Hopewell Amusement Corporation defaulted on its loans. The new owners changed the name to the Beacon Theatre. It remained open, though business decreased until it closed in 1981. As Hopewell began to revitalize the downtown area, the Beacon Theatre was rescued. A group of local citizens formed the nonprofit Hopewell Preservation, Inc., in 1987, with the purpose of restoring the theater and providing performance and meeting space. By 1999 they were ready to begin a rehabilitation of the structure. Major alterations include the removal of the original seats at the orchestra level and most of the balcony-level seats. "Now, no one is going to go and sit in the peanut gallery," Juanita Chambers declared. Now, the Beacon Theatre has become a true beacon in the community.[43]

Courtesy of Bob Sheppard

Hopewell Municipal Building
Lot 10, Block 11, "B" Village[44]

On April 7, 2007, The Martin Luther King Jr. Memorial Foundation, Inc., sponsored "A Legacy of Hope" program.[45] Longtime activist the Reverend Wyatt T. Walker, a close associate of the late Martin Luther King Jr., recalled the past and offered encouragement for the future. The Honorable Donald McEachin donated a granite bench that can be seen in the Ashford Civil Plaza.

"Beginning at the intersection of First Street and 'B' Street; thence running along 'B' Street in a westerly direction" read the descriptive boundary lines of the parcel of land bought by the city from the Tubize Corporation on October 10, 1924. The boundaries include the Hopewell Municipal Building, its annex, and the immediate surrounding landscape of the city block.[46]

Hopewell's first official court building is virtually at the center of the original streets of the city. The Hopewell Municipal Building sits on an entire city block facing the junction of Main, Broadway, Randolph, and a triangular park. The original section was built in 1925 and has two entrances. Carved into a stone frieze above the portico are the words MUNICIPAL BUILDING. The portico feature was a typical trend at the time; between 1900 and 1937 architects designed nineteen court buildings in Virginia with porticos.

The Council-Manager form of government was adopted by the city on September 1, 1924. Known as the "Lockport Plan," this form of government vested the governing power in five men elected for a term of four years. One of those five would be elected for a term of two years. Currently, a seven-member council determines the structure of the city's operations through policy and selects and supervises the city manager. As chief executive, the city manager administers the programs and policies approved by city council.

During World War II, registration for civilian defense work was entirely voluntary although everyone was encouraged to sign up. In January 1942, a one-day registration for African American women was held at Carter G. Woodson School. The Reverend Harry E. James, principal of the school, worked with the Hopewell Defense Council, which sponsored the registration. Black men were also encouraged to register. James Jones volunteered. Four more — John Harrison Jr., Garland Webster Hudson, William Shirley Brown, and Caspar Johnson — were sent by the local Selective Service Board to the army induction station in Richmond.[47] A month later eight more men were drafted. Wilson W. Creighton, Louis Barnes, John H. Ward, Richard A. Clark, Vernon L. White, Pete Jones, Will Robinson, and Hezzike Palmer enjoyed an informal ceremony in front of the Municipal Building before they left for the induction station in Richmond.[48]

The Municipal Building was also the site of the Carter G. Woodson High School commencement exercise in 1942. The commencement address was delivered by Reverend James, principal of the school; the audience and graduating class met in the courtroom at 8:00 p.m.[49] Some of the graduates furthered their education, most often attending Virginia State College (VSC). The students usually returned home for the high school homecoming games. Among the returning Woodson alumni were Miss Ruby E. Wynn, member of the Arlington Heights School faculty and alumna of VSC; Miss Bessie Carter, member of the Carter G. Woodson School faculty and alumna of VSC; Mrs. C. A. Robbins; and Mr. F. Bernard Eppes, member of the Arlington Heights School faculty and alumnus of VSC. Miss Rebecca L. Powell, Miss Mary L. Henson, Miss Lillian Washington, Miss Thelma Gilliam, Miss Julia G. Gilliam, and Mr. Reuben L. Gilliam were all students at the college.[50]

In 1960 only 23 percent of Virginia blacks of voting age were registered to vote. By 1966 the poll tax was banned from state and local elections. By 1968 the proportion had increased to 58 percent, largely as a result of the Voting Rights Act of 1965. It provided federal oversight of voter registration in counties where racial discrimination was proved to have existed. It also effectively abolished literacy tests and the poll tax in federal elections. The Equal Pay Act of 1963, Title VII of the Civil Rights Act of 1964, and the Higher Education Act of 1965 enabled blacks to enter occupations largely limited to whites and to be paid equally in those jobs. Women also had the opportunity to enter previously male-dominated positions.

Throughout the South, tensions grew. Martin Luther King appeared in Hopewell District Court on March 29, 1962, to lend support to the struggle. Kenneth Harris remembers marching, when a child, during the civil rights movement. His father, the Reverend Curtis Harris, led many marches and the participants ranged in age from young people to the elderly. When asked how he was treated during the era of segregation he recalled:

> Well, you could go in there and buy anything you wanted to buy, but you couldn't set at the lunch counter, like W. T. Grant's and Woolworth's, some of the drugstores, you know, they had lunch counters. And I can remember when we went in Woolworth's, and I am a little guy, this is maybe '61, and I could see underneath the lunch counter, that's how tall I was, and it was chewing gum from one end of the lunch counter to the other and I had never seen anything so filthy in my life, and I said, I don't want to come down here anyway. It's filthy. Why would I want to sit here?

DR. LEE: And so you didn't?

KENNETH HARRIS: No ... I did what ... you know, I was in the group, what we had ... you know, I was doing what we were supposed to do, sit down there and wait until the policeman come, and then the police arrested all of us and marched us across the street to the jail.

DR. LEE: How old were you then?

Courtesy of Carmela Hamm

KENNETH HARRIS: I must have been about 12, 13.

DR. LEE: Okay. And so was that the first time that you were arrested?

KENNETH HARRIS: That was the first and only time.

DR. LEE: Okay. What was that experience like, at the age of 12?

KENNETH HARRIS: It was ... it was ... to me, it was boring because as a child I wasn't involved in really what was going on. I just was with the group, and the group went down there, and the group got arrested, the group went over to the jail and somebody did paperwork as far as doing our bond so that we could go back home. You know, I was never behind bars. And then after I can recall later on that we went to court, and I don't even remember what happened at court. But I remember that because of that getting arrested, when I was 15 and wanted to get my driver's license, and it's a place on there that would ask that have you ever been arrested before, so if you checked yes, you needed permission from the judge to get your driver's license. Then I had to take the papers back up to the judge downtown to sign it. And I can remember him looking at me and he asked me am I going to do this anymore. And I said, no. If I said, yes, I wouldn't be able to get my driver's license.

The quest for freedom took on many forms, from sit-ins to a driver's license. Young black people walked a tightrope as they negotiated the shifting southern terrain. Across Virginia tensions erupted in the summer of 1963. Protestors in Danville, Virginia, for example, demanded school integration, political representation, and an end to hiring discrimination at Dan River Mills, a textile manufacturer that provided fully half of local employment and effectively controlled local government. Participants in a sit-in at the mayor's office were forcibly evicted, beaten, thrown down the stairs, and jailed. A law dating to John Brown's raid on Harper's Ferry in 1859 made it unlawful for anyone to incite blacks against whites; it was used in 1963 to indict black leaders. Danville became a national focus of the civil rights movement until the March on Washington in August diverted attention away from Danville. Yet, the underlying motivations for change remained relevant.

The *Hopewell News* photographed the Klu Klux Klan and civil rights activists when they met on the steps of the Municipal Building in Hopewell. For nearly forty minutes on August 8, 1966, approximately two thousand people observed the encounter. The Klansman, lining the north side of the sidewalk of the Municipal Building, were robed and waiting for the activists who had walked two and a quarter miles from Rt. 156. Protesting a proposed landfill in the Rosedale district near the homes of five families, the African Americans, led by Curtis Harris, submitted a typewritten protest to the acting city manager, Torsten Peterson, asking council to stay its action with reference to locating the landfill in Rosedale, an area zoned for industry. He also requested that a committee be appointed to locate another area for the landfill. He protested that "it is regrettable that in this enlightened age 20 percent of any community could be systematically excluded from every committee and commission of any significance within the community."

Courtesy of James Willcox

"Freedom, freedom now," activists chanted while the Klansman responded with "Never, never." Prior to the encounter, when a reporter asked a Klansman to explain their position further, he was told, "Never, never accept integration; never submit to Communism." When the activists knelt in silent prayer, a Klan leader motioned for his members to cease their protests. "Every man has his right to pray to his God." His own prayer, which the newspaper carried, highlighted the perceived threat many whites felt when faced with racial equality.

James Willcox, originally from South Carolina, relocated to Hopewell in 1962. He worked as an engineer for Hercules until he retired. Willcox witnessed the encounter between the civil rights activists and the Klansman at the Municipal Building.

DR. LEE: Okay. So the first time that you saw or heard of the Ku Klux Klan?

JAMES WILLCOX: The first time I ever … and only time I've ever seen it was here in Hopewell in '66. I never saw it in South Carolina.

DR. LEE: And what was your feeling at that time?

JAMES WILLCOX: I'm not sure that I remember that much about it.

DR. LEE: Where did you see them first? Let's set the scene.

JAMES WILLCOX: Down at the Municipal Building in downtown Hopewell. And the Reverend Curtis Harris had a group that marched from one direction and the Klan in their robes marched from the other direction. And I think Curtis Harris's group went up on the top of the municipal steps, Municipal Building steps. Then there was a row of police and then there were the Klan and the mob. And both groups were very orderly. Both made a few comments. Both had a prayer. And then they dispersed and went in opposite directions.

Courtesy of Carmela Hamm

DR. LEE: How did things change after that, or did they?

JAMES WILLCOX: I don't think they necessarily changed that much after that. I don't know that the event had a big impact one way or another. It mainly, I think, gave the two parties a means of expressing their opinion a little bit and then they went off.

On other fronts, progress was being made and noted in the *Hopewell News*.

On **May 3, 1966**, the Knights Social Club honored the Woodson High School basketball team for an outstanding season. In its first year in Group I of the VIA league, Woodson won third place in the state cage race. Woodson's coach, R. J. Hayes, was presented a trophy by Charles W. Smith, superintendent.

May 10, 1966: Bill Russell of the Boston Celtics was named the team's next coach. He's the first of his race ever chosen to pilot a major pro team.

May 30, 1966: Barbara Wyche received the Davis and Elkins College Award. The principal at Hopewell High School, F. Carroll Alexander, presented awards to Wyche and another to a white male, Robert Poole.

June 3, 1966: Both George Kinchen and Rosa Goodwyn, citizens of Hopewell, were recognized for their thirty-five years of service. Goodwin, the head cook at John Randolph Hospital, had been employed there longer than anyone else. Kinchen also had been at the hospital thirty-five years, working in the operating room as an orderly.

June 8, 1966: Prodding Congress for swift action on President Lyndon B. Johnson's proposals to stamp out racial violence, a group of GOP lawmakers asked the House judiciary subcommittee to act immediately on the racial violence section also known as "Title V." In addition, the measure would also ban discrimination in the sale and rental of housing, seek to ensure fair selection of state and federal court juries, and provide new legal weapons against school segregation.

June 9, 1966: "Negro March Proceeds through KKK Territory" screamed the headline. Above, a photograph of Martin Luther King Jr. and a Mississippi state trooper captured a tense moment. Two days earlier, James Meredith had been shot. He had begun a march to encourage voter registration. Both black and white marchers trekked down a relatively desolate road on U.S. Route 51 following the shooting. The Mississippi Freedom March led by King continued Meredith's trek through active Ku Klux Klan territory. Fifteen to twenty pellets were lodged in Meredith's neck, shoulders, and back as he crossed the state line from Tennessee into Mississippi. Meredith recovered.

June 15, 1966: In the first elections following removal of Virginia's poll tax of $3.50, African American candidates won in Richmond, Petersburg, and Fredericksburg. Under the federal Voting Rights Act and court rulings, Virginians were allowed to vote for free and could register up to within thirty days of the election. In Norfolk and Portsmouth, however, blacks lost in municipal elections.

On that same day, the *Hopewell News* carried on page 1 an article entitled "Negroes Urged Not to Serve in Armed Forces." Stokely Carmichael said, "Any black man who fights in this country's army is a black mercenary." As the leader of the Student Non-Violent Coordinating Committee (SNCC), Carmichael spoke to a crowd of 600 attendees at a rally of the Congress of Racial Equality (CORE).

Then, in 1968, the classic civil rights movement ended with the assassination of Martin Luther King Jr. on April 4. The civil rights movement of the 1950s and '60s became a chapter in the larger and longer struggle for equality. King's "I Have a Dream" speech, delivered at the Lincoln Memorial, challenged America to live up to its founding ideals. During his lifetime federal government discrimination ceased; major league sports were integrated; the armed forces were desegregated; legally mandated school segregation was outlawed; the SCLC, CORE, and SNCC were founded; equal access to public accommodations was guaranteed; voting rights were assured; numerous black officials were elected; and King himself won the Nobel Peace Prize at age thirty-five. However, not everything he sought was accomplished.

The "Poor People's March on Washington" in 1968 was the last major demonstration planned by Dr. Martin Luther King Jr. After passage of the momentous civil rights legislation of 1964–65, King began to focus his attention on economic injustice, arguing that blacks needed guaranteed employment, guaranteed annual incomes, and subsidized housing. King's assassination in Memphis in August delayed the march, but his lieutenant, the Reverend Ralph Abernathy, carried out King's plans.

On April 4, 2004, a seven-foot bronze bust of Dr. King was dedicated in the Ashford Civic Plaza in Hopewell. As the keynote speaker, Dr. King's son Martin King III encouraged the audience to continue pressing for full equality and justice.

Courtesy of Paul Di Pasquale

End Notes To Section I

[1] The final draft of the Declaration of Independence was adopted by Congress on the morning of July 4, 1776. To see the evolution of the document from rough draft to final version see the American Treasures of the Library of Congress website: www.loc.gov/exhibits/treasures.

[2] Taylor Branch's trilogy provides a comprehensive national overview of the years 1954–68. For insight into Martin Luther King Jr. through his inspirational sermons see Clayborne Carson and Peter Holloran's compilation in *A Knock at Midnight*.

[3] See Forrest K Lehman's *Settled Place, Contested Past: Reconciling George Percy's "A Trewe Relacyon" with John Smith's Generall Historie*. See John Smith's *General History of Virginia, New England and the Summer Isles, together with the True travels, adventures and observations and a sea grammar*, vol. 1, chap. XII, The Arrivall of the Third Supply, p. 222.

[4] Bermuda Hundred was registered as a Virginia Historic Landmark on September 6, 2006. For the archaeological and architectural resources see Department of Historic Resources (hereafter DHR) file #020-5370; see file #020-0064 for the historic district of Bermuda Hundred. Also see Julian Walker's March 26, 2007, article in the *Richmond Times-Dispatch* regarding Virginia's oldest incorporated town, Bermuda Hundred.

[5] John Smith's *General History of Virginia*. Also see Mark Nicholls, "George Percy's 'Trewe Relacyon': A Primary Source for the Jamestown Settlement," *Virginia Magazine of History and Biography* 113, no. 3 (2005): 212–275.

[6] Flowerdew Hundred in Prince George County is one of the earliest original land grants in Virginia. It was registered as a Virginia Historic Landmark on May 20, 1975 and listed on the National Register of Historic Places on August 1, 1975. See DHR file #074-0006. See James Deetz, *Flowerdew Hundred: the Archaeology of a Virginia Plantation, 1619–1864*.

[7] After Virginia, the colony of Maryland had the largest population of blacks (43,450), followed by South Carolina (39,000). See *From Slavery to Freedom*, pp. 57–58, 65. Also see *African American Odyssey*, pp. 54–55, 100. The United States Department of Commerce, *Historical Statistics of the United States: Colonial Times to 1970*, part 2. Bureau of the Census, Washington, D.C., 1975.

[8] See *From Slavery to Freedom*, pp. 84–86, 99. Also see *Negro Population in the United States, 1790–1915*, p. 57. The numbers for the enslaved population vary. Authors of the *African American Odyssey* state that there were 293,427 slaves in Virginia in 1790; see p. 99. Also see Robin L. Ryder's thesis, "Free African-American Archaeology: Interpreting An Antebellum Farmstead," The College of William and Mary, Department of Anthropology, 1991.

[9] See *The Guide to African American Manuscripts at the Virginia Historical Society*. The information in this section was from research on the 2006 exhibition, Safely Harbored: New African American Acquisitions, which was installed at the Virginia Historical Society from February 11–August 6, 2006.

[10] See *A Pictorial History of Hopewell, Virginia*, by A. V. Carey.

[11] Other companies replaced DuPont; they include Allied Signal, Firestone, Goldschmidt, Hercules/Aqualon, Honeywell, and Smurfit-Stone.

[12] In addition to the city of Hopewell, the Appomattox River runs through the cities of Colonial Heights and Petersburg and the counties of Amelia, Appomattox, Buckingham, Chesterfield, Cumberland, Dinwiddie, Powhatan, Prince Edward, and Prince George. Prince George is also one of the counties in which the James River flows. See *The Hornbook of Virginia History*, edited by Emily J. Salmon and Edward D. C. Campbell, Jr.

[13] Martin Luther King, Jr., "I Have a Dream" speech, 1963, Lincoln Memorial, Washington, D.C.

[14] See the *Town Site Construction and Cost Estimate, 1915–1916 regarding The Building of the City of Hopewell* by the DuPont Company by F. W. Foote. The original was presented to Historic Hopewell Foundation

in June 1998 by the grandson of F. W. Foote, a draftsman and engineer for the DuPont Company. Copy located at Appomattox Regional Library System.

[15] The above text regarding slavery was revised from the 2002 Virginia Historical Society exhibition Enslaved: Life on Virginia Presidents' Plantations, which was installed from October 2002–January 2003. The literature on slavery is voluminous. Classic examples are: Lawrence Levine's *Roll, Jordan, Roll*, and Elizabeth Fox-Genovese's study, *Within the Plantation Household: Black and White Women of the Old South*. Regarding the lives of enslaved children see Wilma King's study, *Stolen Childhood: Slave Youth in Nineteenth Century America*, as well as Marie Schwarz's *Born in Bondage: Growing up in the Antebellum South*. See also Helen Bradley Foster's *New Raiments of Self: African American Clothing in the Antebellum South* regarding expressive culture in the public realm.

[16] Andrew Price, "Plantation preservation under way," *Richmond Times-Dispatch*, January 4, 2006.

[17] See Donald W. Linebaugh, *Kippax Plantation: Traders, Merchants, and Planters: An Exhibit Celebrating the Families of Pocahontas*. Center for Archaeological Research at the College of William and Mary, Williamsburg, Virginia, 1995.

[18] Donald W. Linebaugh and Gary G. Robinson, "Five Artifact Studies from the Heretick Site, Introduction." *Quarterly Bulletin of the Archeological Society of Virginia* 39, no. 1 (1984): 1–3.

[19] Philip A. Bruce (editor), "Will of Colonial Theodorick Bland." *Virginia Magazine of History and Biography* 3 (1896): 315–316.

[20] Gary G. Robinson, "The Glass Bead Collection from the Heretick Site (44PG62)," *Quarterly Bulletin of the Archeological Society of Virginia* 39, no. 1 (1984): 14–23. Kippax Plantation Archaeological Site was added to the Virginia Landmarks Register on June 6, 2007. See the Virginia Department of Historic Resources file #116-5021. The property was listed on the National Register of Historic Places on August 9, 2007.

[21] Appomattox Manor was listed as a Virginia Landmark on November 5, 1968; national status was achieved on October 1, 1969. See DHR file #116-0001.

[22] Prince George County was named for the husband of Queen Anne of England, Prince George of Denmark. See *Hornbook of Virginia History*, p. 168.

[23] Anonymous, *Plantation and farm instruction, regulation, record, inventory and account book…by a Southern planter.* See Eppes Papers, Virginia Historical Society (MssEP734d293).

[24] Dr. Richard Eppes, January 15, 1853. Virginia Historical Society, MssEp734d291. Also see Michael L. Nicholls, " 'In the Light of Human Beings': Richard Eppes and His Island Plantation Code of Laws," *Virginia Magazine of History and Biography* 89, no. 1 (1981): 67–78; Marie Tyler-McGraw, Slavery and the Underground Railroad at the Eppes Plantations, Petersburg National Battlefield (Special History Study, National Park Service, 2005).

[25] See John Michael Vlach, *Back of the Big House: the Architecture of Plantation Slavery* as well as the *Planter's Prospect: Privilege, and Slavery in Plantation Paintings*, also by Vlach. An exhibition entitled Children of Hope: African American Childhood in Virginia, curated by the author, was installed at the Virginia Historical Society from January through July 2005; it explored the world of the enslaved and freed child.

[26] African American soldiers, under the command of General Edward W. Hinks, captured City Point on May 5, 1864.

[27] See A. Wilson Greene's *Civil War Petersburg: Confederate City in the Crucible of War.*

[28] See Calos, et al., *Old City Point and Hopewell: The First 370 Years*, pp 17–18, 29 and Frances Lutz, *The Prince George–Hopewell Story*, pp 170–172.

[29] Eppes papers, Virginia Historical Society, 7 October 1869; 4 December 1869; 8 August 1870. Also see Jeffrey Kerr-Ritchie, *Freedpeople in the Tobacco South: Virginia, 1860–1890*.

[30] See Evelyn Nakamo Glenn, *Unequal Freedom: How Race and Gender Shaped American Citizenship and Labor.* Also see Carole Shammas, "Black Women's Work and the Evolution of Plantation Society in Virginia" in *Labor History* (Winter 1985), pp 5–28. For a treatment of domestic work during a later time period see Elizabeth L. O'Leary's *From Morning to Night: Domestic Service in Maymont House and the Gilded Age South.* Also see Elizabeth Ross Haynes, "Negroes in Domestic Service" in *Journal of Negro History.*

[31] Western Manor was registered as a Virginia Historic Landmark in November 1971 and received national designation in April 1972. See DHR file #116-0002. Regarding the Virginia Declaration of Rights see www.constitutioncenter.org/explore/FoundingDocuments/. See June Purcell Guild, *Black Laws of Virginia.* Also see Philip Schwarz, *Twice Condemned: Slaves and the Criminal Laws of Virginia, 1705–1865.* In Schwarz, *Migrants against Slavery: Virginians and the Nation* he discusses the Gilliam family. Regarding freed blacks see Ira Berlin, *Slaves without Masters: The Free Negro in the Antebellum South.*

[32] City Point National Cemetery was registered as a Virginia Historic Landmark in April 1995 and registered as a national site in August 1995. See DHR file #116-0008. Regarding the establishment of national cemeteries see the United States Department of Veteran Affairs/Office of Construction and Facilities management: Historic Preservation at www.va.gov/facmgt/historic/civilwar. asp#establishment. See the U.S. National Archives & Records Administration's website regarding black soldiers in the Civil War: www.archives.gov/education/lessons/blacks-civil-war. The style of the entry gate, constructed in 1941, reflects the changing times when automobiles became larger and wider gates were created to accommodate them.

On 5 May 1868, General John A. Logan, commander of the Grand Army of the Republic issued Order No. 11, designating May 30 as Decoration Day; it later became known as Memorial Day. It was first observed on May 30, 1868, when flowers were placed on the graves of Union and Confederate soldiers at Arlington National Cemetery. The first state to officially recognize the holiday was New York in 1873. By 1890 it was recognized by all the northern states. The South refused to acknowledge the day, honoring their dead on separate days until after World War I, when the holiday changed from honoring only those who died fighting in the Civil War to honoring Americans who died fighting in any war. It is now celebrated in almost every state on the last Monday in May (passed by Congress with the National Holiday Act of 1971 (P.L. 90 - 363) to ensure a three-day weekend for federal holidays).

[33] Pelham Avenue is located south of City Point at the edge of a ravine. The ravine precluded continuous residential development during the nineteenth century. Pelham Avenue is included although most of the structures do not contribute to the historic character of the district.

[34] The Battle of New Market Heights was fought in September 1864. The Tenth and Eighteenth Corps, including fourteen regiments of United States Colored Troops attacked the outer defenses of Richmond. Fourteen black soldiers and two white officers earned the Medal of Honor, the nation's highest military accolade. Over the course of the war, 1,520 soldiers and sailors were awarded the Medal of Honor; twenty-four of those recipients were African Americans; seven were Virginians.

Five of the Virginians received citations for their roles at Chaffin's Farm on September 29, 1864. Two received citations for their roles at Fort Wagner, South Carolina, on July 18, 1863, and on board the U.S.S. *Brooklyn* on September 1864. The seven Virginians include:

First Sergeant Powhatan Beaty, Company G, 5th U.S. Colored Troops. Beaty took command of his company at Chaffin's Farm on September 29, 1864. He led the men after all the officers had been killed or wounded. The Powhatan Beaty Memorial Bridge in Charles City on Rt. 5 commemorates his bravery.

Sergeant William Carney, Company C, 54th Massachusetts Colored Infantry was issued a citation in 1900. When the color sergeant was shot down at Fort Wagner, South Carolina., on July 18, 1863, Carney grasped the flag, led the way to the parapet, and planted the colors. When the troops fell back he brought off the flag under a ferocious fire in which he was severely wounded twice.

On September 29, 1863, at Chaffin's Farm, Private James Gardiner rushed forward in advance of his brigade, shot a Confederate officer who was on the parapet rallying his men, and then ran him through with his bayonet. The Gloucester native was issued his medal of honor on April 6, 1865.

Born in Princess Anne County, entering service at Norfolk, and serving as corporal in Company B, 36th U.S. Colored Troops, James Miles faced the foe on September 30, 1864, at Chaffin's Farm.

James Mifflin served as an engineer's cook in the U.S. Navy. On August 5, 1864, Mifflin was on board the U.S.S. *Brooklyn* during attacks against Fort Morgan and Confederate gunboats and the ram C.S.S. *Tennessee* in Mobile Bay. Stationed in the immediate vicinity of the shell whips, which were cleared twice of men by bursting shells, Mifflin stayed at his post and performed his duties in the powder division throughout the action, which resulted in the surrender of the *Tennessee* and in the damaging and destruction of batteries at Fort Morgan.

Edward Ratcliff was a First Sergeant in Company C, 38th U.S. Colored Troops. After the commanding officer had been killed, First Sergeant Ratcliff commanded and gallantly led his company. He was the first enlisted man to enter the enemy's works.

Private Charles Veal, Company D, 4th U.S. Colored Troops, of Portsmouth, Virginia, seized the national colors on September 29, 1864, after two color-bearers had been shot down close to the enemy's works. He bore the colors through the remainder of the battle.

See *Black Confederates and Afro-Yankees in the Civil War* by Ervin L. Jordan, Jr. for a detailed rendering of the role African Americans played in the Civil War. See also David Crane and Elaine Crane, *The Black Soldier: From the American Revolution to Vietnam.* See also John S. Salmon's *The Official Virginia Civil War Battlefield Guide.*

[35] Governor Westmoreland Davis appointed sixteen citizens to the Virginia War History Commission with the charge to collect, edit, and publish source material concerning Virginia's participation in WWI. On September 10, 1919, the General Assembly appropriated $10,000 enabling the commission to discharge its duties. The commission received financial support through annual appropriations from 1919 to 1928. During that time seven volumes and several magazine supplements were published. Volumes 1–4 summarize source material compiled by the commission. The volumes include lists of soldiers; newspaper clippings; a guide to war letters, diaries and editorials; and a series of sketches of civilian war agencies. In addition, magazine supplements also provide lists of collected source material. Volumes 5–7 chronicle specific wartime activities in Virginia; they also include military unit histories and locality histories. These volumes describe the location of the communities, their resources, prewar conditions, economic conditions, and relief and institutional war work. See: Library of Virginia, *War Commission Histories and Narratives,* Record Group 66, Box 29.

[36] *The Hopewell Record,* February 11, 1918.

[37] Twelve of the buildings are noncontributory. See DHR file #116-5031. Downtown Hopewell Historic District was listed as a Virginia Landmark in June 2002 and listed on the National Register in September 2002.

[38] See Mary Mitchell Calos, Charlotte Easterling, and Ella Sue Rayburn, *Old City Point and Hopewell, The First 370 Years,* p. 10. Also see James H. Blankenship, Jr., "Notes on City Point, 1607–1865," typescript copy, n.d., n.p.

[39] Department of Historic Resources, file #116-5031, section 7, p. 4.

[40] For a compilation of laws pertaining to free and enslaved blacks in Virginia see *Black Laws of Virginia* by June Purcill Guild. See the 1939 *Guide to Prince George and Hopewell* by the Works Projects Administration. See The Meiklejohn Civil Liberties Institute Archives, Bancroft Library, University of California, Berkeley, *Civil Liberties Docket,* Volume X, No. 1, November 1964, 522, Va. 30 *Gilliam v. Hopewell School Board;* 522. Va. 35 *U.S. v. Prince George County Board of Education* and 522 and Va. 35a *Hill v. Prince George County School Board* Also see the oral interview of Patrice and Joy Gilliam, June 21, 2005.

[41] The Beacon Theatre was registered as a Virginia Landmark in June 2000 and registered as a National Historic Place in November 2000. See DHR file #116-0010.

[42] Tubize *Spinnerette*, January 1938, vol. 6, no. 8.

[43] Interview with Juanita Chambers, July 27, 2005. See also J. Douglas Smith, *Managing White Supremacy: Race, Politics and Citizenship in Jim Crow Virginia.*

[44] See Tubize *Spinnerette*, January 1930, vol. 5, no. 1, p. 12; December 1930, vol. 16, no. 12, p. 12, Appomattox Regional Library System, Hopewell.

[45] The committee members include the Reverend Curtis W. Harris, chairman; Herbert Bragg, vice chairman; Avon L. Miles, treasurer; Iris J. Walker, assistant treasurer; Belinda S. Piercy, secretary. A reception followed at the Beacon Theatre.

[46] An annex to the Hopewell Municipal Building was erected in 1957. Within the Municipal Building, facing the front doors, is a mural depicting the history of Hopewell created by Jay Bohannon in 1989. In 1994 a courthouse was built and all court facilities were moved into the new building.

[47] *Hopewell News,* May 15, 1942.

[48] *Hopewell News,* June 16, 1942.

[49] Members of the 1942 graduating class were: Helen Baumon, Roberta Cunningham, Ida O. Epps, Annie M. Robinson, Edith Watkins, Harry D. Hatcher, Howard Jones, Vernon Jackson, Willie Matthews, and Leroy Wyche. See *Hopewell News,* June 12, 1942.

[50] *Hopewell News*, October 29, 1940.

Above: *Note City Point on this early map. West of there is Broadway, now within the city limits, just east of the I-295 bridge. Detail from a map drawn by Joshua Fry and Peter Jefferson in 1751.*

Below: *A detail from an 1864–65 Confederate map of the area. The City Point Railroad took supplies from City Point to Federal troops besieging Petersburg, and River Road served as a conduit from the massive Union supply depot at Broadway. Detail from: "Preliminary map of a part of the south side of James River … made under the direction of Capt. A.H. Campbell, … Top. Dept. D.N.V. …"*

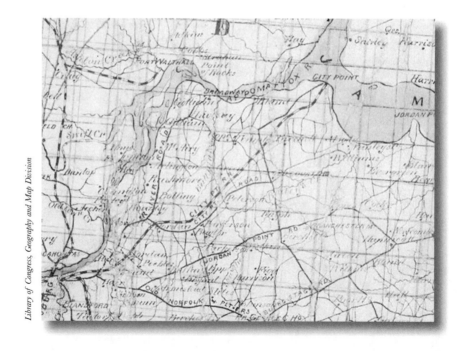

Section II

Introduction to Oral History Section

During the spring and summer of 2005 I conducted ten interviews. I visited churches and libraries and sat in private homes. It is one of the times in my life I will look back on with great joy. In many ways it was a bittersweet time. My mentor, Ed Toppin, had been deceased since December and I was still grieving. For the first time since I had entered the study of history I was without that listening ear and kind word. Yet, when I began to meet people and tell them what I was doing, I was met with open hearts.

The interviews are listed in alphabetical order. I debated about the order as some interviews lent themselves to a chronological retelling of Hopewell's history. In the end I decided that it was better for each interviewee to tell his or her own story and let the reader learn about Hopewell through the words of each individual.

Juanita Chambers recalled her youth in Hopewell during the Jim Crow era. She attended Virginia State College and became a teacher in Prince George County and Hopewell, dedicating herself to the education of young minds.

The Reverend Barbara Crosby also recalled her youth and a time when grandparents figured prominently in one's life, where church and school was an extended family. Her determination to overcome stereotypes enabled her to become a professional nurse, administrator, and entrepreneur.

The Reverend Rudolph Dunbar, originally from South Carolina, devoted nearly twenty-four years to military service. His perspectives on international relations during the mid-1950s and Hopewell during the 1960s and '70s sheds light on attitudes toward race.

Patrice and Joy Gilliam shared their family history as free blacks. They also recalled their experiences during the desegregation of schools in Hopewell. Joy Gilliam was a teacher who lost her job as a teacher. Her daughter, Patrice, was on the front line. She was the infant plaintiff in *Gilliam v. City of Hopewell School Board*, decided by the United States Supreme Court on November 15, 1965. She recalled those first painful days in the school building after she gained admission to previously all-white Patrick Copeland School.

The Reverend and Mrs. Curtis Harris recalled their early days as children, teenagers, a young married couple, and a public couple. As a civil rights activist, minister, councilman, and former mayor, Curtis Harris was well accustomed to being interviewed. We begin to see him from a different perspective through his wife. Mrs. Harris graciously shared her story, helping us understand what it's like to tend to the domestic world while helping as many as possible in a time of reaching to realize the dream of full equality.

Kenneth Harris, their son, shares his memories of growing up in Davisville. He also recalled marching during the civil rights movement, returning home after the Viet Nam War, and race relations in Hopewell.

Jeanie Langford has such a passion for Hopewell. As a librarian at Appomattox Regional she introduced me to the Tubize *Spinnerette*, numerous photographs, and so much more. Her interview speaks about the richness of local history.

Florine Martin is the consummate volunteer. Where there is a need she will fill it. As a wife, mother, and church member she has dedicated her life to helping others.

James Willcox worked as an engineer for Hercules for many years. As a native of South Carolina, he came to Hopewell during his early twenties. He recalled a moment during the civil rights movement when civil rights activists, led by Curtis Harris, and the Ku Klux Klan met on the steps of the Municipal Building.

Maza Wilson, known as "L'il Bit," is packed with power. Her work with youth in the field of recreation encourages them to learn sportsmanship and cooperation. Her own experiences as a worker at Fort Lee and as a karate student highlight the character of someone determined to help the next generation live better lives.

There are so many more I wish I could have interviewed. I did manage to interview by telephone former councilman and mayor James Patterson. He, too, recalled growing up in Davisville. Now he lives right at the edge of Hopewell. He quotes Proverbs 29:18 as one of his favorite passages from the Bible: "Where there is no vision the people will perish."

The interviews were recorded on tape and video and copies of each interview are deposited at the Appomattox Regional Library as well as the Curtis Harris Library in the Carter G. Woodson School. Halasz Reporting and Video transcribed the tapes and copies of the transcriptions have also been deposited in the libraries.

This is not a complete rendering of African American history in Hopewell, Virginia. It is a beginning. For every interview that has been completed here, there are others waiting to be heard.

Editorial Note

The excerpts included in this text have been reformatted, edited, and compiled for publication. Where an insertion is made, brackets [ ] are employed. Where a word was inaudible from the tape, it is so stated: (*inaudible*). Rarely are full interviews included; pre- and post-interview conversations are deleted as are specific sections per the interviewees' request. The words and the conversational tone are unchanged. Our interviews were very much relaxed and down-home in that sort of way where you just feel good to have this time together. If anything, an oral history project such as this illustrates the meaning of living history. The historian Carl Becker wrote, "The history that lies inert in unread books does no work in the world. The history that does work in the world, the history that influences the course of history, is living history, [a] pattern of remembered events."

Juanita Chambers, July 27, 2005

Courtesy of Carmela Hamm

On July 27, 2005, I interviewed Juanita Chambers at her home. She is a retired educator and administrator and a long-time member of the Hopewell School Board in addition to holding various other civic positions. Mrs. Chambers talks about her family background, education, segregation, and social changes in Hopewell during her lifetime. She remembered when Carter G. Woodson School was built near Davisville in the 1940s.

The headline on the front page of the *Hopewell News*, July 17, 1942, declared "Contract is Let for New Negro School." The city manager, W. Guy Ancell, was instructed to purchase from the Tubize Chatillon approximately 3.441 acres across from Davisville housing project at a cost of $500 per acre. Upon this site would be built a one-story, ten-classroom, fireproof building with a brick face and concrete block foundation. It was estimated that the building would cost $42,000.

JUANITA CHAMBERS: I am the granddaughter of Maggie and John-Thomas Briggs. As far as I know we were all Hopewellians. We lived on Arlington Road. My grandparents were born in this area. As far as we can remember … that's on my mother's side. They were living in Hopewell. I was raised on Arlington Road, my sisters and brother were all born there, with the exception of my oldest sister, who was born in Duquesne, Pennsylvania. My parents left here many years ago, and they returned in 1932, the year I was born, and returned to build a house on a plot of land that was left to them by my mother's father. In fact, he had six children, and he was able to leave each of his children enough land to build a home.

DR. LEE: What was his business?

JUANITA CHAMBERS: They tell me he ran a store, like a grocery store, and he also made bricks. They ran a brickyard. He was here when DuPont came to town, and he was by trade a surveyor and he surveyed for the coming of DuPont. When these people came to town, they were looking for people to work, and one of the interesting things that happened, as my mother said, that they wanted him to survey on Sunday. And of course, you know, he didn't ... work on Sunday; but he did do work. He went out and helped to survey. And he also made a business out of it, because on this tract of land that we lived on Arlington Road, he built bunkhouses, long houses, and had bunks, individual bunks where the men would come from different places. You will find this city is made up of people coming from everywhere, and they came in here to work at DuPont at this new plant. So he used that as a source of making money. Men would leave their wives and come to town and they would get a job, and then they would reside in the bunkhouse, and they would pay a fee for living there. So this is the same tract of land that he left to his children because eventually that was not proper anymore, you know, they brought their families in, and then they started sleeping in individual dwellings and places to live. So he was quite a gentleman.

DR. LEE: What kept you here?

JUANITA CHAMBERS: I was able to work. A job. I graduated from Carter Woodson High School.

DR. LEE: What year was that?

JUANITA CHAMBERS: 1949. And fortunately, I got the four-year scholarship to Virginia State, tuition fee paid only. So I rode the bus from Hopewell to Petersburg on Adams Street, and I walked to Virginia State College from Adams Street in the morning, and I walked coming back to Adams Street and caught the bus for four years. I had a brother, of course. Well he went to the Air Force and stayed for four years, and so he left that way. One

---

See next page. *By 1916 DuPont had installed a 7-plus-mile sewer system with 100,000-gallon disposal plant in Hopewell, for Mr. Eppes, from whom they had purchased land for the DuPont plant in 1912. As the commercial center in the downtown area developed, DuPont focused on simultaneous residential growth. The company built villages for its employees "to accommodate about 200 families of the higher class and 1000 of the working class." In addition there were to be "200 bachelors of the higher class and 400 of the working class." The company villages "A" and "B" welcomed the large influx of people from around the world. By 1915, there were twenty houses and a hotel in "A" village. A year later there were 140 houses, two hotels with a dining hall between them, a schoolhouse, a clubhouse, a railroad station, planted trees, and concrete roads and sidewalks. "B" Village began in March 1915 and by January 1, 1916, there were 60 permanent homes, 400 one-family temporary houses, 310 one-family apartment units, a schoolhouse, a welfare building, and plank walkways. Plans were underway to build a county jail to handle increasing incidents of rowdiness.*

"DuPont Powder Plant, City Point, VA" DuPont Hopewell Works provided substantial support in the World War I effort. The company was engaged in the manufacture of guncotton, an element of artillery ammunition.

sister tried to stay here and do clerical work in the school system and she finally left.

During my time, it wasn't much for women to do in this area if you weren't going to teach school. I became a schoolteacher in 1953.

DR. LEE: 1953, here in Hopewell?

JUANITA CHAMBERS: It was Hopewell. Hopewell … see, Hopewell and Prince George were combined. They had one superintendent. The superintendent was housed here in Hopewell. And so all of my time counts with Hopewell, but I actually taught in the county, Prince George County, for five years prior to coming here. I'll tell you the reason. When I graduated from high school … I mean from college, I was 20 years old. We had a principal in town, Mr. Epps. He was a very nice gentleman, and he was my high school principal. He told me it is not wise for you to come into the city and teach now. You are too young, because see, some of my peers and neighborhood friends were still in school. So he intervened and got me a job in Prince George. And I worked out there for five years. After five years he said, you are ready to come back. When I came back, the Carter Woodson that's over on Winston Churchill Drive now was opening. It was a new school being opened, first grade through high school. I came back into Hopewell, and I continued to teach, so I stayed as a teacher and a principal and as an administrator for 35 years.

DR. LEE: Okay. What are some of the changes that you have noticed in your time in the school system here?

JUANITA CHAMBERS: Too many to mention. However, with whatever changes that might come to mind I can still say that the same goal for education is to teach people how to survive. I told somebody recently, when they were saying, "my daddy didn't finish high school" or something. I said, but he's doing what education is supposed to do for you. Education has one main goal as far as I'm concerned and that's to teach you how to survive, and if you learn how to survive and live in the community and be a good citizen, then you are an educated person. That's why we go to school, to get those survival skills that we need for better living.

There were many, many changes. The racial thing, of course. When I started teaching it was all black everywhere. Of course, it is different now. We pretty well integrated it. I'll now talk a little bit more about the school board and my participation if you would like. Maybe not at this … not at this point because I was instrumental in helping to get this place, you know, kind of together. When I say get it together, I mean simply this, we have three elementary schools, one middle school, one high school. You don't have much choice. You don't have much choice here. We have the city so divided that you have to go to one of those three elementary schools depending on where you live. No issue at all about the middle school. [If] you [are] going to stay here, you are going to that school if you want public education. And one high school, because that wasn't always the case.

Tubize Spinnerette *Jan. 1929, v.4 #8 (pg. 5)*
Maude Langhorne Nelson Library, Hopewell

Solemn faces but happy hearts.

Tubize sponsored Christmas parties for the children of Hopewell. Here, the children are standing on the steps of the Carter G. Woodson Junior High School holding their gifts. Once inside the little boys would receive toy trains while little girls would get dolls, and all the children would have their pick of dogs, cats, books, and a variety of toys. During the party the children sang Christmas carols, recited poems, and made other Christmas presentations.

Some other changes, in facilities. The old black school was horrible. The first school that I worked, I taught in a Quonset hut.

DR. LEE: A what?

JUANITA CHAMBERS: A Quonset hut, a metal building. A metal building with a stove in there that you had to put wood or coal or something in it. I had never learned how to keep a coal stove burning. The children taught me more that first year than I had ever dreamed of, because I was in the rural area. They knew a lot of things about keeping that room warm; when to open the windows and when not to open the windows so we would be safe and what have you.

So it's been a lot of changes. Curriculum, a lot of curriculum changes. Of course, through my role and by being here so long I went from a teacher to supervisor of secondary education for the whole city. So I saw a lot of changes in curriculum. A lot of changes in basic human relations among people. I've been from the era when whites didn't speak to you nor recognize you or try to identify you differently from another black, to now when I go downtown and I meet people on the street, most of them know I am Mrs. Chambers. So that's been a great change and a desirable change.

DR. LEE: Okay. The school that you went to, your public school education …

JUANITA CHAMBERS: Public school was over in Davisville, over on Terminal Street.

DR. LEE: Was that Harry E. James or …

JUANITA CHAMBERS: It was Harry E. James, but see, it was Carter Woodson first.

All right, first, I started school at old Carter Woodson School behind the firehouse.

We all had to go there (blacks). That was about two, almost three miles that we'd walk to school. I started to school in the first grade. I could read when I got there. We didn't start school until six years old.

No kindergarten, I believe. After … they had a divided year, L and H; L the lower grade … lower of the grade, and H, the higher. So I was in first grade, 1 L. I could read. So they decided that I no longer had to stay in that first grade, and they put me in the second grade at the half year.

I guess I tell you, it's interesting how I learned to read. My parents were not educators. My mother finished school … finished her schooling in the seventh grade. She went to school in City Point. That was as high as that school went to … seventh grade. If they wanted to do anything else in education they had to go to Peabody; had to go to Petersburg, and you know how far Petersburg is from here.

So out of her family, only one, which was the youngest one of them, had the opportunity to go to Peabody; and he was the youngest, a man.

But back to Carter Woodson. I stayed there and at the end of that second grade they had built a school up here, up the hill, which was Arlington School. All of us on this side of town went to Arlington School, grades one through seven. A wood building, outside wood toilet, outside pump … you pumped … primed the pump with water, with a trough, it was like a pig's trough, and the principal was also a teacher. Arlington School had one to seven grades and that meant that it probably was seven teachers, and the principal was one of the seven teachers.

All right, so I stayed there until the spring of '45, 1945, and the school burned down. When the school burned down, they separated us and they spread us around anyplace they could find, basically to the churches. I had two sisters that went to school at Friendship Baptist Church on Arlington Road. I had a brother that went to school I believe at the House of Prayer. I was in the seventh grade, and I went to school in the community center in Davisville. It's a little building in Davisville off of Terminal Street; and the teacher was the principal. See, the seventh grade teacher was always the principal. I finished my last year of elementary school there. I was there just a few months, because it was in the spring, I would say about the first of March because we were planning for a May Day program coming up. And so I only went from March until June, and then school closed. Then next year, just across the street, I started in September 1945, at Carter Woodson High School.

Now, my brothers and sisters stayed in the churches two to three years before they could get that school (Arlington School) built again. It was ridiculous, because they were in the main sanctuary of the churches and, you know, children running all over the place. They were damaging the inside, not intentionally, and ... because the churches agreed to take them just on a temporary basis to finish out the school year, it caused their parents to get together in groups and just go down and demand that we get another school.

DR. LEE: To city council?

JUANITA CHAMBERS: Well, they were at that time ... I don't know. They might have gone to city council, but I could hear around the house, I could hear my father saying, I'm going to see the superintendent. So I would think they were negotiating more with the school board than downtown, but you know, of course they are a unit, they worked together, but I was so young I didn't know really what was going on. But finally they rebuilt Arlington School.

And when they did that, they shifted several times with that. They cut Arlington School back to one through five, and then ... well, let's put it this way, it took a long time. Arlington School stayed one through seven for a long time, but after they built Carter Woodson, and remember Carter Woodson opened in '58, they shifted Arlington School to one through five, and then they housed all of the black, I'm talking about the black kids at Carter Woodson. So when you finished Arlington School in the fifth grade, then you came to Carter Woodson, and then Carter Woodson also housed a lower grade because, you remember, it was another population over in the Davisville area, and it was another place called Georgia Hill, and another place over there, DuPont City, and every little neighborhood had its own names. I don't know where all these names came from, but the students came to Carter Woodson. If you were black you came to Carter Woodson.

DR. LEE: Do you remember when Arlington Road School burned? Was it Arlington Road?

JUANITA CHAMBERS: No. Just Arlington, Arlington School. 1945.

DR. LEE: And then Carter G. Woodson opened in 1958?

JUANITA CHAMBERS: The Carter Woodson that's on Winston Churchill Drive ... now, it's Carter Woodson ... I left a big piece out. In 1941 ... now, I'm not sure, it might be '40 or '41. In 1941, then came the housing project, the housing project in Davisville. When they did that they put that school across the street from the housing project, down the street from Reverend Harris. I don't know whether you have been over there or not. They put that school there. That then became one through high school. Mind you, that's eleventh grade. Now, we were cheated a whole year out of school because the other school system was running one through twelve. We were running one through eleven. And they closed up this big, old, raggedy building behind the firehouse, moved everybody into Davisville that was in high school.

Now, let's just get this … let's smooth this out. Let's make it make sense. The first Arlington school was put up there around 1941, so was the Davisville School 1941. They shipped all of the elementary students in that area to the new Carter Woodson. Everybody in the whole city that was from eighth grade through eleventh grade had to go to Carter Woodson in Davisville. This school (Arlington Elementary) was built over here to house one through seven on this side of town. You understand me?

DR. LEE: Yes.

JUANITA CHAMBERS: Okay, so all that did, the project was coming, the new school was coming and it didn't have a gym. It only had one long building with classrooms on the hall. So when we went to the eighth grade … now, it was … we were small, small. Big numbers for the population in elementary school. They get to high school, the boys could get on at the plant. They could drop out of high school, know somebody at the plant, no entrance exam, nothing like that, and most of them were doing menial work, custodial work and what have you, and they could drop out in the eighth grade or ninth grade, and most of them, you know, were behind anyway. It wasn't anything to retain kids then. You had no remediation, no nothing like that. And they would drop out of school and go to the plant. And you would find that you had some … I have some friends in their early fifties that have been at the plant thirty-eight years almost. I mean, they went that early.

And so the enrollment continuously … continued to decrease, decrease. What made me think of that, we had like a block, everybody was in the eighth grade. You go together for the English, you go together for the math, you go together for your science, you go together for everything.

Then they decided they would bring in home economics, and for some reason they thought that that was an ideal vocational skill for black people. And they removed the old church from behind the old raggedy Carter Woodson School and brought it over to Davisville, so it's the center building in there. If you have gone over there you see the old gym building …

DR. LEE: … it's a mattress factory.

JUANITA CHAMBERS: Yes. Yes. And then it's another building, I don't know what they use it for, and the long building. Now, they didn't have the gym building when I was there. That gym building didn't come onboard until possibly 1951, I would say

'50 or '51. I left there in 1949 and they hadn't started building it. But they built it right after I left.

So the only elective course we had, if you want to call it, was to take home economics, I guess. No typing. No typing whatsoever. I work at the computer right now, and I do my banking and do all my correspondence and keep up with everything on the computer and I don't know the keyboard. The reason I don't know the keyboard is because we had no typing. There was one typewriter in that school. This is a school from the first grade through the eleventh grade, and that typewriter was in the principal's office,

Courtesy of Carmela Hamm

and my sister was the secretary. So I never did (learn the keyboard) … and then I'm a science major, and I taught chemistry, biology, and general science, so when you go to Virginia State, and you are a science major, you don't have time to take typing. You stay in the lab. So I mean, that's just been my life. And I could have done it along the way, but I find that I can do the computer, I know where the keys are, and it doesn't matter where my fingers are so I mean, I do it.

DR. LEE: Now, when you were coming up everything was segregated?

JUANITA CHAMBERS: Everything.

DR. LEE: Were you aware of the difference …

JUANITA CHAMBERS: Yes.

DR. LEE: … between blacks and whites …

JUANITA CHAMBERS: Yeah. Yeah.

DR. LEE: … the accommodations?

JUANITA CHAMBERS: All my life I have known that. I have known that. I guess … I hear a lot of people say they weren't aware. We were aware. And I would imagine this might have been a little more prevalent in my home because, I mentioned earlier, and my parents left here and went to Duquesne, Pennsylvania, in the Pittsburgh area. Now, that's another part of the story. The steel mills opened up up there, and my daddy was from Dinwiddie and my uncle owned the same plot of land

I mentioned, you know, before, my uncle had a barbershop in there, and my daddy and three of his brothers left the rural area of Dinwiddie and came to Hopewell to be barbers in my mother's brother's barbershop, and that is where my mother met my father.

And then when a lot of black people started going to the Pittsburgh area to work in the steel mill, my daddy left. He decided he didn't want to be a barber, he was going to work in the steel mill, and he went to Pennsylvania. And my mother just followed him up there. They were courting. And they got married, and they remained in Duquesne for sixteen years. My mother went up and lived on the lot. If you don't know what live on the lot means, it means simply this: When she went up there she knew some other people and worked for white people. And she got a job working for the Carnegies. You know the Carnegie Library? She lived and worked for the Carnegies.

And I'm back to the white/black thing. She worked for the Carnegies. And she learned a lot of social graces. Her reading and writing skills were excellent. I don't know what they taught her at one through seven, but her reading/writing skills were perfect. And she worked for them and learned a lot of social graces, a lot of things.

And when she returned home she came home because Depression came, and like when she came home, she was pregnant with me. Depression came. They start laying off people, you know, in the steel mill. She and my daddy had bought a home. They sold the home. She had what people call now a yard sale, and she sold all of the furniture and she came home with one little girl, almost four, carrying me, and the only thing she shipped home was a trunk and a sewing machine.

Well, she was ahead of the game. She was ahead of the game. They had a Metropolitan insurance policy for $2,000. They cashed it and came home and built that house down on Arlington Road, and you should see it, for $900, and we never had a house payment. So this was smart. This was smart.

And so having had the experience of the so-called integration in the city, she kept us forever warned, you are here, you are in the South, and you are a Negro. Not black. You are a Negro. Black just come on the scene here lately. You are Negro, so behave yourself, you got to ride the bus, go to the back of the bus. Sit back there, because if you didn't, you go to jail. And no one wants to go to jail. I don't want you to go to jail. So we were very, very aware of who we are, but still she taught us how to be gracious and to remember that you might be a Negro, but you got to be a smart one. So, yes, I was always aware, always aware of who I am.

DR. LEE: What are some of the places that you all could go here?

JUANITA CHAMBERS: Oh, church. Church. The center of our lives was the church. That was the center, the church. We went to the church. Church services, Sunday school, regular service. What was it … BYPU something, but anyway, something they had for young people.

DR. LEE: Youth?

JUANITA CHAMBERS: Youth something, yeah. In the evening on Sunday. Bible class on Wednesday. But it was a thing to that, too. It was an advantage. That was when you could see your boyfriend. So we used church to our advantage. Now, the Beacon Theatre was there. And I have a thing about that Beacon Theatre. We had a retreat down there the week before last; now, the school board did. That was the second time I'd ever been there. I went there when we had the sensitivity … sensitivity … well, anyway … training. We had a lot of training, you know, getting the black/white relationships and what have you when we did integrate, and we went there to see some movie that I guess it was supposed to tell us how we can survive, you know, in a different culture or something. But the Beacon Theatre was open, but it had a balcony to it, and momma said her children couldn't go down there and sit in the balcony. Never, never, never go sit in the balcony, so we weren't allowed to go to the Beacon Theatre but other children did go. They could go, you know, and buy the ticket and go … oh, shoot, momma called it the peanut gallery. Now, no one is going to go and sit in the peanut gallery. And I didn't ever go.

And when this project started out I have always had an unusual feeling about it, but I had to let the baggage go, and go on and contribute and do what I had to do about the Beacon Theatre. I had to let the baggage go sometimes, but I never had a very good feeling about the Beacon Theatre because we weren't allowed to go see the movies. And let's see, where else did we go?

DR. LEE: Where did you go see movies?

JUANITA CHAMBERS: Petersburg. And the market … of course marketing hadn't come about, the word "marketing," but they did a wonderful job with the Petersburg situation. When you buy a ticket, a round-trip ticket, go to Petersburg and come back, you got a movie ticket on certain days, especially on the weekend. So we wanted to go to the movie … they had three movies in Petersburg. They had … what was it … Barney Theater, the Gem Theater and Idlehour, I guess … Idlehour I guess that's what it was. And you could go to either of these movies with this ticket that you would get with your regular ticket going to Petersburg.

And I remember it used to be thirty-five cents. Thirty-five cents got you to Petersburg, back, and you had the movie, movie ticket.

DR. LEE: So a round-trip ticket…

JUANITA CHAMBERS: …and the movie ticket was thirty-five cents. But thirty-five cents was difficult to get, now. It was difficult to get thirty-five cents. But we could go to Petersburg and come back, and we went on Sunday. You know, sometimes after we go to church, if you get up and go to Sunday school, go to church, you might get permission to go to the movie.

And I left out something there. My … the sister that's older than I am, I'm the second child, she's four years older than I am, and when I was talking about this reading and going to school, I would imagine that I learned how to read from her.

DR. LEE: Okay. And so all of you all grew up with this sense you were living in a segregated society but you were no less than anybody else?

JUANITA CHAMBERS: Oh, yes. We knew that. And a proud family, too.

DR. LEE: Other places like Jones Lake or …

JUANITA CHAMBERS: Yeah. We … when you could, when you could get out there you go out there, but most the time that I went, it would be like church activity, you know, they would have church bus and we go out there to Jones Lake. And we went to the beach in Norfolk once a year. That was always a big time, you know. Tyler's Beach, Sea View Beach. Oh, I don't remember all of them. Tyler's, Sea View …

DR. LEE: Bay Shore?

JUANITA CHAMBERS: Bay Shore, yeah, that's it. Bay Shore. And then we had relatives. Let's see. I had an aunt in Hampton, and so we used to get to Bay Shore a lot. And let's see. I don't know. We went to the movies. It just wasn't too much to do.

DR. LEE: Playground?

JUANITA CHAMBERS: Playground. Well, see, the playground to me, I worked on a playground. I worked on a playground. I worked on a playground for, I don't know, it might have been while I was in college, but every year, just about, while I was in college I went to Philadelphia to work; had aunts in Philadelphia, so all during the school year I would go, you know, when the kids go home, I'd go to Philadelphia. …

But back to the playground. Somewhere in there, either latter part of high school, somewhere in there I worked playground, I worked South B Village and City Point. That was for the city. They had a recreation department, and so I just sat on the playground, you know, in the heat, and we had a box we locked, and so we would do things with the kids.

Now, that is something that might be noted here that's interesting. I believe we had more togetherness with the recreation department than any other place. We had a lady, and she was like my boss, Mrs. Ida Cooke, and Ida had come here from York, Pennsylvania. And she was the first (black) person that I had been aware of to do that type of work, you know, for the city, and she retired from the city, from that community center. And Ida came in, and we really would go to another white playground, and have activities or they'd come over to our place, we would have a square dance. And we did arts and crafts and all that stuff.

And on Monday, we would go for staff meetings, and we met with the white folks for the staff meeting. And that is … it's been little note about that, but it was one of those things that just happened, like we had like a jamboree over at the ballpark, and each playground set up, and we had like … well, I don't know, Arlington didn't have one then I think … might have been three areas that were black, but many more, you know, that were white operating under the recreation center, and we actually had a jamboree. Everybody … because I know my kids they did an Indian village. They did a teepee, and they made a covered wagon. And the parents helped, and you know, the parents didn't have anything to do, they'd come out there, you know, and they would help. So that was a mild kind of integration and one that was really worthwhile. And so I did that. I was working, though. Working. But when I was younger (preteen), there was no such thing as a playground.

DR. LEE: So are we looking at the early fifties?

JUANITA CHAMBERS: You are looking at the early fifties.

DR. LEE: Let me go back to something, you talked about work in Philadelphia. Had you thought about working here in Hopewell, or could you make more money in Philadelphia? Is that the reason you went there, aside from the fact …

JUANITA CHAMBERS: No choice to work. Nowhere to work. Nowhere to work. I mean, it's … this was pennies at the recreation center. So it definitely was pennies there. See, the money was better. More pennies. Yeah, it was nothing for us to leave home and go to the beach, work for the beach … you know, work at the beach for the summer or something.

Everybody was always looking for somewhere to go so they could make, you know, some money, but there was no work here, not for … especially for a girl. And the boys that went into the plant, they went into the plant for permanent jobs. They didn't go in the plant for temp jobs, so it was no … I tried working at the cleaners, and things like that. I tried everything, you know. I've been working all my life. In fact, I've been working since I was nine years old. It was a lady up the street that made clothes, and in the evening I'd come home and I'd go up there and sew with her, and that's my hidden talent. I sew. And I did that as a part-time job while I was teaching, and for years at night I taught ladies how to sew. And my husband and I worked five jobs. But that's not part of the history.

DR. LEE: Did you notice segregation there in Philadelphia or was it integrated?

JUANITA CHAMBERS: It was still there … it was there. The only difference was … for me, that I saw, was transportation. You could get on the EL or the sub or ride the bus and sit down anywhere you want, but in most cases, not all, in most cases you had a concentration of black people in certain areas that lived in certain areas, you know. There were spots here and there, but when I went there I didn't … I didn't feel much different. The only thing I really recognized was that I was … I could ride the bus or public transportation. Maybe I wasn't in the right area, but I didn't stay in the same place every time I went, because I had an uncle and three aunts there, and they graciously moved me from one house to the next house. In other words, I could stay here one summer, and the next summer you come you had to go to another house to stay. And when you come to visit, then you go around and they would call around and somebody would fix dinner, and you know, would all get together. And so I didn't see much difference, but you got to remember I was not there all the winter. I didn't go to school there. And I'm just there to work, and if you work in the summer, that's all you can do is get up in the morning and get a ride, transportation to work, and then come back. And that was just about the size of the activity. Nothing out of the ordinary.

DR. LEE: Were the restaurants integrated?

JUANITA CHAMBERS: Yes. Yes. Anybody could go in there. Yeah. Anybody could come in.

DR. LEE: And blacks were not relegated to a specific area of the restaurant?

JUANITA CHAMBERS: No. No. No. No. It was … yeah, I worked down near Market Street, down in the city hall, and the population down there working mostly was white and, you know, it was kind of weird to see us come in, but that's where I worked.

DR. LEE: And so the summers were spent there during college. When you graduated from Virginia State …

JUANITA CHAMBERS: '53.

DR. LEE: '53, just before *Brown versus Board of Education*?

JUANITA CHAMBERS: Yeah.

Dr. Lee: What was the feeling like here in Hopewell regarding changes, social relations, blacks and whites mingling?

Juanita Chambers: Well, let's see. We … it didn't get here on time. You know, it came like in 1954 but it took a long time to get to Hopewell. Well, the first … maybe I should say when Carter Woodson was built, it was built because of pressure, pressure, separate but equal, separate but equal. And they realized I think … they, they the school board, they the city council, they the administrators in the city, they realized they had a problem after that decision, and so they tried to cling on to separate but equal. And as a result, Carter Woodson was built.

And they put the campus-style school there, and we had a lot of issues going. The regional plan had an auditorium, and so we reviewed the project. They didn't have enough money to build the auditorium, so it took another group of people to organize and go in and demand the auditorium. Demand the auditorium. And they got the auditorium.

And the building was not built as solid as it needed to be, and it was a campus style, and so that's why, you know, since I'm on the school board, we'll get to that, on the school board, it was so important that we tied the old building together and make an adequate structure. And as a result, that's what you have there on Winston Churchill Drive there now. But that took years to do.

But I'm saying that that was the main issue. Hopewell tried to get to where they could cling … we had separate and equal facilities. They did the same thing in the county. The first school was like old Disputanta Training School with a red tin Quonset hut, as I told you, so they built in 1957, they built J. E. J. Moore School, which is the older one, right at [Route] 460.

… It is named after an old black principal that had been at the old school for years. And I was there teaching and so I had seniors, I had seniors that year, and so …

Dr. Lee: What years were you there?

Juanita Chambers: Oh, let me see. I stayed … we came in that school in 1956, 1956, and so they named the school after him. And so my class did the first yearbook, the very first yearbook that was done at that school, and it was for the Class of 1957. And by the way, Friday night, we're having a class reunion, too, at the Elks Club. But that class … I followed that class from eighth grade through 11th grade, and we had the same homeroom. In other words … that's nice, when you got good kids, and I did have good kids, but if you got bad kids, it's not nice, it's not nice. So it was forty-five of those kids in that class and do you know, just about every one of them have done so well, and so that, that's the main thing after '54. All right. When that didn't work, they started … I wish I could explain. I can't get it together, because Reverend Harris and his group and his organization …

DR. LEE: Is this the SCLC or NAACP?

JUANITA CHAMBERS: I don't know. I don't know whether it was SCLC or the NAACP, but you know, the group … they are the same people in this neighborhood. If you belong to one, you belong to all.

But anyway, they started off by putting about, I guess, around fifteen kids or something like that at the old Hopewell High School. And some of them couldn't cut it. They had to come back. And so I guess they left … I don't know how many. Reverend Harris could tell you exactly, but around ten or less, and they went up there, and they were the good students, and they did fine, they did excellent as far as academics are concerned, but they had hard times. All right.

Like the next year, I think they took … I don't know, ninth graders, they took them … but in other words, took about four or five years to get this little handful of kids in the high school integrated into the school system. And finally the last year they said, those that want to go, go. And it didn't make sense because they could have done it like this haste. When school ends and it starts the next year, well all of those move together. So we were left with … I think the last class didn't get up there, honest, I might be wrong, I don't think that last class got away until 1968.

DR. LEE: So it started about 1963?

JUANITA CHAMBERS: I don't know. I don't really know, but it took … yeah, about that time, or '64 or something. It just took little bits, and little bits, and little bits like that, and then finally that last class left us. And at that time then we got switched around.

DR. LEE: The teachers?

JUANITA CHAMBERS: The teachers. I was teaching then. Yeah. We got switched around and we went everywhere. Some went to the high school. Some went to Mallonee, which they then developed, they turned Mallonee into junior high. I believe the high school must have opened around '64. You know, they built the high school, the one on Mesa Drive. Yeah. Yeah. High school. And I think the kids went out there for the first time in '64.

I left the … I didn't leave Carter Woodson even though the high school was gone, I stayed there for a while. I didn't leave Carter Woodson until maybe 1971, around in about '71. So maybe I should say that it really took the teachers and everything to '71 to really get spread out. And my husband was different. He's one of the first persons to teach in the integrated school.

DR. LEE: What was his name?

JUANITA CHAMBERS: Wilson Chambers Jr. And it's an issue. You got four, five people that lay claim on that title. When we were in the all-black school, you know, the state turned over the driver education to the schools, and the state paid for the driver ed. And he happened to have been one of those persons that had come out of the military, Korean War, and he came out in October, and from October until the next school year he had to find something to do, and he went to school at A&T. He's from Greensboro, North Carolina, however. And he went to A&T to wait until school time to open to get his first teaching job. And he got a certification in driver ed. And I don't know whether he had a hunch about it or what. I don't know what made him do that, because I didn't know him at that time. And so when the state says that you are going to teach driver's ed, he was ready. So he took … he taught driver's ed for them thirteen years part-time. Part-time.

So this is where I am going. He did it like one school year. At the end of that school year they wanted to continue that because in the summer school, summer school was at Mallonee, the building up by the school

Below: *James E. Mallonee School, on Curt Teich & Co. postcard, postmarked in Hopewell in 1937.*

From collection of Bob and Susan Sheppard

board office. They put him on the summer school's staff and he taught driver ed. That's why I am laying claim on the first black teacher to go into the system. However, right after then, right after then, they ... I think it was two of them, a lady that taught French, and Chambers, sent one to Mallonee and sent Chambers to the high school, not full-time, sent him up as a social studies teacher and sent him up there to do social studies for two periods in the morning, and then he'd come back to Carter Woodson and do the rest of his teaching day. Now, in between there, in shifting around people, they sent three or four other people into the other schools, into the other schools, and that is the confusion. It is not a confusion, but that's why we can't explain it, because they never got together and said exactly who went first into the regular school, but he went first by going into that summer school. Do you understand me?

DR. LEE: Yes.

JUANITA CHAMBERS: And so he did that, and that was a good source of income, because, see, that was being paid for by the state and he did that as part-time. By the way, he was an administrator in the area, too, for many years.

DR. LEE: Administrator in public schools?

JUANITA CHAMBERS: Public school here in Hopewell, uh-huh.

DR. LEE: In Hopewell, not Prince George, but Hopewell?

JUANITA CHAMBERS: Well, that's how I met him, when I was at Moore. He came to teach in 1957. He came to teach, 1957. And let's see, we courted from whatever time school opened, and when July came, we were married, and we stayed married forty-six years. He just died one year ago. One year this past 18th of July. Forty-six years. ...

DR. LEE: [He] went to AT&T?

JUANITA CHAMBERS: No. He graduated from Shaw, in Raleigh.

DR. LEE: Shaw, yeah, I have heard of it.

JUANITA CHAMBERS: Full football scholarship.

DR. LEE: How did he end up here in Hopewell?

JUANITA CHAMBERS: Well, he told me that was when he came out of the service. He got out of the service in '56, and he told me just some friends told him that, you know, "just plot a plan," and this area was one he applied in, and he came up here to Prince George, and he got hired.

He still was hired by the same superintendent that was in Hopewell, do you understand, because this was Hopewell, Petersburg ... I mean, Prince George, Hopewell schools. And he stayed there one year, and he didn't like it. He left, and went back to Greensboro, North Carolina, and stayed two ...

two years, I think, and then he came back here and, you know, stayed for years, maybe twenty-eight years in the system. But I think he went a year … but now, he has over a period of years, thirty-two years' worth of … he had thirty years' worth of, you know, educational experience. Well, I think he went downtown in the administration in 1974, I believe, he went down there to work as director of Student Services.

. . .

DR. LEE: Black and white at that time?

JUANITA CHAMBERS: Yeah. … It was black and white.

DR. LEE: And when you went into administration, what was your …

JUANITA CHAMBERS: Principal first.

DR. LEE: Principal. Where?

JUANITA CHAMBERS: Hopewell Occupational Work Center. Now, where was the Hopewell Occupational Work Center? Right there where the old Carter Woodson was.

. . .

[V]ocational education got to be a push like it is right now, and so I went over there and I stayed over there fourteen years and ran that.

DR. LEE: When did you first go over there?

JUANITA CHAMBERS: '72. I believe '72. And I stayed there until '86. I am telling you, I don't know what I'm doing with these dates. That's why I said this is just as I can remember.

DR. LEE: Okay.

JUANITA CHAMBERS: Yeah, I think from '72 until '86. Then when I left there, I went down to the administrative building and I was supervisor of Secondary Education.

DR. LEE: And how long … '86 until …

JUANITA CHAMBERS: '88 I retired. Both of us retired together in 1988. Same time, same service.

DR. LEE: What are your hopes for Hopewell?

JUANITA CHAMBERS: I was reading the paper a little while ago. We need development of the business area in Hopewell. We need revenue, tax revenue, more homes to be built, especially now that, you know, for the involvement in BRAK [Base Realignment at Fort Lee], you know, around 7,000 folks will be coming here, some of them are already coming I think. And people're going to be walking the streets trying to find living quarters. We need more homes.

I believe the city is planning and going in the right direction, and maybe it will all come together one day, but we have a lot of public housing in this city, and it was needed then to have it, but we are landlocked by the rivers, and we weren't successful about annexing Prince George and so we can't look forward to getting any territory that way, so we [are] really landlocked, but we need to use the resources that we have now in a much better way. We still have vacant lots, and areas in the city that's all grown up, and we have some land over by the plants and things that we need to negotiate in getting in here so that we can have more building, and we need to build quality homes, quality homes.

We made some mistakes in the city by building … I don't know what they might call them … they might be … call them affordable homes. Some of those are built, and they are very nice, and then some of these things they are putting up, I don't think council should approve. I don't think they should approve that type building. So with that, we can get some revenue in the city, and when we get revenue in the city, then it means that the schools can have more money for education and also the other needed … especially the police force and social services and all these other things that they have to take care of. But that's what we need.

I think it is coming together. I have not lost hope, but we see a few new things coming up, so that's a good thing.

DR. LEE: You've been on the school board for how many years?

JUANITA CHAMBERS: Sixteen years. This is my seventeenth year.

DR. LEE: And what's the reason you stayed on it?

JUANITA CHAMBERS: Because I know about schools, and that is a fact. I've been doing this fifty-two years. And I think that that age is not a barrier with me. I think that when you stay mentally alert, and you take care of your health, it's no reason to stop if you feel like you are doing a job that needs to be done. I like giving services, and that's why I stay on the school board. I have three years now left, and of course I have said this over, and over, and over again, when the three years up, I'm going to stop. I have to have something to do, and why not do something that I know how to do.

DR. LEE: I know that Hopewell residents really benefit from the experience that you have, particularly in the school system. How would you say your involvement impacts the lives of children?

JUANITA CHAMBERS: It has to have its impact because I live in a community of my former students. I got them all around. My husband stayed in the hospital for a long time. When I would go down to John Randolph Hospital, and it is just amazing, I would have them down there (in the hospital room) from food service to healthcare. Mrs. Cooper runs 2B, she supervises it. And they are all over the hospital, they are nurses, they are doing all of the different jobs in the hospital. The head … the person that runs the whole maintenance crew, it's a white-collar job, is one of my students.

I look all around, I have two over here, and living behind me and all around. And so I feel that they have been successful and I feel like I had a part in it.

The Reverend Barbara Crosby, September 3, 2005

Courtesy of Carmela Hamm

The Reverend Barbara Crosby was interviewed at her church on September 3, 2005. She recalls growing up in Hopewell as well as the interconnectedness between family, church, school, and community.

DR. LEE: And where did you live in Hopewell?

REVEREND CROSBY: On Wakefield Street. Wakefield Street is still there. The house I was born in my mother is living in now. And my grandparents had it, and then my mother has it, and it's part of the family now.

DR. LEE: What's that section called?

REVEREND CROSBY: Arlington Heights.

...

DR. LEE: All right. What are your earliest memories of growing up in Arlington Heights?

REVEREND CROSBY: Earliest? I can remember that I lived with my grandparents. My grandparents raised me on Wakefield Street right here in Arlington Heights, and both sets of grandparents were next door, so I had my father's people next door and my mother's people next door, and I ran from house to house. And I was from house to house, and they took care of me, and I just remembered a happy time. I remembered my grandmother would take all of the furniture out of the house and put it on the porch and we had to clean every Saturday, a spotless house, you know. And we waxed the floors. You know, had linoleum on the floor, and we would wax the floors, and we would do a dance, so we used to do ... the ladies danced. And when I became a teenager, I was a really good dancer. I learned it from my mom cleaning house and waxing the floors.

We put that paste wax on the floor, and then when it dried, you had to go and, you know, you had to either do it with your hands ...

Dr. Lee: Rub it in.

Reverend Crosby: ... or we were young enough to do it with our feet, you know.

Dr. Lee: Okay.

Reverend Crosby: So that was a happy time.

Dr. Lee: How many brothers and sisters did you have?

Reverend Crosby: It's five of us. I have ... my oldest sister, Mary Lewis, I mean, she was well known. Nice, pretty girl, long hair. And she was very popular. I'm saying that. And she was older, two years older than I. She has passed now. We lost her. She was born in, you know, it was about '40 or '41, November of '41. And ...

Dr. Lee: And then it was you?

Reverend Crosby: And then, yes. I was the next one. And then my mother remarried, or married to Isaiah Grant, you know, prominent family in the community. They used to live in the house next to Mt. Carmel.

     ...

That the family was there. And she had three children by him. He has passed. Emily Grant, Calvin Grant, and Isaiah Grant. And they are still around.

Dr. Lee: And where did you go to school?

Reverend Crosby: I went to Carter G. Woodson.

Dr. Lee: Did you go to the one ...

Reverend Crosby: Arlington ...

Dr. Lee: ... over by the old fire station, behind the fire station?

Reverend Crosby: I started out there like ... somewhat like the eighth grade I went over there, and then the school was completed the next year and I came here.
     ... Came to ...

Dr. Lee: The new one?

Reverend Crosby: Winston Churchill. Yeah, the new one. And I graduated from there.

Dr. Lee: What year did you graduate?

Reverend Crosby: '0 ... I was ... '61. 1961.

Carter G. Woodson School

DR. LEE: What are your memories of Carter G. Woodson?

REVEREND CROSBY: Mr. Thomas, if I would think of a person it would center around him. Mr. Carter was assistant principal during that time, and he was a friend of my family. My grandparents and … his parents and my grandparents were real good friends, and so I knew of him, you know, let's say in the community as well he lived in. And I believe … he tried to keep me straight, per se, so he kind of looked out for me and every time I got in trouble, you know, he would be there, and chastise me, you know, and keep me going, you know, even after my parents or my grandparents died, you know, he was still around.

DR. LEE: Would you say he was a favorite?

REVEREND CROSBY: I think he was a … I looked up to him as … not as a teacher. He wasn't a teacher. He was the assistant principal, and he ran … you know, walked around (*inaudible*). It's fine memories of him being there, I guess as a disciplinarian more than … and encouraged me, but … he encouraged me a lot, you know, talking to me and just stuck with me, you know.

DR. LEE: What were your dreams and hopes at that time for yourself?

REVEREND CROSBY: I think probably getting out of school, getting out of high school was the biggest thing. And I think that around about the time I guess the last year you began to think, what are you going to do, I thought about being a mortician. I don't know, for some reason I wanted to be in business for myself, even during that time, I wanted to be a mortician. But I had some prerequisites to get, you know, that I didn't have, the school didn't provide me. I guess they said just general courses, get out as fast as you can. I think they kind of put me on the track of not being able to go into the sciences so, you know, and the math that some people had. And I don't think it was too much of a push during those days for us to go into like medical school and, you know, having all the chemistries and, you know, and trigonometries and all that, you know, they didn't require that. So I just took general courses. I got ... it was predicted for me that I would be blessed if I got a secretarial job somewhere or something like that. That's the impression I got.

DR. LEE: Was the school segregated at that time, in Hopewell ...

REVEREND CROSBY: Yes.

DR. LEE: ... and in school?

REVEREND CROSBY: Yes. Yes.

DR. LEE: So it was all black?

REVEREND CROSBY: All black.

DR. LEE: Was anyone really encouraged to go to college or to pursue anything out of the ordinary?

REVEREND CROSBY: That would be just the servant role I call it. Yes, I believe there were a few families of achievers in the community. I think they encouraged them to go forward, but the average person, we were like average, you know, average family, not educated, you know, first one I believe ... I'm thinking right off now, first one to finish high school, I was, you know, in the immediate family, anyway. My parents ... my mother went to the tenth grade. My dad, about ninth, even though he was really brilliant, you know. You know, I think that it went by families as far as encouragement, who would do well.

DR. LEE: Okay.

REVEREND CROSBY: Like the superlatives in the high school, and the yearbook, you know, they predict what families are going to do well. And I'll be honest with you, we had a color thing going among the black people, you know. It seemed to me that, you know, if you were lighter, you were expected to get further than if you were dark.

DR. LEE: Okay.

REVEREND CROSBY: You know, and if you were light with nice hair, you were expected to get further, you know. So the more you were like white, I said ... these are my opinions, okay, I want to bring that to you ... the way I felt, you know, so it just seemed they were the ones that were more, you know, encouraged to do ... to go on forward, become teacher ... to become a teacher was a big encouragement, and something that we could achieve, at least that's what they felt like as, you know, a career. Secretarial work, or a good job in the plant, you know, something like this was okay.

So we had a lot of people, young people getting out of high school getting into plants, and the few that were able to get grants or to go on kind of left the city almost.

DR. LEE: It's interesting that you should mention that color issue because in fact history does bear out that those with lighter skin and long hair generally were encouraged to really push and reach for that American dream.

REVEREND CROSBY: Yes.

DR. LEE: And they were like part of this ideal.

REVEREND CROSBY: Yes.

DR. LEE: Would you say that the city had some of that color issue going on as far as residential settings, like light people lived in one particular area or went to a particular church or …

REVEREND CROSBY: You saw a bit of that, you know. It wasn't as bad as I heard talk of, and it was … but it was acceptable, I mean, you know, it was a fact happening, but I don't know how overt it was, you know, current I should say, in everybody's sight, but if you really stopped to think about it, you know, that's what happened. If you were light, you know, your opportunities … you had better housing, better, you know … the white people treated you better.

Now, my sister that was older than I, two years older than I, she was light, and had long hair, and she was accepted by inner … you know, the race, the black race, she was accepted, and I think it spoiled her to the point that she didn't achieve because they gave her so much without work. And I found that everything I got I had to work for it, and I also had to work against negative feedback, you know, like some people say, oh, she's not going to be anything, you know, she's not going to do anything, so they wouldn't even try to … that's within, you know, our community or … she's not going to be anything.

DR. LEE: When did you first notice that?

REVEREND CROSBY: '78, '9, somewhere even that far back. Why I can say that is because my grandmother died when I was thirteen, and before that I can remember coming home to her crying about negative conversations, you know, talking to me, and the difference between my sister and I. And I used to lay on her stomach and I can remember her just hugging me, you know, encouraging me on, oh, you are going to be somebody.

And I think that I can accredit even minor degrees and my push and my life accomplishments to the fact that when I was so young it could have been the other way if I didn't have the encouragement of her, it would have been to the point that I would have felt like, no, I couldn't do it.

Dr. Lee: Right.

Reverend Crosby: I would have been brainwashed, I think, to say that, no, you can't accomplish this, but because of my grandmother taking me, and my grandfather and my grandmother, they sensed the difference, and … they sensed the difference, and they tried to, you know, baby me, so they kind of took me as favorite since so many other people had taken, you know, my daughter and other people in the community like that as favorites.

Dr. Lee: You mean your sister?

Reverend Crosby: They took … yes … they took me as a favorite, and so they … and the only way they could do that is by words and encouragement. It wasn't a financial, it wasn't an educational … they didn't have an educational push for, me but they had that encouragement that, yes, you are somebody and, you know, you are going …

Dr. Lee: You can do?

Reverend Crosby: You can do.

Dr. Lee: And so when they died how did this impact your life?

Reverend Crosby: Oh …

Dr. Lee: How old were you when they …

Reverend Crosby: Thirteen. Well, when my grandmother passed, I was thirteen and I was entering in high school during that time. I remember the morning she died. I didn't want to go to school, you know, and I kept hanging around, hanging around, and being late. And we had to walk through a path, you know, across the railroad tracks, through a path to get to Carter G. It was all paths going through there during that time at the old Carter G., you know, and that's where I was, so it was about the eighth grade or something like that when she passed.

　　　And I went to school that morning, I end up going, and the minute I got there, they called me to come back home. And she had passed next door at my other grandmother, my father's mother's house. It was really a devastating time, and that was the time that I went to start going to church myself.

Dr. Lee: You had not to that point?

Reverend Crosby: I was going to church, but I started going for myself.

Dr. Lee: Okay. I see.

REVEREND CROSBY: You know …

DR. LEE: Yes.

REVEREND CROSBY: … I started going to church for myself. She made me go.

DR. LEE: Yes.

REVEREND CROSBY: You know.

DR. LEE: And after that you wanted to go for yourself?

REVEREND CROSBY: Yes, after that, I … I wasn't made to go by my mother, by my father, but I chose to because of my, of course, background. And I wanted to see her. I wanted to see her again. And everybody could see her, and they were seeing ghosts and all this. I wanted to see her, grandmother again. I was afraid of ghosts. And I think that's probably why I had a desire for the undertaker, to be an undertaker, and also to just inquire, you know, what happens after death, because I wanted to see her. I wasn't afraid at thirteen. And it impacted my life. I stayed with my mother for two years after that, and my dad, I went to live with my dad for two years.

DR. LEE: And where was this?

REVEREND CROSBY: He was … at that time he was in the family home. He was … I stayed with my mom two years, and then I went to stay with him, and they're side by side.

DR. LEE: Okay. Okay.

REVEREND CROSBY: Okay. And he was there, and you know, after that I left, and after I graduated from high school I left. Went to Washington.

DR. LEE: Okay. So in '61 you left?

REVEREND CROSBY: Yes.

DR. LEE: Okay. And went to where, again?

REVEREND CROSBY: Washington. I went there, and I started the school, the best I know, from … in secretarial science. It was decided I didn't want to scrub no floors, I can tell you that, and so I had to go to school for that, and it didn't work out. I didn't have the money to finish, and I realized I had an inferior education, and so I had a problem keeping up with the studies, anyway, and I was struggling with it, and I had to drop out because lack of money. The family couldn't support me here.

DR. LEE: Until that time had you thought that you'd had an inferior education or was there any …

REVEREND CROSBY: Yes, I had that because I found out when I really inquired about becoming a mortician, community college, I found out, you know, that I didn't have the prerequisites out of high school that would enable me to go straight into, you know, a program.

DR. LEE: Okay.

REVEREND CROSBY: So I didn't have what it takes … what it took to get what I wanted … where I wanted to go, however, you know, I didn't have the money to, you know, take the courses to get myself prepared to do and stay here. We didn't have money at that time.

DR. LEE: I need to go back just a little bit. Which church did you all attend?

REVEREND CROSBY: Friendship.

DR. LEE: Okay.

REVEREND CROSBY: Uh-huh. My mother was … she's known now on the record for being faithful to Friendship.

DR. LEE: Okay.

REVEREND CROSBY: And we … my grandmother … I'm sorry … my grandmother, see, she has a block in there and even in the new Friendship, and during my childhood and days coming up we had the old Friendship and that was a wooden … little, wooden building.

DR. LEE: Was it further up this end?

REVEREND CROSBY: It sit[s] right where it is.

DR. LEE: Okay.

REVEREND CROSBY: Right in that … right there where it is now.

DR. LEE: All right.

REVEREND CROSBY: I think they … I don't know if they kept a little bit of it and had church. I can't remember that, when they started building. But it was right there close, really. I think … they probably had church and start building the large one a little further over, but those were good days at … man … every summer we would go to the beach, you know …

DR. LEE: Which beach?

REVEREND CROSBY: Tyler's Beach was one I remember, then it's …

DR. LEE: Where is that?

REVEREND CROSBY: I'm not good at names.

DR. LEE: Tyler Beach, where is that?

REVEREND CROSBY: It's down near Hampton.

DR. LEE: Okay.

REVEREND CROSBY: Somewhere down in that way, Tidewater area. And it was several little beaches we went to I can remember.

DR. LEE: Bay Shore?

REVEREND CROSBY: Yeah, something like …

DR. LEE: Buckroe? Jones? Jones would have been around here.

REVEREND CROSBY: Would have been around here.

DR. LEE: Uh-huh. But you remember Tyler?

REVEREND CROSBY: But we get on the bus … yeah, I remember Tyler about … we used to get on this bus and go, and every year we work harder. And then we had … in the summertime we had Bible study on the outside.

The kids would come down and we had Sunday … you know, Vacation Bible School and stuff, well, we would be running around on the outside doing arts and crafts. And sometimes we would have picnics, you know, picnics out on the grass.

And my grandmother was faithful to the revivals and all that. I know I had an aunt that migrated up here because of my grandmother, right …

DR. LEE: From North Carolina?

REVEREND CROSBY: From North Carolina. And she was in Holiness. So she would go to some of the little Holiness churches and invite my mother's … my mother, when they had … when they had a revival, say, maybe some Sunday evening they had special services, so my mother would go with her a lot, you know. And I used to go, too, and we used to beat the tambourine, and I tell you, we had fun. And they would let … allow the kids to shout. We would be shouting and having churches and they'd be falling out. And that's when I introduced to, you know, the Holiness Pentecostal Apostolic, I am telling you it was … I was introduced to that faith, those faiths, but we would always go back to, you know, Friendship, their duties and work with Friendship Baptist Church.

DR. LEE: Well, the church has been a central part of your life?

REVEREND CROSBY: Oh, of course.

DR. LEE: Early on?

REVEREND CROSBY: Early, early, early, early.

DR. LEE: And the extended family is also a central part of your life. Would you say that you saw your grandmothers like mothers? Were they like mothers to you or were they ...

REVEREND CROSBY: My grandparents?

DR. LEE: Yes.

REVEREND CROSBY: My mother's mother was my mother.

DR. LEE: Okay.

REVEREND CROSBY: And if I'm not careful, I start calling her my mother instead of my biological mother. Might get you confused there, so straighten me out because she was that ... I called her Momma, my grandmother.

DR. LEE: Okay.

REVEREND CROSBY: And very, very much part of my life, even now, even though I was thirteen then, so it's been forty years ago.

DR. LEE: And what did your call your mother?

REVEREND CROSBY: Called her by her name, Madeline.

DR. LEE: Oh, okay.

REVEREND CROSBY: And my daddy, I called him by his name, Charlie, and they allowed that.

DR. LEE: So your grandparents were ... you thought of them like parents?

REVEREND CROSBY: They were parents.

DR. LEE: Uh-huh.

REVEREND CROSBY: They were the role of parent for me. And I was aware that my mother was ... you know, my mother was my mother, my biological mother was my mother.

DR. LEE: Yes. And so in '61 when you decided to go to Washington, who did you talk this over with; your grandparents, your parents?

REVEREND CROSBY: My grandfather was still alive.

DR. LEE: That's right. Your mother ... your grandmother had ...

REVEREND CROSBY: Had passed. My grandfather was still alive, which was very much part of my life. So he explained to us, you know, when my grandmother died, my grandfather said that she set on his knee the night before she died and told him if anything were to happen to her to always take care of me, take care of me. And that's what he did. You know, he ... right at the store, he got a bill, and if ... so that I would not go hungry or want for nothing, so I would go there and walk in, and Frances Dureski ... the store, right ... you know, right there next door, that little store.

DR. LEE: Oh, okay.

REVEREND CROSBY: Uh-huh. We used to go in there, and I would walk in there and anything ... he carried me in there and say, now anything that little black one want ... now, this is what he said ... you give it to her. And when she come in here, anything that little black one say she want, you give it to her. So I would go there and get potato chips, junk after school, and he would pay the bill, at the end of the month he would pay the bill, never complain. Sometime I used to go down there and get steaks and anything else, you know ... you know, I'm not going hungry ... be hungry, you know. And certain foods I didn't like. And you couldn't get me into a fish, because it just seemed like they never could get the scales off fish, so when they had fish for supper every Friday, hmm, I had my own food. They used to gave me anything I wanted.

DR. LEE: Did you feel special?

REVEREND CROSBY: Special by my grandparents.

DR. LEE: In the larger world, how did you feel?

REVEREND CROSBY: I felt that I had to work for what I got in the larger world, that no one is going to give me anything.

DR. LEE: Did you feel spoiled?

REVEREND CROSBY: Only, only by ... I felt spoiled by my grandparents, you know what I'm saying? They were the center of my life, the background of everything I get.

DR. LEE: And so when you moved to Washington you are leaving everything behind that is dear to you?

REVEREND CROSBY: Yes.

DR. LEE: What was that like?

REVEREND CROSBY: Oh, life in Washington was like ...

DR. LEE: Because you were eighteen, nineteen?

REVEREND CROSBY: Uh-huh, yes. Seventeen, I believe I got out of school, and, you know, I was born in March, I was seventeen that summer. I believe that's the way it was.

DR. LEE: You went to the twelfth grade; did they have a twelfth grade then because I know …

REVEREND CROSBY: No. It stopped at twelfth.

DR. LEE: Okay. I know at some point they only had the eleventh grade.

REVEREND CROSBY: Right.

DR. LEE: But you had the twelfth?

REVEREND CROSBY: They stopped it somewhere in there. Yeah.

DR. LEE: Okay. And so … and Washington at that young age away from everybody …

REVEREND CROSBY: Eighteen, I guess.

DR. LEE: What did you notice was different between Washington and Hopewell?

REVEREND CROSBY: Besides the size of the place, I felt like I was, you know, kind of dumb, you know. I felt inferior in terms of wiseness, you know, getting around. I found out that all that cleaning my grandmother made me do, I didn't know how to clean, because I went to get a job, and I couldn't find anything except for somebody said live-in job like. So I tried that, and went there, and I guess I stayed awhile. I don't know if it was a month. And I dropped the … I was cleaning the bathroom and whatnot, nice things in there, dropped a couple of those, and then I had to pay for them out of my pay, so I didn't … I didn't get anything. And then I didn't clean good enough, you know. So that was a bad experience, because I couldn't find a job I could do.

DR. LEE: And what did you do then?

REVEREND CROSBY: Well, you know, I kept trying, kept looking, and I went through a lot. I lived with a lady that gave me some food, a little bit of food, and let me stay in her basement, and she helped me some look for a job so I had food. And then I went down to … you know, I was trying school, and it was really rough.

DR. LEE: How long did you stay there?

REVEREND CROSBY: I stayed there maybe about, off and on about three or four years. I would stay there. I finally got a job in a tall girls' … a tall girls' boutique like, and I was just cleaning, dusting, and you know, putting things away, as they say. You know, people come in, try something on, and I would put it back on the rack, you know, just basically working …

DR. LEE: Was it retail or …

REVEREND CROSBY: It was … I wouldn't call it retail. I was just the maid.

DR. LEE: So you couldn't even have that opportunity to be a salesperson?

REVEREND CROSBY: No. No. No. No. No.

DR. LEE: Okay. All right. Things still segregated then?

REVEREND CROSBY: Yes. Very much so up there, down here.

DR. LEE: And here?

REVEREND CROSBY: Oh, yes. They had it rough up there and down here.

DR. LEE: Would you say that was up to that point in your life the hardest time of your life?

REVEREND CROSBY: Of course, uh-huh. That was the hardest time. It was shortly after that … you know, I would come home, of course, often as I could down here, and I think … the things got better for me when finally a friend of mine or acquaintance … you know, around here in Hopewell there were a lot of soldiers from Fort Lee, that is the history of Hopewell, so it seems like most of the girls were dating people from Fort Lee, the different people come in. They were marrying and dating, and going on post, and you know, they were entertaining them.

And I kind of promised myself from seeing some of the results of them that I was not going to become involved with an Army person, a person that is in the Army.

Well, it was one young man that I end up talking to, and I was in between here and trying to make a way in Washington, and he told me that I should go to school, why don't I try to go to school for LPN since his wife was an LPN, and everywhere he went his wife had an opportunity to get a job and go with him.

And I said, oh, oh, okay. Well, let me try that, since I can't get into the school for mortician, let me try. And so I got into that program in Washington, D.C., as an LPN, as a Licensed Practical Nurse. And after that I began to get jobs, and I got jobs, government jobs, good jobs, you know, I did well in it. And you know, and my life went like I wanted it to go.

DR. LEE: What schools did you attend for the LPN training?

Courtesy of Carmela Hamm

Reverend Crosby: Washington Hospital Center. It was ... so I end up going there. That was the program.

Dr. Lee: Okay. And had you any thought of coming back here to get a job prior to that?

Reverend Crosby: Yes, I did. Prior to that, no.

Dr. Lee: Okay. It was just out of the question to ...

Reverend Crosby: Well, it just wasn't my thought to go into the plant.

Dr. Lee: Because that was the only thing you could do, either that or domestic work?

Reverend Crosby: Yes.

Dr. Lee: Okay.

Reverend Crosby: That or domestic work was about the size ... for me. You see, for me. Like I said, you know, you had to be of a family, pretty nice, decent looking, and this kind of thing, you know. And I just felt ... that's what I felt. That's what I ran into.

Dr. Lee: So you felt the opportunity was not here for you to ...

Reverend Crosby: It wasn't here.

Dr. Lee: ... do what you wanted to do?

Reverend Crosby: Yes.

Dr. Lee: Okay.

Reverend Crosby: Or to move into any area that I wanted to, would be interested in.

Dr. Lee: And with the LPN credential you saw a change in your life financially, economically?

Reverend Crosby: Yes. Yes. And fulfilling, you know, and I became very good at it because I was able to help people, you know, and I felt myself work, like, oh, man, I have found something that I can do that people can look at me, you know, and say, you know, I achieved it, you know, it's ... you are not giving me anything. I'm working for it.

Dr. Lee: Right.

Reverend Crosby: So I did very well. You know, I got all kinds of awards and recognition, saving people's lives, and you know, and I had these things in writing, you know.

Dr. Lee: Uh-huh.

REVEREND CROSBY: I applied to Fort Lee before I came back home and got the job right away as an LPN. So I was kind of, you know, into it.

DR. LEE: Okay. And so what year was this that you got the job in Fort Lee, and did you move back here to Hopewell?

…

REVEREND CROSBY: I would say about '60 … it may have been '64, or '5, somewhere like that.

DR. LEE: What changes have you noticed from '64. From '61 to '64, '5, have there been any changes here?

REVEREND CROSBY: The change … not really a change. I found that the people … I compared I guess what had happened between the people that I went to school with, what they had accomplished, and where they were at the time. And I found that most of the people were employed at the plant, that they remained in Hopewell, that they were in the plant. During that time the plant was paying the most money. And they were paying sometimes ten, thirteen, fourteen dollars an hour or something like that after you got in there. And they had nice cars, nice homes, you know, and they were doing just fine.

And the other half that remained in this area was on social help, so they were in the projects and getting income from that and having children. And they had nice … projects were fairly new or renovated or new during that time, so they were nice dwellings for the blacks. And so, you know, that's just about the way it was, either you are on social service doing well, or you are in the plant or wherever. Very few people were professional, you know, in the area. They seemed to have gone or stayed where they went to college. The college professionals, you know, seemed to have gone other places to pursue professions.

DR. LEE: Okay. And so working at Fort Lee, what did you notice … was that segregated also as far as working with patients …

REVEREND CROSBY: No.

DR. LEE: … cafeteria?

REVEREND CROSBY: No. No.

DR. LEE: By then it was integrated?

REVEREND CROSBY: It was integrated by then.

DR. LEE: Okay.

REVEREND CROSBY: And it was integrated by then, but as a civilian, you know, of course, you were ... you were not ... you were just a worker, you know. I mean they gave all their attention to their own ...

REVEREND CROSBY: ... 1984, I did my own ... I started my own business for home health care.

DR. LEE: In the tri-city area of Petersburg, Hopewell ...

REVEREND CROSBY: Yes. Hopewell ... I actually started off an office in Hopewell.

DR. LEE: Okay.

REVEREND CROSBY: And then I moved to Petersburg.

DR. LEE: Uh-huh.

REVEREND CROSBY: And then I created locations throughout, you know, different offices, you know.

DR. LEE: And so '84 you became a business owner?

REVEREND CROSBY: Uh-huh.

DR. LEE: How did this change your life, because you had a family now, also?

REVEREND CROSBY: Uh-huh.

DR. LEE: How many children did you have at that time?

REVEREND CROSBY: When I start ... I had all my children when I started business.

DR. LEE: And how many children do you have?

REVEREND CROSBY: I have four. ...

DR. LEE: All right.

REVEREND CROSBY: Two girls and two boys.

DR. LEE: And their names?

REVEREND CROSBY: Terence, David, Candice, and Belinda, two girls, two boys. They ... when I started business it just ... I mean, you know, I just added on, added on, did well at that, very well. I was one of the largest what they call personal-care providers with a contract for the government in the area, had the largest amount of patients at one time, at one time. And different locations everywhere. And then I got this call into the ministry, that's what happened, and ...

DR. LEE: What year?

REVEREND CROSBY: ... I just stopped ... I started in ... it was in '90, '90, '91.

DR. LEE: So four years after you had opened your business?

REVEREND CROSBY: It was a little longer than that.

DR. LEE: Okay.

REVEREND CROSBY: It was about … you know, seemed like it was about ten, almost ten … around '84.

DR. LEE: You opened business about '80 … okay.

REVEREND CROSBY: Yeah. And I started about, you know, '91, '90, '91, started going back to school again.

DR. LEE: And where did you go to school?

REVEREND CROSBY: I went to Virginia Union and worked … took three years, a three-year course at Virginia Union I finished in two.

DR. LEE: All right. Okay.

REVEREND CROSBY: Just by the grace of God, I have to confess. I'm not smart at all. Some people tried to say that. And then when I finished there, I went to Howard and I did in two years what I should have done in three.

DR. LEE: So had you given up your business at this time?

REVEREND CROSBY: No. Business still going. And that, you know, it declined, you know, in membership because I wasn't hands on, aggressively hands on like I was before, so I gave all kinds of time, you know, to school, and other people kind of running it, and it dropped a tad bit, but it supported … I had two daughters in college at the same time.

DR. LEE: Where did they go to school?

REVEREND CROSBY: St. Augustine or St. Augustus, North Carolina, Raleigh, and three years … my baby girl … three years, Candice completed hers, UVA, four years UVA, and then she has her master's from MCV in hospital administration.

And now she … both of them are anticipating going into nursing to take on the business. Candice got a program at MCV which she's entering for RN in which they are going to give her, two years, she gets her … I think it is a bachelor's/master's program in nursing, and with all of her prerequisites and all that kind of stuff she is ready to go on this pilot program for nursing.

DR. LEE: So they are following in your footsteps and carrying on the business?

REVEREND CROSBY: Yeah, the business. And my daughter Candice is running the business in Petersburg. And now I am reworking the business which started in Emporia, and my baby girl is deciding she's going to Southside Community College. She's started her associate in nursing, and it shouldn't take time, and she's going to be running and working with the business during that time.

DR. LEE: You are fortunate.

REVEREND CROSBY: They are going to take over the business.

DR. LEE: That's wonderful. That's wonderful.

REVEREND CROSBY: It has done very well, educated, and we've had nice things to do sometimes, and income multimillions of dollars in years, I mean, the income (*inaudible*), so I'm just helping them to carry it to another level, you know, in Emporia, separating Petersburg and Dinwiddie.

DR. LEE: Now, when you started your church, what year was that?

REVEREND CROSBY: In '98, '98 and '99.

DR. LEE: Was this a dream of yours, to have your own church or …

REVEREND CROSBY: No. It was never a dream, and it is not … it is still not a part of a dream. It wasn't a dream. It's just a sense of feeling of calling.

DR. LEE: Okay.

REVEREND CROSBY: Okay. And I felt I'm a serious teaching … I'm a teacher. You know, I do have … the nursing, I taught nursing, you know, in my career, teaching nursing, I still have a school for nursing assistants as a part of my business. So I like teaching and spiritually, you know, I like Biblical teaching, and I just know I'm a teacher, and a worker, and so … but I found I went to my church body, and my body didn't believe in women, you know, being active in the church, you know, the one that I have been faithfully working with, and so I had to, you know, I had to make a big step, and it was very devastating to step out from that church and go to school, go to, you know, through milieu, and it was a whole different world and milieu, and … but I had to follow suit on what I felt the Lord was leading me to do.

So after I finished … it was after I finished, you know, the doctorate, you know, I finished that, then here I am a teacher, but who would let me teach? You know, where you send the people if you teach them? Who is going to let you teach the people? And so it kind of led into the fact that, well, you need to start, you know, your own and work from there in the teaching. So I did, set up the Bible college, you know, through that, and …

DR. LEE: And what year was that?

REVEREND CROSBY: '99, 1999.

DR. LEE: Okay.

REVEREND CROSBY: So we went through a process for the Department of Higher Education to offer degrees. And now, you know, it's up and running, you know.

DR. LEE: How did you decide to locate here in Hopewell?

REVEREND CROSBY: Hopewell is my hometown, and I felt led because of the need. I looked at it as a social ministry. Now, where am I going to help, you know? I was going into it with … I started off, I had a development center. I incorporated that, and I got a couple of grants here, you know, I got a CDD: GE (*inaudible*) downtown grant to help the poor people in the area. What we did, we helped them pay their rent, we got food from the Food Bank, and we had a clothes closet, which people donated to us. We fixed it up and we gave clothes. We still have some of that here, but it is not popular. We gave a lunch, you know, kids lunch bags after school, you know, between the time of supper and afterschool snack. We had children to do that, so we were doing a lot of outreach ministry, and you know, helping.

So it was a social ministry. We were just helping. And I was doing that mainly out of my business, retired from my business, you know. You know, one year I spent about $70,000 in setting up and giving and doing, you know, of my own money, and doing ministries, and I was still doing, you know, just working out of the church name and setting up the schools.

But I found that people began to become very dependent on you giving them something. If I help you with your lights, they owe a three or four hundred dollar light bill, then you know, it's still didn't bring you closer to God, and that was the ultimate theme for you to come into church and become, you know, thankful, and then get yourself on your feet and then go out and help someone else.

That was my goal. But they would get it. Some of them were very demanding, you know, like … and especially when they saw that I got a grant to help underprivileged people like that, and the money wasn't all that, and I had to match it, and they didn't pay anything for administration fees, so I had to hire somebody myself to be there and available, you know, to do it on a daily basis, you know. So it was very expensive for me, but then when they come in saying you got that money from the state, you know, and the people start telling you that, you got that money from the city, and you got to, and I'm going to report you, and all this, you know, when they start saying that when they would come in and want … they wanted the help, but they didn't want to tell the truth, and fill out the paperwork, you know, they don't want you to track them down, and it became … it became a problem, a big problem, so eventually I just slowed up. I gave up a little bit. I was losing and going down, you know, and people weren't being appreciative.

So I found out that my teaching gift is exactly what needs to be … you teach the people, and then they get out and go, and they do for themselves. So that changed. That was my view of Hopewell, they were just underprivileged, nobody gave them a chance, but I know myself I have given a lot of people chances. You know, I have some homes, some houses around here, and for the homeless, and I knew that they were … they were in there in the wintertime, you know, and I would just pray on the fact they wouldn't burn the houses down, but I knew that they would go in there and sleep. And I would have … I would say nothing because they would be out in the car, you know.

And I have done all kinds of things to help the city, you know, out, as far as poverty is concerned. We did a survey on … it was backing up with the city, what city council did on people that were homeless, and somehow I got to the real homeless situation, you know, that was in the city, and it is a homeless problem, you know, in the city. And it's going to become another problem. It's going to become a larger problem unless we kind of deal with it because in this area they are building up houses, they are doing … they are fixing up houses, but the rent is going up and a lot of these people are not going to be able to pay the rent, you know, on the houses.

Courtesy of Carmela Hamm

So here they are again, you know, into a poverty situation, creating homelessness, you know. And it can end up being a problem where you are building up and it's looking great and everybody has to take care of their property, and you are doing good on one side, but it's going to create another problem with people without homes.

DR. LEE: Do you see an increase within the last few years of homelessness, like since the '90s, or since 2000, or is it decreasing?

REVEREND CROSBY: Surely … it surely it's not decreasing. I mean, you know, decreasing. It is more or less … it is on the rise where, you know, because for one thing the city was not aware of this homelessness problem in the first place. When I got into it, I could see it, because they would allow me, you know, the people would allow me to get close enough to see this homelessness, and by the same token, me having the houses, you know, that … in the area, I have about six houses, you know, in this area …

DR. LEE: Arlington Heights?

REVEREND CROSBY: Arlington Heights, and all of them are … you know what I'm saying? Well, I purchased them because they were on sale, and they was going … what was going to happen is the people were going to come in and fix them up just like they are doing now, and then the rent was so high that the average person could not afford it. You see, all the people that make the money, it seems, you know, you are in a little corner of Hopewell, or you know what I'm saying, all by yourself, you are not aware of what is going on, and everybody respect you, they don't go over here and mess with this set of people that we all know, and they don't mess with that set, but then all the rest of the people that are doing well can't look out and see the need of the people that are right next door on the other street. You know what I'm saying?

DR. LEE: Uh-huh.

REVEREND CROSBY: So … and it's a problem. Talking about future in Hopewell, there's something that … it's some way we're going to have to get to the people that … they don't want to be called poor, you know. I don't want to call them poor. I have heard people say, I haven't been given a chance. You know, nobody give me a chance. If they give me a chance I will do, if they give me a chance. And I have given a lot of chances. You know, I have given you a chance, and they don't do … I'm not too sure where we are going with that.

       I think that one of the best ways to do is the church is the best resource for us to get to the underprivileged, and it's the best way for us to get to them, and I think to teach and to get them to work.

       It is amazing, the mentality of the people that are in the area. They think they know … they think they know the law, and they think they know how to get around and get what they want. You see, once you survive, you barely survive, you know, it becomes a routine for you, and it works on this person, it works on that person, then you know, that's a way of life. It's a way of life. And if you are not in it, you know, you just don't think like they do. You just don't … you know, I mean your mind is just totally different, you know. I don't know how to explain that, but that's a problem in my hometown.

The Reverend Rudolph Dunbar, August 18, 2005

Courtesy of Carmela Hamm

After twenty-three years, nine months, and eight days in the military, the Reverend Dr. Rudolph Dunbar now invests his time in church, community, and family. Indeed, they are his earthly trinity. Dunbar provides an overview of the progress Hopewell is making and believes progress is accelerating.

RUDOLPH DUNBAR: I am originally from Hampton County, South Carolina, a little town down there by the name of Varnville, South Carolina, a couple miles from Hampton County seathouse … or Hampton County seat, that is, in the lower … they refer to … thirty miles from there they refer to it as Geechie Country, so I'm just about thirty miles from Beaufort, South Carolina, which is the real lowland of South Carolina, right on the coast, the Atlantic Coast.

DR. LEE: How long did you live there?

REVEREND DUNBAR: I lived there until I went to New York City.

DR. LEE: How old were you then?

REVEREND DUNBAR: I was about … in my late teens. And I was drafted in the military. As a matter of fact I came into the military out of New York City.

DR. LEE: Okay.

REVEREND DUNBAR: And after coming in the military, I stayed in the military because I elected to stay in the military. The point of the whole issue is that I was requested to be a male secretary for a school in Varnville, South Carolina, because of the acquaintances of my father and the principal of that school, he requested me by name because he knew that I possessed some good qualities as far as administration was concerned when I was young, real young. And he requested me by name. And I got a call that there was a job waiting on me if I wanted to come back down there. And I said, well, I'll go back and try it for a little while. I went back and tried it for three months, I guess, and that's when the draft came for me up here. So I had to come back and answer the draft.

In the meantime, my sister, who was studying the same that I was studying in school, basically, she took over the job, and after pulling my first two years of military service as a draftee, they had to guarantee me that job after getting out of the military service, but since my sister was doing such a wonderful job, I said, well, being a male specimen, I would say, I can get a job anyplace even if it's digging a ditch, so I let my sister have that job, she can keep that job, so that's what I did, and I went back in the military.

DR. LEE: How many years did you stay in the military?

REVEREND DUNBAR: Twenty-three years, nine months, and eight days.

DR. LEE: So you had an opportunity to travel the world?

REVEREND DUNBAR: Yes.

DR. LEE: What did you notice was the difference between … with places that you traveled in the military and here?

REVEREND DUNBAR: One of the main things that I noticed that was different w[as] the educational process. Every student that was in school wore identical uniforms, outfits, if you will, to school so you could not identify a poor person from a rich person in a school setting, and I was very impressed by that. In addition to that, their educational process was different in that they went to school most of the year round. They didn't have as much time to throw away as our American folks did, particularly during the summer months. I think at that time there was something like three weeks they had out of school between … or three weeks break they had out of school in the summer, and of course two weeks during the winter months, which entailed the Christmas season, the Yuletide season and all that, but I was very interested to realize that. And I learned to understand that it was the same thing in other foreign countries that I hadn't been to yet, but I did get to them eventually, and witness the fact that they had the same kind of program.

DR. LEE: What is the time period that you were in the military?

REVEREND DUNBAR: I was drafted in 1954, December 4, 1954, and I retired in … on September 8, 1978. 1978.

DR. LEE: And three tours during this time?

REVEREND DUNBAR: I had three tours in Germany. I had one in Japan mainland, one on the Okinawa Island of Japan, one in Korea, and one in Vietnam. So ...

DR. LEE: So when you entered in 1954 the Supreme Court had just handed down the decision of *Brown versus Board of Education*?

REVEREND DUNBAR: Uh-huh.

DR. LEE: And then when you ... and so the school system was completely segregated at that time, conditions were very untenable. When you went to Europe what was the situation like there?

REVEREND DUNBAR: Well, there was still some lingering ideas in the people's heads that the typical I will say Caucasian or European American had more or less distributed to the people about African American people, and you would find periodically that people who were not directly affiliated with the military having these strange looks about African American people because of the rumors that had been spread and all this.

Many of them who were not so closely associated with them were still reluctant to become associated with African Americans. So my understanding was that they were required to have so much training in American history, and particularly black American history, African American history, and they came to know out of those three times I was over there, they came to realize that information that they heard was false, and as it is in most foreign countries, they don't want to be listed or titled or labeled racist.

So when that happened they became to be very, very closely concerned, connected with and of course affiliated, if you will, with the African American, and I was able to experience and witness the relationship through handling all of the marriage applications for African Americans to Europeans while I was over there, especially the first two times. As a matter of fact, my first time over there that was one of my primary responsibilities to process applications for that.

DR. LEE: What time period was that?

REVEREND DUNBAR: This was '55 ... from April of '55 to November of '56, that entire period of time. My primary responsibility was to process marriage applications. Most of those marriage applications were between African Americans and Europeans, Germans. And I learned to know a lot about their culture through the processing of those applications, and I learned a lot more about African Americans as a result of that, and the relationship between the African American male and the European female. Very interesting. Some experiences that I don't think I would ever be able to exchange for anything else.

Dr. Lee: Did you notice the difference in residential arrangements, blacks and whites living together or in the same neighborhood, as opposed to here?

Reverend Dunbar: As far as ... well, no. The blacks and whites living in the same area over there, naturally there would be some blacks living on the economy, most of the blacks were living on military installations, those who lived on the economy they didn't have any problems mingling with the European population at all, and the European population, from what I saw and what I heard, had no problems living in the community or having blacks live in the community of the European. They got along real well.

But in any case you see like that you are going to find someone who is going to upset the applecart, you know, because they want to prove themselves being so macho and to prove themselves what they are really not to further impress other nations or other nationalities or whatever, but other than that, the relationship between the Germans and Americans were good. I had the opportunity of being exposed to many of the German nationals because when I wasn't busy processing marriage applications, I was doing stenography work with the court section, and I traveled all over the area recording court proceedings and all of this nature. And I had a good rapport with the Germans because I learned to speak a little bit, you know, broken German, you know, just enough to get a point across or whatever. I learned to speak it, because I had to, being in the position I was, as more or less a temporary or part-time court reporter. And the relations got to the point where many activities were requesting my presence for the purpose of recording a court proceeding from cities as far away as a hundred miles. They had to provide me transportation for that purpose. But the rapport was a great rapport between me and the German nationals. I never had a problem with them, and from what I understand, they never had any problem with me. I have never given them any reason to have a problem with me, anyway.

I have always been one, and I have always been taught by my father that whenever you see another individual, you don't see color. He taught me that from being knee-high to a duck. I can never understand why he, from South Carolina, never having been out of South Carolina, would teach his children this. And to the best of my knowledge I am probably the only one who accepted it from him. The rest of them declared never ... I'll never be able to work with them, or never be able to live near them and all this stuff, you know. And they are still that way. But I learned from him that human beings are human beings. All of us are human. The art of the whole thing is to treat people like you wished to be treated, and I practice that, and believe me, it got me through a lot of stuff even while I was in the military.

While I might be jumping the gun, but while on that subject, when I was in Vietnam, I mean mortars were raining down around us practically every night in Vietnam. I was responsible for five local national secretaries. The chief secretary of those five was straight out of Hanoi. And she told me, she said, I never had anybody to treat me like I'm a human being. She said, so I'm going to tell you something. She said if you see me reach down and pick up my purse from beside the desk, and I go outside of the office, she said, you make it to the bunker. You go to the bunker.

I said, why are you saying that? She said, if I pick up my purse from beside my desk to go outside, that means that Hanoi is going to strike Tan Sun Nhut. Tan Sun Nhut was one of the main airports … right there in Saigon. And many days, many days I followed her instructions, and many mortars came in, right in the building we were in after she picked up her purse. She said, I didn't tell anybody else this because everybody treat me like I'm a dog, like I'm not a human being, because she is out of Hanoi, North Vietnam. And all of those things came back to me that my father taught me, regardless of who they are, treat people like you want to be treated and that, you know, maybe that got me through Vietnam in the midst of all those mortars that were falling down around me, because the target was Tan Sun Nhut, which was right across the street. Tan Sun Nhut was the air base, military air base, and was right across the street. And I give thanks to having a concerned father for me in the future, and I try to pass it on, you know, but some people will accept it. Some won't because of their machoism.

DR. LEE: So when you came out of the military, seventy …

REVEREND DUNBAR: '78.

DR. LEE: '78?

REVEREND DUNBAR: Uh-huh.

DR. LEE: Where did you go from there?

REVEREND DUNBAR: Right here.

DR. LEE: What were conditions like here in Hopewell?

REVEREND DUNBAR: Hopewell, I was living in Hopewell since '70. As a matter of fact, when I came back from Germany the last time we came into Fort Lee, so I was living in the Hopewell community since '70, more or less. And when I came here in '70, the population of Hopewell was just under 10,000. It was 9,000 and a few.

People didn't seem to be so overly concerned about African American progression. They didn't seem to be overly concerned about advancement and all this. Many of them would ... they attend the schools and all this, but they didn't allow the, this is from my observation, they didn't allow the education that they received to be used for advancement, and many of them sat around on their education and didn't do anything. But ...

DR. LEE: Like (*inaudible*)?

REVEREND DUNBAR: Particularly black. There was still a little racial friction around ... of course, there still is a little racial friction around ... during that time. You had to be careful with who you associated with. You had to be careful with what you patronized, or where you patronized and all this stuff, because a little bit of that stuff was still in them, kind of like I said, some of it is still in them. During that time when I first came here, Dr. Harris was a good man to know, you know, because he didn't ... as a matter of fact, that's when I started working with him with the SCLC.

DR. LEE: Southern Christian Leadership Conference?

REVEREND DUNBAR: Right, Southern Christian Leadership Conference. I also was active in the NAACP over there, the NAACP, and Dr. Harris believed in ... one of the first things he told me was ... he said, I am an activist. And he said it so calmly, and yet so seriously. He said, I am an activist, and I believe in getting to the source of things. And I'm thinking all the time, you know, here I'll only be working with Dr. Harris. And he came to us with a statement at a meeting once, and said that he was going to be going down in North Carolina where they were doing some construction work down there, and apparently there were some African Americans' property that were being damaged and all this in the process of this construction, and he was going down there to do something about it. And when he told me what he had to do, I told him, I said ... well, that was the time when he placed himself in front of dump trucks and all this, you know. And I told Reverend Harris, I said I've been in the military and all this, as a matter of fact I was still in the military then, I said, I don't know anything about combat. I said, but now, I'm going to support you all the way, but I'm not going to go lay down in front of bulldozers and dump trucks and all this stuff. So he said, fine. I know where you are coming from. If you support me, that's fine. That's fine. So I supported him through all those things and many other things have transpired. Fort Lee was one of his main targets. He loved jumping on Fort Lee, jumping into Fort Lee's case because there was some stuff going on at Fort Lee that was ... I considered really inhumane.

DR. LEE: Such as?

REVEREND DUNBAR: Racial issues and stuff of this nature, you know. And it is still going on. It is going on right now, as a matter of fact. Only if … as a civilian … military didn't have any problem … as a civilian if you were seeking advancement in certain areas and you weren't hooked up with some of the uppers on Fort Lee, you weren't going to make it, regardless of how many degrees you had, you weren't going to make it. You might want to close that door. It might not keep out a lot of the noises, but it will keep out some of it. So you just didn't advance if you were an African American civilian and you were trying to do the best you could possibly do for advancement if you were not hooked up and had some kind of relationship with those people who were in higher positions.

Courtesy of Carmela Hamm

DR. LEE: Who were usually white?

RUDOLPH DUNBAR: Yeah, who were usually white. You could forget it.

DR. LEE: Did most black people know this?

RUDOLPH DUNBAR: Yes, they knew it. But most of them would sit there and choose not to rock the boat, yet they wanted advancement, but they would choose not to rock the boat. And that's the kind of stuff Dr. Harris liked to attack. He got a lot of enjoyment out of attacking those kind of things. And they would make it appear as if they were changing a little for a period of maybe a year or two, and they would revert right back to the old … same old process. Whenever one left out of a position with what we call authority, they had already trained one to take over that position when they leave to carry on the same type, the same type of mannerism I'd say, and it was in the system. It was in the system. If you found it in one agency, it was in all the other agencies on the post. So many times I referred many people to Dr. Harris knowing that those were his types of things that just made him joyful, if you will.

DR. LEE: People who were seeking advancement or … wanting to be involved?

REVEREND DUNBAR: Those who were really concerned about advancement and was not … they were not going to …

SECTION II

DR. LEE: Back down?

REVEREND DUNBAR: … back down, and they didn't find any problems in rocking the boat, you know. Others who had problems with rocking the boat, they would sit there and just sit through the whole thing and suffered the case to be so.

DR. LEE: So you were like a confidant, in a way?

REVEREND DUNBAR: More or less, yes. A lot of people would come to me. They looked at me as if I was a character guidance professional, because I always voiced my opinions. If you are right, I am with you, but if you are wrong, then I'm going to have to try to show you where you are wrong first so you can right yourself and then step forward. You know, and they appreciated that. Apparently they did, because I had people coming to me all the time for advice and suggestions and recommendations and all this stuff. And in most of the cases I was fortunate enough to refer them to Dr. Harris and he took on their cases.

Along with him was Mr. Raymond Tucker, out of Prince George. You probably heard a lot about him. Have you heard of Dr. Sylvia Tucker? This is Dr. Sylvia Tucker's husband. He is also a military retiree. He was the president of the Prince George Chapter of the SCLC. And eventually as Dr. Harris got older, he kind of shifted off most of his responsibilities to Brother Raymond Tucker, who was the president of the Prince George Chapter. So the Prince George Chapter and the Hopewell Chapter worked closely together. So since that time I've had reason to refer people to Mr. Raymond Tucker. He's good, too, but he wasn't as … he wasn't as forceful as Dr. Harris. Dr. Harris would threaten you in a minute, you know. He would threaten people in a minute. And they were afraid of that, so he got much of what he wanted done, he got it done by virtue of the fact that he didn't mind threatening, you know. He still doesn't mind, either.

DR. LEE: Are you a member of SCLC?

REVEREND DUNBAR: Of the SCLC?

DR. LEE: Yes.

REVEREND DUNBAR: Yes. I support the SCLC and the …

DR. LEE: NAACP?

REVEREND DUNBAR: … and NAACP.

DR. LEE: When did you become a member of the SCLC and the NAACP?

REVEREND DUNBAR: I became a member of the … I was a member of the SCLC before I was a member of the NAACP, and that was … a member of the SCLC somewhere around '73, I guess. '72, '73, in that area.

DR. LEE: So prior to discharge from the military?

REVEREND DUNBAR: Uh-huh. ... And I became a member of the NAACP, I think it was in '76, something like that '75, '76.

DR. LEE: Other than Fort Lee, what causes have you fought for or activated for?

REVEREND DUNBAR: Well, fighting for civil rights, really. Well, I will tell you what, I'll tell you one thing we did here, since I've been here, and this kind of hinges on my training from my father to treat other people as they wished to be treated. There is now a predominantly white Baptist association located in Petersburg, headquartered in Petersburg. This is the only African American church in that association.

DR. LEE: City Point?

REVEREND DUNBAR: City Point. Another church has been accepted into it, which is Lebanon Baptist Church in Surry County. However, they haven't gotten to the point yet where they participate in any of the activities. But I became associated with the pastor of First Baptist, the big church down here on Second Avenue. He calls it a barn, you know, the big barn. Willie Cromer was his name. Willie Cromer was a native of Greenville, South Carolina. When he discovered that I was from South Carolina, he seemed to kind of just reach out and latched onto me, more or less. As a result of that, he asked me one day why aren't you a member of Petersburg Baptist Association? And he gave me all of the goodies that they had to offer out of the Petersburg Baptist Association that our black association didn't have to offer.

And he said, would you be interested in getting your church into the association? I said, well, what do I have to do? He said, see the director of admissions. I said, okay, who is the director of admissions. So he took me and introduced me to the director of admissions. As a result of that, when we united with the Petersburg Baptist Association we caused them to change their constitution and bylaws completely, and now they are reaching out, they are reaching out for African American churches, but the African American churches are withdrawing. They are not coming forward.

They have some property down here south of here at a place called Camp Kehukee, where you can have retreats. If a church belongs to the association you can have retreats out there. You can go swimming out there, fishing out there. You can put on any kind of services you want because the facilities are there, any kind of services you want, and you don't have to worry about being bothered.

You can take your entire church out there. You can invite people from other churches to go along with you and all of this. And the main thing about it is that unlike the American–African American associations they don't beg for money. They don't beg ... if you give them ... if they get $100 a year from the church, $100 a year, they are happy, satisfied. You are still entitled to the same privileges as those churches that throw in $100,000, $200,000, or whatever.

And I have developed a rapport with all of the white ministers, pastors, that pastor the churches in that association. And I have been called upon to refer African American ministers to the association for pastorate consideration. And here again, you know, we don't believe in ... when I say "we," I'm talking about the typical African American, typical African American says if you are called to minister, you don't have to go to school. That's what they say. You don't have to go to school. So the ones that went to school I have referred about maybe eight different ministers, but what kept them from getting the positions that I referred them for was either they had been married too many times, or they didn't have the required education, had not been to any type of seminary or anything of that nature, or they, themselves, the ministers, didn't like the congregation that they were interviewed by. So with that, when it comes to community activities, working in the community, as far as the faith community is concerned, I am the only African American representative in the city of Hopewell other than Dr. Curtis Harris, and he doesn't work in the areas I work in.

DR. LEE: Was that a conscious decision that you all would work in different areas of faith?

REVEREND DUNBAR: No. It just happened. It just happened. I guess it was one of those things where I won't trod on your territory, you won't trod on my territory. It was just ... it just happened.

DR. LEE: Well, actually it works well.

REVEREND DUNBAR: It does.

DR. LEE: You cover more ground?

REVEREND DUNBAR: Yes. It works very well, as a matter of fact. And beside that I am engaged in ... I am on ... one, two, three, four, five ... about five different boards of advisors, right here in Hopewell, on one in Petersburg, on one in Richmond, and I am also a member of the African American Church Leadership Conference in Richmond.

Now, the African American Church Leadership Conference in Richmond comes under the Richmond Baptist Association, which is a sister association to the Petersburg Baptist Association. There are many, many, many, many churches in Richmond that belongs to the Richmond … Baptist Association, which is a subordinate of Southern Baptist Convention. So … and they are doing the very same thing that I've been doing. They are reaching out, trying to pull these pastors in so they can be representatives of the Southern Baptist Convention and the Richmond Baptist …. It is hard when you can't get members onboard, but even in the Richmond Baptist Association there are churches from Norfolk, Newport News, Hampton. Some even come as far as from Danville into Richmond to go to meetings. And it makes for a good relationship and good ecumenical services.

DR. LEE: Hopewell is coming up fast.

REVEREND DUNBAR: Well, it is speeding up now. It took a long time for it to take off, you know, like … the one problem now with Hopewell is that it is landlocked.

DR. LEE: So you cannot grow.

REVEREND DUNBAR: Yeah. In order to … in order to improve … to be considered would be either digging, going up or going down or both because Prince George is not letting up any land, you know. Chesterfield either. So there is no expansion for Hopewell. No more. And Hopewell would probably still be down there in that nine, ten, eleven thousand population bracket had it not been for that last annexation that they permitted to go through with. I don't think they are going to allow any more.

DR. LEE: I'm fairly sure about that, but you are doing a lot with what you have.

REVEREND DUNBAR: Oh, yes. And you know, with the planning commission, you know, we come up with a lot of ideas and all this, and many of those ideas are accepted by the director of development.

DR. LEE: How long have you been on the planning commission?

REVEREND DUNBAR: I've been on there now nine years, nine years. Right about '96, yeah.

DR. LEE: A lot has been done in that time.

REVEREND DUNBAR: Yes, a lot. A whole lot has been done.

DR. LEE: What are you most proud of?

REVEREND DUNBAR: I think that I am most proud of the fact that I have a hand in the doings of whatever is done in Hopewell as far as development is concerned. I can reach back and pat myself on the shoulder and say, yes, I was instrumental in these happenings.

DR. LEE: Well done. Well done. Thank you. Thank you very much.

Mrs. Joy Gilliam and Patrice Gilliam, June 21, 2005

On June 21, 2005, I arrived at the Gilliam home to interview Patrice Gilliam; when I arrived, her mother, Joy Gilliam, was there. When asked, she initially declined to be interviewed. She relented, however, and her comments shed light on hidden areas of Hopewell's history. She passed away on February 10, 2007.

Patrice recalled those painful first days of desegregation in Hopewell as well as her hopes for the future. Patrice Gilliam's interview provides insight into the experiences of students on the front lines of the desegregation struggle. In many ways they were soldiers who were following orders, from their parents, the courts, and the schools. Their stories demand a study in itself. While some later

Left: *Patrice Gilliam.* Below: *Joy Gilliam*
Courtesy of Carmela Hamm

rebelled, others continued holding their positions on the front lines of the battle for equality.

DR. LEE: This is June 21st, 2005, Tuesday evening at the home of 1108 Maplewood in Hopewell. Thank you so much. I appreciate this. This is a part of the Hopewell African American Oral History Project. And I would like to get a sense of what Hopewell was like as you were coming up. And I also want to get a sense of your family place in Hopewell's history, also. Would you like to start with your grandfather, George Washington Gilliam, or yourself?

Patrice Gilliam: Well, I never knew George Washington Gilliam. He died when my father was seventeen years old, but I …

Dr. Lee: Your father's name?

Patrice Gilliam: My father's name is Reuben L. Gilliam.

Dr. Lee: Okay. So you never really knew your grandfather?

Patrice Gilliam: I never knew my grandfather, but I have been told about him, and the fact that he was a riverboat pilot. He was the first African American riverboat pilot east of the Mississippi, that he ran an excursion boat from City Point, and it would go to Richmond, and from Richmond it would come back through City Point and go to Norfolk.

Dr. Lee: And the name of the excursion boat?

Patrice Gilliam: It was entitled the *Pocahontas*.

Dr. Lee: Now, that seems unusual for a man, an African American man in the 1930s to have that kind of mobility and opportunity. Do you know what it was that led him to this occupation?

Patrice Gilliam: I don't. I get a sense that during that time African Americans in the city had been pushed to the river, to the riverfront. At that time Hopewell was beginning to become industrialized and it was growing a little bit west of City Point. And the town itself was beginning to build up. This area of City Point is the oldest section of the city, and it was a river port area. And as I indicated, African Americans had been relegated to this end of town. And if you didn't have a general store to operate, then from what I understand they made their living from fishing, and I imagine that the river was their work ethnic, their occupation dealt with working around the waterfront and fishing and whatnot.

There was a gentleman here who owned a general store down the hill on the waterfront.

Dr. Lee: Do you remember the name of the store, the owner's name?

Mrs. Joy Gilliam: All I know is that it was Mr. … was it Arthur Jackson?

Patrice Gilliam: Arthur Jackson's grocery store.

Mrs. Joy Gilliam: May I interject this, because I talked to her father a little bit more than she did. During the time, during the early … the early part of time the Gilliams were free Negroes. They were never slaves. They were free Negroes. And you have some of them already named in the previous history that was done.

DR. LEE: By?

MRS. JOY GILLIAM: Back in the thirties, I think. They were … one of them was in the legislature. They were farmers. And you see, all of this deals with probably how he became a pilot, because of the fact that they were always free and there is a great deal of white blood in their, in their family.

DR. LEE: Okay.

MRS. JOY GILLIAM: And we have just recently found out there was an area in west Hopewell that was called …

PATRICE GILLIAM: Broadway.

MRS. JOY GILLIAM: … Broadway. This is where Patrice's great-grandfather is buried. They had a family cemetery back there, and the property was over near what is now the federal reformatory.

DR. LEE: And what's his name?

PATRICE GILLIAM: His name was Reuben.

MRS. JOY GILLIAM: His name was Reuben, too.

PATRICE GILLIAM: Reuben Montezuma

MRS. JOY GILLIAM: Reuben Montezuma, I guess.

DR. LEE: Do you know his birth and death dates?

PATRICE GILLIAM: No.

MRS. JOY GILLIAM: Huh-uh. What I'm trying to say is that …

PATRICE GILLIAM: The Gilliams had a social …

DR. LEE: Network?

PATRICE GILLIAM: Yeah. They were considered a step above most of the black …

MRS. JOY GILLIAM: They were considered the affluent.

PATRICE GILLIAM: The affluent blacks in the area.

DR. LEE: Due in part to their family relationships with the white Gilliams.

PATRICE GILLIAM: With the white Gilliams.

MRS. JOY GILLIAM: Probably. Probably.

DR. LEE: So we're looking at patronage ties between the white Gilliams and the black.

PATRICE GILLIAM: And there were some that acknowledged the fact that they were related and there are some that didn't want to acknowledge the fact that they were related.

DR. LEE: Okay. All right.

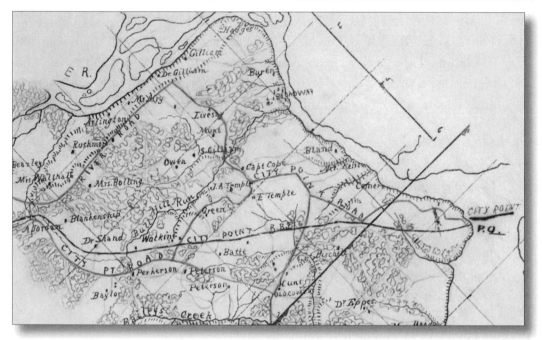

Section of a map, created in 1864, of Prince George County, Virginia, "made under the direction of A. H. Campbell," head of the Confederate Topographical Department. Roads, railroads, waterways, place names, and residents were recorded. In upper left are the homeplaces of "Gilliam" and "Dr. Gilliam," and east of there, Broadway. To the far right is City Point.

Broadway, once the largest town in Prince George County, was in the eighteenth and part of the nineteenth centuries a major port and transportation center. Town resident William Gilliam was mentioned in a 1780 record. In 1862 one of the five inhabited buildings in the town was owned by Reuben Gilliam, free black. Shortly thereafter, Broadway again was of major importance, serving as a massive supply depot for the Union army besieging Petersburg.

MRS. JOY GILLIAM: And this property, which was Broadway, we're told, we've been in the … process of researching it ourselves, but we were told that they had a plantation back over there, and the government wanted their land. They had a rifle range and all of that, and they wanted them to get out, and they refused to get out, so they shelled the house and everything. And they finally forced them to move.

So Patrice drives out there now talking about, I want to see my land. And I tell her, there's no way under the sun she is going to get her land back, but she drives out there looking for her land. Now, as late as about five years ago someone called here from the library here in Hopewell and asked me if we had anything to do with Broadway. And I told them, I said, I married into the family. You'll

Below left: *A small section of a Union map (of Bermuda Hundred, 1864–65), surveyed and drawn by Major J. E. Weyss and assistants. At center is visible Union-held Broadway Landing, with earthworks protecting it and still in evidence a few of the buildings that had once populated the town of Broadway. Also visible, crossing the Appomattox, is the Union army's pontoon bridge, a major link in its supply line to aid in the siege of Petersburg.*

Below: *The pontoon bridge, and a view of Broadway Landing, on the south bank of the Appomattox.*

Left: *Library of Congress, Geography and Map Division*
Below: *Courtesy of Library of Congress*

have to talk with my husband. Well, they never called back. And my husband just was never the kind to pay too much attention to history. He didn't care for that. So he never called them.

But when they called me, they told me that there was a group from William and Mary who was doing excavation out there, and they wanted to know if he had anything to do with that property. Well, he was the youngest in the family. Now, she tells you that she never knew her grandfather, but she did know her great uncle, her grandfather's brother, and he told us when he came back here, he told us that his mother had sold that property when he was still a minor, and he was trying to reclaim the land because it had been sold without his signature or anything. But it was going to cost a whole lot of money, and he didn't … he didn't have that money, plus the fact that none of these white people around here wanted to even discuss it.

So that's how we really and truly found out about Broadway, was when he …when he came, when he came home.

DR. LEE: Okay.

MRS. JOY GILLIAM: Now, he was an Episcopal minister.

DR. LEE: And his name again?

PATRICE GILLIAM: His name …

MRS. JOY GILLIAM: His name was William Edward Gilliam.

DR. LEE: And he was the brother …

MRS. JOY GILLIAM: Uh-huh.

PATRICE GILLIAM: Brother to George.

DR. LEE: … Washington Gilliam.

MRS. JOY GILLIAM: Uh-huh.

DR. LEE: Okay. And we're talking about the area called Broadway. The area where we are now, what's that called?

PATRICE GILLIAM: This is City Point.

DR. LEE: City Point. And so you all have been affiliated with City Point for how long?

PATRICE GILLIAM: For me, fifty-two years.

DR. LEE: Since you were born. Since you were born.

PATRICE GILLIAM: Uh-huh.

DR. LEE: Okay. So we have got some background information on the family now. You grew up in this home right here?

MRS. JOY GILLIAM: Uh-huh.

PATRICE GILLIAM: Uh-huh.

DR. LEE: And you started at Harry E. James Elementary School?

PATRICE GILLIAM: Uh-huh.

DR. LEE: Where was that located?

PATRICE GILLIAM: It is located in a section of Hopewell called Davisville.

MRS. JOY GILLIAM: It's in the projects.

PATRICE GILLIAM: It's in the projects.

DR. LEE: Uh-huh.

PATRICE GILLIAM: And my mother was a teacher there, at Harry E. James, and she taught me in the fifth grade. And she was hoping not to teach me in the fifth grade, but it didn't turn out that way. Growing up and going to school at Harry James meant that … there used to be some steps that led down the hill toward to Water Street, and Water Street leads up to an industrial road, because down on Water Street was a sand and gravel pit as well, and it is in a residential area. As I indicated, black folks in City Point, this is where they lived, although where I live is bordered three sides in a white, residential area. But the Gilliam family has been on this dead end or the Maplewood extension ever since I can remember and prior to that, as well.

> We traveled, we walked to school, and we traveled an industrial route because the industrial trucks went in the back way to what used to be Allied Chemical plant. And we had to cross Route 10, which is also known as Randolph Road, to get to school. We had no school buses that we could ride to school. We had no school guards that stood out at Randolph Road. And you would have had to have watched us crossing the street. It was like chickens trying to cross the street in the middle of rush-hour traffic trying to get to school. When it rained, we took the Yellow Cab taxi would come and pick us up.

> There's a school that the children in the next block went to that's entitled Patrick Copeland. From my door to the door of Patrick Copeland Elementary School, where there are sidewalks that you can travel if you had to walk is one mile. From my front door to the school Harry E. James was one mile and five tenths, and because we lived in a neighborhood one block away where the children who lived in the next block went to Patrick Copeland my parents thought that it might be a better idea to make application for me to go to Patrick Copeland.

> And the secondary reason was, and my mother really did not wish to teach me in the fifth grade, that was going to be a hard issue.

DR. LEE: Was there one teacher?

PATRICE GILLIAM: No. There were two teachers, but there was a high group and a low group, and she had the high group, along with the fact that I was a pretty good student, I was a high achiever at the time. And just knowing because of dealing with other children who had gone to school there, their parents had worked there, too … in fact, one student's father was the principal. Not only was he a principal, but his mother taught the third grade, so I'm sure that Bernie Epps had as equally of a hard time as I had.

But it wasn't bad at Harry E. James. I had lots of friends and I thought I was popular and whatnot. I sang in the choir. Not because I was Joy's daughter, but because I had my own identity.

DR. LEE: Right.

PATRICE GILLIAM: But when I got into the fifth grade I got my first F, because I had something I had to prove. My mother had a project that we would have to do, all fifth graders had to do the second semester, and it was a social studies project, and the project was outlining the fifty states. And you had an outline that you had to follow, you had to come up with a picture of the state. My mother was a creative teacher. She didn't always have the tools that she needed to teach the classes. My mother taught social studies without maps, without a globe, and that's kind of difficult. She bought a book of maps and they had a thing, it was called a ditto machine, and she made dittos of maps and passed dittos out to the students. That's how we learned about states. Used the map that was in your textbook to locate countries and rivers and landscapes. And creativity, I guess my being a teacher now, I learned a lot from her because you had to be creative and you had to be innovative back in those days, and you didn't have the textbooks and all the tools you needed to teach, yet we had a first-class education and we were nutured.

DR. LEE: And so in this environment you got your first F?

PATRICE GILLIAM: I got my first F because I did not do the project. And I didn't do the project because I had several students who said, oh, you know you are going to get the A. And I had to prove that I was not going to get the A. And at the end of the nine weeks I had an F on my report card for that nine weeks. I had a C out of the course, but I had an F for that nine weeks because I did not do the project.

And my father was furious with me, but I never told either one of them. And I guess if I had told them maybe there would have been a way that they could have worked with me or I would have had some other redress with the class, but that's when I got the first F. And that summer … well, for two years of that time during the summer I would spend six weeks at Virginia State in a reading clinic. And the summer that I had finished the fifth grade they were kind enough to give me a break, and I didn't have to go to summer school or … it was basically for enrichment, but they didn't think I needed to go for enrichment because I knew that I was going to be going to Patrick Copeland in September, and it was under court order.

DR. LEE: Okay. And so at that time you are entering the sixth grade?

PATRICE GILLIAM: Entering the sixth grade.

DR. LEE: Twelve years old?

PATRICE GILLIAM: Eleven years old.

DR. LEE: And you know at that age, eleven, twelve, you think all eyes are on you or whatever. What was it like to go into that school?

PATRICE GILLIAM: I was a very timid child, scared of my shadow. I remember being told that we were going thirty minutes ahead of time. I remember my grandmother, because she was a domestic worker and …

DR. LEE: And her name?

PATRICE GILLIAM: Her name was Mary Bowman Gilliam. She was married to George.

    …

    I remember when the court order came that we would go to Patrick Copeland, I remember her saying that she didn't think she'd ever live to see black children go to a white school, and she didn't believe it.

MRS. JOY GILLIAM: I told her emphatically that they was court ordered or they wouldn't be going there to school.

PATRICE GILLIAM: And rather than go with us, grandma called Yellow Cab, and I thought she was going to work. Usually she would walk to work, or she might catch the bus up here and go wherever, but she called the Yellow Cab. And it was about a quarter of 8:00, and we left here at about three minutes to 8:00, and when we drove up in front of Patrick Copeland and got out, there's a building right across the street from Patrick Copeland. It used to be a dance … here of late it was a dance studio, but it used to be Appomattox Cleaner, and grandma was standing in the doorway of Appomattox Cleaner dressed with an umbrella to get … keep the morning sun off of her because she wanted to see us walk into Patrick Copeland because she did not believe that it was going to happen. And mom and dad …

MRS. JOY GILLIAM: No. I wasn't there.

PATRICE GILLIAM: You didn't go with us the first day?

MRS. JOY GILLIAM: I went to work. Your daddy took you.

PATRICE GILLIAM: I thought you went with us.

MRS. JOY GILLIAM: Huh-uh. I did not go. I went to work.

DR. LEE: Your presence must have been strongly missed since she remembered you being there.

MRS. JOY GILLIAM: Well, we had been told that they had to be there for half an hour before any of the rest of the children. Now, from the time that they went into Patrick Copeland for I guess the first three years, my husband took his vacation at the beginning of school. I would go to work, but he was the one who saw to it that particular morning that they went into school. And you see, this was the strange thing about it, there were seven children involved in the desegregation of the schools. And all seven of them … well, all of them weren't in Patrick Copeland.

PATRICE GILLIAM: No, but …

MRS. JOY GILLIAM: The ones who were in Patrick Copeland, I think it was about four of them, they went into the school.

PATRICE GILLIAM: We went two weeks ahead because they transferred.

MRS. JOY GILLIAM: Yeah. I know that. I know that. I know that. But what I'm trying to say is there was another group of children that the NAACP worked with Curtis Harris and the superintendent to determine whether they would go into the schools, into the schools. But my two children had to go two weeks before any of those children did, and if they didn't get killed or nothing would happen to them, then the rest of these children went into the schools. So I have always felt that the seven children who were involved in the desegregation suit was really … they were really the ones who desegregated the schools and everybody else was a Johnny-come-lately, that's the way I felt about it, because they made sure that if nothing happened to these children, then the rest of the children that the superintendent and Curtis Harris had worked with their parents and whatnot to get them to put their children in the school, then they would go to the school.

DR. LEE: Do you remember the names of those children or family names?

MRS. JOY GILLIAM: I can give you all of their names but I would prefer … I would prefer not to because you have no idea what these kids went through and how the other parents of the children who went into the school, how they honestly felt about these children. And when I tell you that the principal under whom I had worked when I first started teaching was the principal of the school Carter Woodson called all of his faculty together the morning those kids went into school, and this is what he told them, he told them that his children would never go to the integrated school. He told them that by my putting my children into the white school most of the teachers in town were going to lose their jobs, and I was the one who would be responsible for it.

Now, I wasn't there, but I had friends who still worked there and this is what they told me. And I also want you to know that for two years … I had worked here eleven years. The year before they went into the schools I was declared teacher of the year, and for the next two years my telephone never rang except for one particular friend who lived in Petersburg, and she would call every day. If she didn't call me, I would call her. But for two years my telephone never rang, not from a white person, and not from a black person.

PATRICE GILLIAM: She lost her job.

MRS. JOY GILLIAM: And many times my husband came in from work, and I'd be cuddled up in the corner of the sofa crying my heart out. And he always walked in and he said … he'd come in and he'd say, what's the matter? And I wouldn't even be able to give it out. And he'd come over and he'd put his arm around me and he said, don't take it like that, Joy. They aren't giving you anything. And we have each other, we have the children, and that's all we need.

DR. LEE: So what year was it you got the teacher of the year award; do you remember?

MRS. JOY GILLIAM: Well, it wasn't … you know, it wasn't an award like it is now where the school gives it to you and everything. This was an award that the children voted the teacher of the year and …

DR. LEE: That's even better.

MRS. JOY GILLIAM: And this was 1963, wasn't it?

PATRICE GILLIAM: Sixty …

MRS. JOY GILLIAM: 1963. '62, '63.

PATRICE GILLIAM: Yeah, '62, '63.

MRS. JOY GILLIAM: 1962, '63, because you went into the school in '63.

PATRICE GILLIAM: '63, in August … in September, '63.

MRS. JOY GILLIAM: Yeah.

Courtesy of Carmela Hamm

DR. LEE: Did you have a brother or sister that went in with you?

PATRICE GILLIAM: I have a brother.

DR. LEE: And his name?

PATRICE GILLIAM: Reuben.

MRS. JOY GILLIAM: His name is Reuben L. III … I mean II.

PATRICE GILLIAM: II.

Dr. Lee: So you two and five other children went into …

Patrice Gilliam: My brother and I went for two weeks before the other five came.

Dr. Lee: Okay.

Patrice Gilliam: They transferred in. My first week was interesting because I had a little boy in the seventh grade who spat on me every day for about four days. And I was going into … I would go in the front door in the morning, but I wasn't supposed to go in the front door in the mornings, and I didn't realize that. You know, that was the way that we had gone in. And there was a door middle way of the school that I was supposed to come out of in the afternoon, and that was the same door I was supposed to go in, but I didn't realize that. And at the time we did not ride the bus. We had someone that would take us, or mom would drop us off in the morning. Someone would pick us up in the afternoon. That first day, I guess I got caught up because the teachers did not walk us to our point where we were supposed to go down the steps, and I went all the way to the end of the hall, because I was on the second floor, and I went down the … and out the door that the seventh grade students went out of, and walked around the back and came to the front.

And I didn't realize that wasn't what I was supposed to do, but every day I did that for about four days. And there was this one boy who would run up next to me and one day he spat in my hair, another day he spat on my shoe, another day he spat on my dress, and the boy just looked familiar. And I came home and I told dad about it. And dad called the principal. And the principal's name was Logan C. Harding, and very kind gentleman, very fatherly. I imagine he had children. But he was very understanding. And he told … he called me in. He told my dad that he would talk to me the next morning. And he called me into his office, and I talked to him. I tried to describe him, the little boy. I hadn't seen him that morning. But he asked me did I pass by his office in the afternoon? And I said, yes. And he said, well, I'm going to be standing at my office window. You point him out to me. And that particular afternoon I pointed him out to him. And he came out and caught him and suspended him.

Well, the little boy looked familiar, and I couldn't remember. It was just something about this boy that looked familiar to me. And Friday I figured it out. He was the *Progress Index* paperboy, and he came to collect. We just happened to be outside that Friday afternoon. I don't remember why my brother and I were outside. And Daddy happened to have been home. And he was home a little early that day and I ran in and I said, "Daddy, Daddy, the boy that spat on me is the paperboy." And he said, "You are kidding." And I said, "No. He's coming, he's coming. He's riding his bicycle and he's collecting for the paper."

And Daddy came to the door when he came to collect and I went to the door with Daddy and Daddy handed him his money and Daddy spat down by his feet. And he said now maybe you will understand what you've been doing to my daughter, because he glared at Daddy.

We found out the little boy lived over on Ramsey Street, which is one of the streets we would have to walk when we were going to Harry E. James, but that little boy moved and he left Patrick Copeland. I don't know if he moved to North Carolina. I don't know where he went. I don't even know what his name was. But that was one of the incidents at Patrick Copeland that I can remember. Another incident was that my class was kept in, and those who rode the bus managed to get out. They kept them long enough, you know, just so that they would get on the bus, but those of us who didn't ride the bus we had to get home the best way we could. And when I came out of school, and I started walking home, I was aware that this light green car was slowly following me. And when the man passed me, and drove on off, I took off running. I guess I … it must have been a mile. I must have broken every track record my grandfather's track team had ever made because I think I got home in about ten minutes. And when the man came back and he was facing me, I was further along than I was when he had passed me before.

And I came home and I told my Dad about this car. And I had managed to get three of the numbers for the license plate and whatnot. And I think Dad called somebody, and they finally found out who he was. And the guy said that he was … he was looking out for me. And I don't know if it was someone that Daddy knew. I don't remember whether it was one of the federal marshals. And that was something else, I was seventeen years old before I really knew that federal marshals were there watching us, because one of the things Mom and …

MRS. JOY GILLIAM: You would be surprised at the number of people that the children didn't even know, but they made a point of being in that area of the school when it opened, and when it closed. They were all looking out for these kids, and some of them I wouldn't know if they walked in the door right now, but all of them knew Reuben because, as I told you, he had carried mail, and some of them were actually winos but they were looking out for these kids.

PATRICE GILLIAM: One of them told Daddy that something was wrong with his daughter.

MRS. JOY GILLIAM: That she run like a jackrabbit. All I was trying to do was see to it that she got home safely.

PATRICE GILLIAM: But one of the things that Mom and Dad had decided once we went to Patrick Copeland was that they wanted us to have as much of a normal life as possible, so we really did … we really were not aware of the federal marshals. The federal marshals were there the day that we went into the school, but I didn't know them. I didn't know who they were. You didn't see them walking around in the school. I don't know if they were outside. I don't know, but we had that protection.

Mrs. Joy Gilliam: And you can say anything you want to, but there was some very, very hard feelings among whites when these kids went into the schools. There was hard feelings among the teachers in the school where they went. Now, my son … of the two children going into the school, I would have thought that it would have affected Patrice much more than it affected my son. He was just in the second grade. And he was a happy-go-lucky kid, and he always had a smile on his face. You never knew when anything was bothering him. And I will be honest, I had no idea how it affected him until he's a full-grown man because he grinned all of the time, and he very seldom let you know when anything was bothering him.

The only way we would know that something was going on with him, she'd come home and tell us. Now, she passed by his classroom one day, and the teacher had put him off in a row all by himself. She had pulled him aside from all of the other children and had him sitting over by himself. And she came home and told us. And of course the next day I had business at school, and I had business in the principal's office with the teacher, and I wanted to know why she had my child, he's the only little black speck in the buttermilk, why she had my child sitting in a row all by himself.

Courtesy of Carmela Hamm

And she said something to the effect that he had a cold, and that I needed to … in fact, she wrote a note. She didn't put any salutation on it. She just wrote a note telling me, take your child to the doctor and have him inoculated for … what was it …

Dr. Lee: Polio.

Mrs. Joy Gilliam: Have him inoculated. And of course I wrote her back and asked her who in the world she was writing the letter to. She didn't address me. But I told the principal, and I told her, I said my children are in here on court order. If I have one more complaint the federal marshal will be sitting in your room from now until school is out. They knew not to fool with me. My husband didn't have to go up there. I was always there, always, whenever there was any, any problem. And I tell people right now, you don't put your children in school and just leave them there. You have to check on them. Now, I don't mean go up there belligerently like most folks do nowadays, but you have to check on your children. It was quite an experience. I tell you one other thing, which was funny. They ate their lunch at school, and they had to take their lunch money. My husband would get them every morning, he'd give them the exact change, and he'd take my fingernail polish and put a dab on each coin. One day it would be on heads, next day it would be on tails, but he had fingernail polish.

PATRICE GILLIAM: And each week it would be a different color.

MRS. JOY GILLIAM: Yeah. And they had fingernail polish on their money. So the cafeteria manager asked Patrice, she said, why is it you and your brother come in here every day with fingernail polish on your money? And Patrice just looked at her and smiled and walked on. But when Boo came along and she asked him, he looked up at her, he said, oh, my Daddy puts that on my money every day so you white folks can't say I stole anybody's money. Patrice didn't tell her what it was all about. But Boo would tell it all. Oh, my Daddy does that every morning so you white folks can't say we stole anybody's money.

DR. LEE: I wish I could have seen her face. It sounds like you all had strategies in place to protect yourself and each other. And did you feel like you were your brother's protector in that situation because you said you walked past the classroom where he was?

PATRICE GILLIAM: I just … we were kind of cohesive at an early age anyway, and that was just normal for us at that time, but things didn't bother him like they would bother me.

MRS. JOY GILLIAM: I think they bothered him, but we didn't know it.

PATRICE GILLIAM: Yeah, we didn't know.

MRS. JOY GILLIAM: But she broke the ice for everybody else.

PATRICE GILLIAM: Yeah. I was the ice breaker. And my classmates … we had a classmate, and we ended it with the Age of Aquarius and we danced to the Fifth Dimension's *Age of Aquarius* and whatnot. And in my last will and testament I left the right … I left my seat at Hopewell High School, and the right for every black child in the city of Hopewell to have an opportunity to attend the public school of his or her choice in the city of Hopewell, and the right to run for whatever office or whatever superlative that he or she felt they were worthy of.

The Reverend and Mrs. Curtis Harris, June 23, 2005

Courtesy of Carmela Hamm

I interviewed the Reverend and Mrs. Curtis Harris in their home in Davisville. Across the street sits Union Baptist Church, where Reverend Harris has pastored generations of families. Beginning in the 1960s Harris mounted seven campaigns for a seat on the Hopewell City Council. After he filed a discrimination lawsuit against the city, which he won, politics changed in Hopewell. By replacing the at-large system with a ward system and thereby redrawing voting districts, Harris became the first African American to serve on the Hopewell City Council, in 1986. By 1998 he was elected the first African American mayor of Hopewell. This is the first time the Reverend and Mrs. Harris have been interviewed as a couple and the first time Mrs. Harris has been interviewed. From their comments we have a better understanding of what it was like to grow up in Hopewell during the Jim Crow era. We can better appreciate the sacrifices activists and public servants make as well as the determination to maintain a family life and why Mrs. Harris's favorite scripture is from Psalm 121: "I will lift up mine eyes unto the hills from whence cometh my help, and where it comes from, knowing that it doesn't come from that mountain, it comes from who made the mountain."

Courtesy of Carmela Hamm

DR. LEE: June 23rd, 2005, in the home of the Reverend Dr. Harris and Mrs. Harris at 209 Terminal Avenue in Hopewell, Virginia.

REVEREND HARRIS: Street. Street. Yes.

DR. LEE: In Hopewell, Virginia. And this is for the Hopewell Oral History Project. And this particular interview will focus more on their life together as a couple working together, raising a family, and overcoming obstacles during the civil rights movement. We'll start with some background information. Where were you born, Mrs. Harris?

REVEREND HARRIS: Dendron, Virginia. Dendron, Virginia.

MRS. HARRIS: 1925.

DR. LEE: All right. What schools did you all attend here in Hopewell?

REVEREND HARRIS: Carter G. Woodson, both of us.

DR. LEE: Okay, Carter G. Woodson. And where was that located at the time that you went to school?

REVEREND HARRIS: Behind the fire station.

DR. LEE: The current fire station?

MRS. HARRIS: The principal was Harry E. James.

DR. LEE: What are your earliest remembrances of your school days?

REVEREND HARRIS: Well, I remember the first day I went to school, my sister brought … took me to school.

DR. LEE: Walking?

REVEREND HARRIS: Walking. There were no buses. And I lived in this area.

DR. LEE: And what was this area called?

REVEREND HARRIS: Davisville. Still Davisville. And my sister took me to school, and the school had a rule that when you come to Carter Woodson, all the girls would go in one door and the boys would go in another door, all the way at the other end of the building.

DR. LEE: What grades did that school go up to?

REVEREND HARRIS: Primmer. I mean it started at a primmer, and it would go to …

MRS. HARRIS: Started at the first grade, and up to the eleventh grade.

REVEREND HARRIS: Mrs. Byas was my primmer teacher, but my wife said it's the first grade. I won't argue on that. I know it didn't go no … beyond the eleventh grade.

DR. LEE: Okay. And that is the grade that most black people at that time would be able to go to in the public school system?

REVEREND HARRIS: Yes.

DR. LEE: If they wanted anything more they'd have to go elsewhere?

REVEREND HARRIS: Well, we graduated. They gave us a certificate, or a diploma, but if you tried to get into college, you had to go through some …

DR. LEE: Remedial?

REVEREND HARRIS: Yeah, remedial classes before you can get in the college on up.

MRS. HARRIS: I didn't have to do that.

REVEREND HARRIS: You didn't?

MRS. HARRIS: I went to Virginia State College, that's what it was at that time.

DR. LEE: Now, on graduation, what were the plans of most of the students and yourselves; go on to college, to work, to stay here in Hopewell, to move elsewhere?

MRS. HARRIS: You know, I really didn't have any plans. I really didn't.

DR. LEE: You all had met by this time, right?

MRS. HARRIS: Yes. Yes. We had met, but my mom said, you are going away from here, so I did go to school.

DR. LEE: At Virginia State?

MRS. HARRIS: Uh-huh.

DR. LEE: And you also went to trade school …

MRS. HARRIS: Yeah.

DR. LEE: … in cosmetology?

MRS. HARRIS: And beauty culture. Yes.

DR. LEE: And attended Virginia Union?

MRS. HARRIS: Yes.

DR. LEE: What were your plans?

MRS. HARRIS: To be a beautician and open up my … a beauty shop, which I did later.

DR. LEE: Harris and Young Beauty Shop?

DR. LEE: And at the time that Mrs. Harris started the beauty parlor, what were you doing?

REVEREND HARRIS: I was a janitor at Allied Chemical.

DR. LEE: What were your plans upon graduation?

REVEREND HARRIS: Well, see, I went … when I finished high school, I went later to Virginia Union. By that time, I done got in love stuff, and when I found out she was going to Virginia Union, I said I better go to college. So we went to Virginia Union for about a year and a half or two years, and then we decided to get married.

DR. LEE: Okay. Let me back up a little bit. When did you all first meet?

REVEREND HARRIS: Well, I had noticed her at the high school and, you know, we were at the same school so …

MRS. HARRIS: We were in high school.

REVEREND HARRIS: We were in high school. We were in high school, and then we had a program, and it was … I was dancing in the program because …

DR. LEE: You used to dance?

REVEREND HARRIS: Oh, I used to cut a rug.

DR. LEE: So now we are hearing about a different side of you. Were there dance contests?

MRS. HARRIS: On Friday. They used to have talent programs every Friday.

DR. LEE: And this was at the school?

MRS. HARRIS: At the school.

Courtesy of Carmela Hamm

DR. LEE: What other recreational activities were there?

REVEREND HARRIS: At school?

DR. LEE: During that time, in the neighborhood, at the church.

REVEREND HARRIS: We had a basketball team at school, and we had a football team. We never won no games, but we had a team. The team was so small, you go to play somebody like Armstrong …

DR. LEE: In Richmond?

REVEREND HARRIS: Yeah. Them big boys knock us down, but we were trying.

DR. LEE: Okay. And so outside of the school, what were you all able to do as far as recreation?

REVEREND HARRIS: We didn't have very much recreation. It was not popular in this area.

They … in the summer they would … they had a little wading pool, but the school was closed.

DR. LEE: Okay. Where would the wading pool be?

REVEREND HARRIS: In front of the school.

… Behind the fire station.

… And they … we could go in … I think they had some swings, and some, merry-go-rounds on that … and so that was the recreation for the whole city, black part of the city.

DR. LEE: Right. Did you want to …

MRS. HARRIS: Where we lived, we made games that we made up, and of course croquet, and baseball and those kind of things we occupied ourselves with, because we were in the county at that time.

DR. LEE: Prince George County?

MRS. HARRIS: Prince George County. It was later annexed.

REVEREND HARRIS: I was in the city.

DR. LEE: You were a city boy?

REVEREND HARRIS: Yeah, that's right.

DR. LEE: You were a country girl. So we are talking about segregation during that time, blacks and whites did not mingle at all.

MRS. HARRIS: Right.

DR. LEE: Were you aware of the kinds of facilities that they had?

MRS. HARRIS: Yes. Oh, yes. Yes, because … the whites that lived over where I lived, they rode the streetcar, and we walked when I went to school, and we were three miles from the school and we walked to school and back for eleven years.

DR. LEE: And the books that you got for school, were they the books that had been handed down from the white school, because I know that's the case in many localities? Is that the case here?

REVEREND HARRIS: Yes. Yes. Not only they would have hand-me-down books, they would use the paper, and you had to turn it over on the other side after the white kids got through with it. And when they get ready to put in some new seats in, we would get their seats, because they would be all … things all written on top of them and everything, the names and so forth on there, so we had hand-me-downs.

DR. LEE: In everything …

REVEREND HARRIS: Yeah.

DR. LEE: ... regarding school?

REVEREND HARRIS: Yeah.

DR. LEE: All right. Was there any interaction with whites at that time?

REVEREND HARRIS: No.

MRS. HARRIS: Fighting.

DR. LEE: Fighting?

REVEREND HARRIS: Yeah, if you run up into them.

MRS. HARRIS: Well, he probably didn't, but it was a white school on our route home.

DR. LEE: Do you remember the name?

MRS. HARRIS: It was ... what was it ... Highland Park ...

REVEREND HARRIS: Highland Park.

MRS. HARRIS: ... Elementary School, it was a white school that we had to pass that school walking, and of course, there have been times when the principal had to walk with us because of ... to keep down the fights from the black and the white fighting.

DR. LEE: Okay. So this was a regular occurrence, these fights?

MRS. HARRIS: Well, it didn't last too long. I don't know what they done about it, but I know it did happen a number of times.

DR. LEE: And you weren't involved?

MRS. HARRIS: No, I was not involved in fighting.

DR. LEE: Okay. What was the feeling during that time, your own personal feelings about the conditions under which you were living, segregation, inequality, injustice? What did you feel?

REVEREND HARRIS: I never accepted second-class citizenship. I didn't know what to do about it, but I never accepted it. And I never had any white friends. Where she lived there were some white folk living close in the community, but there were never any white people living in the community where I lived.

DR. LEE: Davisville?

REVEREND HARRIS: Until I was about ten years old, and there was a community that was in transition, and ... that is, white people were moving out and black people were moving in, and that didn't last too long. I think there were about three or four white families still in the community when I moved into the community.

DR. LEE: What was the name of that community?

REVEREND HARRIS: South B Village.

...

DR. LEE: Which was part of what, DuPont?

REVEREND HARRIS: No, no.

DR. LEE: Tubize?

REVEREND HARRIS: Well, I suppose back in the history that that's the way they identified the different sections of the city, and South B Village. There was also a North Village, and that was a white community.

DR. LEE: Okay.

REVEREND HARRIS: South B Village was originally a white community, but they were in transition when I moved into that community.

DR. LEE: At the age of ten?

REVEREND HARRIS: At ten.

DR. LEE: Okay. And how did this change your feelings about whites, or did it?

REVEREND HARRIS: The two white boys and a white girl, Bobby something and another boy, I can't think of their names now, but we used to beat up on them just because they was white, and ...

DR. LEE: The girl, too?

REVEREND HARRIS: Yeah.

DR. LEE: You didn't discriminate?

REVEREND HARRIS: No. And you know, we didn't just beat them for no reason. If they are trying to play ball with us, then they going to get beat up on because the opposition team will be ... well, they would be helping to deal with the ... in the fight some blacks were sometimes helping the whites if it's on their team.

DR. LEE: Okay.

REVEREND HARRIS: But surely that black boy ... that white boy is going to get beat up on before the game is over. And they come back. They were ...

DR. LEE: To play?

REVEREND HARRIS: Yeah. Yeah. They come back. And we never had no trouble with their parents. Bobby lived closer ... further away from us than the other boy, it was he and his sister. He was down by the dump, so he got to come by my house to go to the store, so he done anything ...

DR. LEE: Anything?

REVEREND HARRIS: ... yeah, he got trouble going to the store. And so that was ... and that didn't last long because they finally moved out of the black community.

REVEREND HARRIS: And we had one man, a white man who lived in the community, and he was an entrepreneur. He was a businessman. He used to make home brew and sell it.

DR. LEE: Bootleg?

REVEREND HARRIS: Yep.

DR. LEE: Okay. All right.

REVEREND HARRIS: They evidently … must not be against … must not been against the law.

DR. LEE: Nobody bothered him?

REVEREND HARRIS: Nobody messed with him. They called him Home Brew Dad.

DR. LEE: Okay.

REVEREND HARRIS: And you ain't know about that? Home Brew Dad was there, he stayed there … I mean he was an old man. He died there. He didn't have no family. And we used to go out and pick up bottles and sell them to him. And I think it was a penny for a bottle.

> …

> And he would wash them out. That's how he put … he … you have a bottle of home brew, might be a Pepsi-Cola bottle.

DR. LEE: Yes. So if you were walking along drinking a home brew no one would necessarily know because it was in a different kind of a bottle?

REVEREND HARRIS: Yes. Yes.

DR. LEE: So you were involved in helping the Home Brew Dad with his business.

REVEREND HARRIS: Yeah.

DR. LEE: I'm just trying … I'm just trying to get the story. So in actuality, you were a contractor?

REVEREND HARRIS: I was cleaning … I was finding bottles, and …

DR. LEE: Just want to make that clear, you were finding bottles.

REVEREND HARRIS: I was finding bottles to sell to Home Brew Dad.

DR. LEE: Okay. A penny a bottle?

REVEREND HARRIS: A penny a bottle.

DR. LEE: How old were you then?

REVEREND HARRIS: When I first got to the community I was ten, and I did it until Home Brew Dad died.

DR. LEE: Okay. So Mrs. Harris, you had a man who obviously, you know, was very interested in making his way in the world and doing something. What kind of work were you involved in; housework, or did you work outside the home?

MRS. HARRIS: Well, I have done some babysitting, yes, outside of the home. And I have ... well, call it domestic work because I have worked on Saturdays to clean up for white people during the time I was in school.

DR. LEE: And who trained you to do this?

MRS. HARRIS: My mother.

DR. LEE: And this was something that most black girls did at that time, or a few?

MRS. HARRIS: A few. A few.

DR. LEE: And so you knew from what your parents said that you were going to college?

MRS. HARRIS: Yes.

DR. LEE: And what about you; you went because she was going? Had you had any aspirations to go?

REVEREND HARRIS: No. I didn't ... I was not geared to go to college. I had talked about it, and even to the extent of what I'd like to be, but ...

DR. LEE: Was Davisville called "The Projects?"

REVEREND HARRIS: It's always been called Davisville, but it is The Project.

DR. LEE: Okay.

REVEREND HARRIS: Because originally ... I mean, originally there was only one project, but there are several projects in Hopewell now.

DR. LEE: Is this the original project?

REVEREND HARRIS: Yes.

REVEREND HARRIS: So we ... my wife went to a meeting and volunteered me to be the scoutmaster and ... because I didn't know nothing about no scouting, but the scoutmaster ... the man that ... the executive invited wives, they didn't invite no men, he invited wives, and when they had the meeting they decided that we were going to have Boy Scouts in Davisville.

DR. LEE: Had there been one before?

MRS. HARRIS: No.

REVEREND HARRIS: Yes, they did.

MRS. HARRIS: Where?

REVEREND HARRIS: Junius Taylor was a scoutmaster before.

Clothing - John			1926		23 10
Mar 10	School shoes	4 50	Dec 23	Over coat	15 00
Mar 15	Black Socks	1 50	Jan 3	Rain coat	5 50
May 14	Rubbers	1 25			
Jun 8	Cap	75		Total for year	43 60
Sept 2	School Suit	8 00		Budget	45 00
Sept 4	3 Shirts	3 00			
Sept 7	4 Underwear	3 20			
Nov 17	6 Handkerchiefs	90			
	Total	23 10			

AUGUST FOOD								$40.00
Days	1	2	3	4	5	6	7	8
			35 70	34 00	32 40	30 60	30 00	28 90
Credit	$40.00							4 80
							60	1 20
Groceries	3 50			50		50		
						1 30		
Meat Fish		80						
Milk			Sunday		20		60	30
Fruit					1 00			
Vegetable				1 10				20
Ice					40			
Oil				1 70	1 60	1 80	60	1 10 6 00
Total spent		4 30		34 00	32 40	30 60	30 00	28 90 22 40
Balance	35 70							

Records in the War Commission provide information about living conditions in Hopewell in the early twentieth century. In the Davisville settlement African American bachelors were provided with living accommodations free of charge. Included were electric lights, running water, bedsteads, stoves, coal, and wood. Single women stayed in several units in the married quarters and were charged $1.50 per person per month. Two women were housed to a room. They were supplied with bedsteads, tables, chairs, electric lights, running water, and stoves. Families rented homes in the allotted family section of Davisville for $3.00 per month; included were electric lights, running water, and stoves. Board at company-owned segregated restaurants was $5.25 and up per week.

Tubize Spinnerette *Volume 2, # 4, p. 14, 15*
Courtesy of Maude Langhorne Nelson Library, Hopewell

Mrs. Harris: Okay. So.

Reverend Harris: You don't know about that.

Mrs. Harris: I really don't.

Reverend Harris: But he had it before. And so they needed to try to get another … a troop in Hopewell. And Reverend Terrence, Reverend Terrence still lives, he is a member of Mt. Olivet Church. He is the interim … he is … what is his … he's retired, and he was assistant to the pastor.

Dr. Lee: Okay.

Reverend Harris: So he's retired, but he's still there. Reverend Terrence came into this area to start a Boy Scout troop, and that's what he did. They had the meeting, then they said, okay, we need a Boy Scout …

Dr. Lee: Excuse me. So you said Reverend Terrence said you needed a Boy Scout troop.

Reverend Harris: Yeah. And he got these women together.

Dr. Lee: So he made sure it happened.

Reverend Harris: I ended up being the scoutmaster.

Dr. Lee: Okay. Now, so this was after you all had married, and you married in 1946?

Reverend Harris: Yes.

Mrs. Harris: Right.

Dr. Lee: So until that time, except for what Junius Taylor had started, there had not been an organized Boy Scout troop?

Reverend Harris: Right.

Dr. Lee: And at this time you had sons yourself that were part of a Boy Scout troop?

Reverend Harris: No. They were little boys.

Dr. Lee: Okay.

Reverend Harris: I think they came …

Mrs. Harris: They were not old enough.

Reverend Harris: They were not old enough. They became Cubs.

Dr. Lee: Okay.

Reverend Harris: Didn't we have a picture with them in the Cubs … yeah, we have a picture of them with the cub suits.

Reverend Harris: She was … she was a den mother.

DR. LEE: Okay.

REVEREND HARRIS: And she was a Girl Scout leader.

DR. LEE: Had there been a Girl Scout troop?

MRS. HARRIS: Yes, there had been a Girl Scouts troop.

DR. LEE: Okay. And you were involved in that?

MRS. HARRIS: Yes.

DR. LEE: Who were some of the other people involved in that?

MRS. HARRIS: Adults, you mean?

DR. LEE: Yes.

MRS. HARRIS: Mrs. Ida Cook.

DR. LEE: Recreation director?

MRS. HARRIS: She was the recreation director at that time. In fact, she was very instrumental in getting the scouting troops, you know, here in our area.

DR. LEE: And where did you hold your meetings?

MRS. HARRIS: Well, to begin with, at my house.

DR. LEE: Okay. So this is seen like a center of activity, community activity, your home?

MRS. HARRIS: For that it was.

DR. LEE: What inspired you to get involved with that?

REVEREND HARRIS: On account I was a scoutmaster.

MRS. HARRIS: Because it was a need. It was a need.

DR. LEE: And what were some of the things you all did?

MRS. HARRIS: Well, we used to camp out, and done so many things to earn badges, you know, different kinds of crafts. Used to do neighborhood chores during that time and …

DR. LEE: What areas were most of the girls coming from; from Davisville and other areas?

MRS. HARRIS: The whole area here, Hopewell, all of blacks and, you know, wherever they were here in Hopewell because in my troop … when I was senior troop leader I had … I was still living here in this area, but most of my scouts were from the other area where I used to live. See, I lived in Arlington Heights. That's where I was reared, in that section of Hopewell, but that was, as I said before, was

Prince George. Well, we had ... I had scouts from there, and from the Dreamland area, from all of the areas because, well, we hadn't had any scouting, you know, in Hopewell for black children.

Dr. Lee: How did you recruit girls and the leaders?

Mrs. Harris: Through the schools, you know, and was active in participating in the school activities.

Dr. Lee: And how long were you involved in this?

Mrs. Harris: I think by the time you had started preaching.

Reverend Harris: It was still ... you were still in scouting when I started preaching.

Dr. Lee: When did you start preaching?

Reverend Harris: 1950 ...

Mrs. Harris: '7.

Reverend Harris: '57 ... '52 ... '55. '55.

Dr. Lee: 1955. Okay. This was after you had been to Virginia Union?

Reverend Harris: Yes.

Dr. Lee: And did some of the professors there encourage you to pursue your calling in the ministry?

Reverend Harris: No. I had ... I was interested ... Dr. Ransome ...

Dr. Lee: Oh, yes.

Reverend Harris: ... was my professor, and he taught me Bible, and ... but I was not interested in preaching. He and Dr. McHall, who was one of my professors also, and he's a preacher ... maybe it did rub off on me, but I didn't know it, because I went to do some other things ...

... too, and then I came back and got into the scouting program.

... That's really what influenced me to be a preacher ...

Dr. Lee: And that was through your wife.

Reverend Harris: ... through the scouting program, and I was always trying to find a way to cause people to function in a positive way. So I ... all of the boys had to have uniforms, and it was difficult because scouting uniforms were very expensive.

Dr. Lee: Yes.

Reverend Harris: And they still are. So I put on a program that on every meeting you'll have to get a piece of the uniform, the neck ... the tie, or the shirt, or either piece. And by the … and then I started to get all of the boys to get a bicycle. If they didn't have one, borrow one. So on Sunday we're going to Sunday school, and you can't go unless you have that piece of your uniform, and so we went to all of these churches around, and the boys were very, very excited about that, and it took twelve Sundays to go to all of these churches, and by this time I had already been baptized …

DR. LEE: Right.

REVEREND HARRIS: … and fallen away from the … my first love, and … but when I … after I stayed for twelve weeks in the church …

DR. LEE: It took hold.

REVEREND HARRIS: Yeah. I ain't never been out since.

DR. LEE: That's how you got in.

REVEREND HARRIS: Yeah.

DR. LEE: Okay. All right. What was the first church you pastored?

REVEREND HARRIS: First Baptist and Bermuda Hundred.

DR. LEE: And what was your role in the church as the first lady? Did you still have the Girl Scouts then?

MRS. HARRIS: Yes … no. I can't remember ever scouting … being in scouting at all after he started preaching.

DR. LEE: After he started preaching.

MRS. HARRIS: Because when he went to First Baptist and Bermuda Hundred I taught Sunday school over there, and organized a missionary circle in that particular church.

DR. LEE: Had they had one before?

MRS. HARRIS: No. They had Sunday school, but they did not have a missionary society.

DR. LEE: And what inspired you to start the missionary society?

MRS. HARRIS: Well, I guess I've been … that's one of my interests, missions, and as much as they didn't have it, and that I was active in my church in it, so I encouraged them to do the same.

DR. LEE: Do you see yourself as a leader?

MRS. HARRIS: No, not really. No.

Dr. Lee: Even with starting the Girl Scout troop and encouraging your husband to start the Boy Scouts and starting a missionary circle as First Baptist?

Mrs. Harris: I don't know. I ... I just ... I've never been able to do what I think leaders ought to be able to do, and I have had roles ... I've had jobs as leaders but I didn't feel, you know, comfortable with it, because I am not a public speaker, and I've never been ... I can remember ... I had ... the Girl Scouts used to be on the radio, and I ... I don't know, I just ... I don't know what happened to me. I just was a loss for words seemingly, you know, but other ... when I am not up front like that I do better.

Dr. Lee: You are a behind-the-scenes leader.

Mrs. Harris: Yes.

Dr. Lee: Okay. Do you see yourself as a leader?

Reverend Harris: Yes.

Dr. Lee: And when did you first start seeing yourself that way?

Reverend Harris: As a boy, when they wanted to start a fight ... I was at ...

Dr. Lee: At South B Village?

Reverend Harris: Yeah. No. Right here in Davisville, before I got ... before I was ten, when someone would fight, I'd lead the fight, and people had began to look at me for leadership. And I didn't know what was going on, why people were looking at me the way that they were looking at me, but that was my time. That's how I functioned.

Dr. Lee: And so leading the fight, when you'd come up against segregation, civil rights, you naturally stepped into that position as a leader?

Reverend Harris: Yes.

...

Mrs. Harris: I helped you get into that.

...

Mrs. Harris: As a leader in civil rights.

Reverend Harris: Well, she's ... what she's ... what she's talking about, I ... see, I was already, before ... she's talking about the sit-in movement, and ... but I had been the president of NAACP in Hopewell.

Mrs. Harris: Oh, yes.

Reverend Harris: Before that.

Dr. Lee: Okay.

REVEREND HARRIS: But what she is … when she got into … involved … because, you see, we never really … we really considered … we never considered the NAACP to be a civil rights organization.

DR. LEE: What did you consider it to be?

REVEREND HARRIS: A social …

DR. LEE: Club?

REVEREND HARRIS: … club. And we used to raise the money and send it to the state or the national and get some memberships, and we didn't want white folks to know nothing about it. So we never … we never considered ourselves …

Courtesy of Carmela Hamm

MRS. HARRIS: Didn't you promote some integration with scouting when you drove for that … drive, the paper drive.

REVEREND HARRIS: Yeah. Yeah. Well, that was not … that was not because of the NAACP. It was because my initiative as a … what I considered a leader, and when we found out … when I found out that the white troop was getting a truck from Fort Lee for a paper drive so that they could go around and get paper, and I don't know what we did with the paper, but when I found that out I said … I showed up with my troop, and they didn't know what to do with me.

DR. LEE: You showed up at Fort Lee?

REVEREND HARRIS: At a place … at the recreation center in Hopewell.

DR. LEE: Okay.

REVEREND HARRIS: They were going … all of the troops, and it's been published that all of the troops going to come up to the recreation center because of a paper drive. I figured we were going to get all of the paper together and sell it at … for some price, I don't know.

So I got my boys together and we showed up at the recreation center. And they had to give us a truck. They didn't know what to do. But by now I am in civil rights, because you are going to have some trouble with me, so they gave me a truck.

DR. LEE: What year are we talking about?

REVEREND HARRIS: That was … that was before the sixties.

DR. LEE: Okay.

MRS. HARRIS: It was in the fifties because Curtis was little.

REVEREND HARRIS: Yeah.

DR. LEE: So *Brown versus Board of Education* was '54. Was it at that time? After?

MRS. HARRIS: It was before then.

REVEREND HARRIS: Before that.

MRS. HARRIS: Before then.

DR. LEE: So it was just unheard of that you all would even come down there …

REVEREND HARRIS: Yeah.

DR. LEE: … and even think about getting a truck?

REVEREND HARRIS: Yeah.

DR. LEE: Okay. So is that when leadership here in Hopewell began to see you as someone who may be forceful regarding their rights?

REVEREND HARRIS: That might be one of the times when that started to happen.

DR. LEE: Okay. Had you joined the NAACP at that time?

REVEREND HARRIS: Yes.

DR. LEE: So this was all working together?

REVEREND HARRIS: Yes.

DR. LEE: All right. And you said that initially the NAACP was seen as a social group.

REVEREND HARRIS: Yes.

DR. LEE: You began to change that here in Hopewell?

REVEREND HARRIS: No. I vanished out of the NAACP. I just vanished out of it because I don't know … I was interested in giving a lot of leadership for scouting. I was interested in baseball. I played baseball, and …

DR. LEE: At the church, also?

REVEREND HARRIS: Yeah.

DR. LEE: Were you involved in the SCLC at that time?

REVEREND HARRIS: No. At the beginning there was no SCLC.

DR. LEE: Okay.

REVEREND HARRIS: We got involved with the SCLC after Rosa Parks.

DR. LEE: All right. So most of your time was spent with the church with recreation, the Boy Scouts, and with your family?

REVEREND HARRIS: Yes.

DR. LEE: At this time, let's say about the 1960s or so, how many children did you have about 1960? You have six all together.

REVEREND HARRIS: I had four.

DR. LEE: You had four at that time, so a lot of your time is spent with family at that time?

REVEREND HARRIS: Yeah.

DR. LEE: Did you start … how did you … because we're talking, things were still very much segregated, how did you raise your children in that kind of environment to believe that they have, you know, every right to be first class, to be treated as first-class citizens?

REVEREND HARRIS: Well, we didn't ever think that our kids were going to ever go to school with white kids. When the *Brown* … the *Brown* case … when the Supreme Court agreed that African Americans can go to the same school with anybody else, so … and a part of that, during that era the black kids … the schools were running … it was raggedy. Schools were just in bad shape. And the white folk were not interested in doing anything about it. The thing that really made us angry and concerned is the fact that the law said that you not supposed to have no separate schools. So finally, in '60 …

DR. LEE: '3?

REVEREND HARRIS: … '60 I believe we filed a suit …

        … to integrate the school system in Hopewell.

MRS. HARRIS: Now …

REVEREND HARRIS: Isn't that '60?

MRS. HARRIS: It was. It was that time. But prior to that, why did we open a typing class here? You know, they weren't even teaching that to our children; is that right?

REVEREND HARRIS: Yeah.

DR. LEE: Was it a typing class here in your home?

MRS. HARRIS: Huh-uh. Next door.

DR. LEE: Okay.

REVEREND HARRIS: We used to have a snack bar next door.

DR. LEE: Reverend Harris' Snack Bar?

REVEREND HARRIS: No.

MRS. HARRIS: Harris' Snack Bar.

DR. LEE: Okay, Harris.

REVEREND HARRIS: So we got the teacher at the school, the typing teacher, to start a class in the snack bar after school, and they learned how to type. Do you know Avon Miles?

DR. LEE: No. I have heard that name, though.

REVEREND HARRIS: Well, he was in that class. Mr. Bernard Epps?

DR. LEE: No.

REVEREND HARRIS: Son, Bernie was in that class, and my son, Michael. And my daughter, Joanne, who was too young to be in the class, she went there and learned anyhow. And all of them now learned how to type. When they got to high school, they could type fast.

DR. LEE: How long did you have this typing class?

REVEREND HARRIS: I think, what, a year, two years?

MRS. HARRIS: About two years.

DR. LEE: Is this during school year, or the summertime?

REVEREND HARRIS: It was during the school year.

MRS. HARRIS: After school.

DR. LEE: Okay. An after-school program, basically.

REVEREND HARRIS: Yeah. We didn't know what we were doing.

DR. LEE: Well, it paid off.

MRS. HARRIS: It did pay off with some of the students that were there.

DR. LEE: Yes. And apparently those in charge of the city didn't know that you all were running that so that you could continue running it?

REVEREND HARRIS: Yes. They didn't care.

MRS. HARRIS: They didn't know. No.

REVEREND HARRIS: They couldn't do anything about it. That was my store.

DR. LEE: So we're at 209 Terminal. The store is ... where was it?

REVEREND HARRIS: Right there.

MRS. HARRIS: 211.

DR. LEE: 211 Terminal Street. Okay. So it was Harris's Snack Bar?

MRS. HARRIS: Yes.

DR. LEE: How long do you own that?

REVEREND HARRIS: Oh, five years.

MRS. HARRIS: Approximately.

REVEREND HARRIS: About five years.

…

REVEREND HARRIS: … We had to close up the snack bar when we integrated the restaurants.

DR. LEE: So we lost something. We lost something. Actually, we lost quite a bit to integration.

REVEREND HARRIS: Yeah.

DR. LEE: And then, you know, there was some good that came out of it, but a lot of the small businesses that we had, we lost. Very much so. And in fact, that's one of the things I wanted to ask you about, small businesses here in Hopewell prior to integration, do you remember any of those?

REVEREND HARRIS: Yeah. Mr. Brown had a grocery store.

DR. LEE: Where was that?

REVEREND HARRIS: Right over here.

DR. LEE: Davisville, off Terminal Avenue?

REVEREND HARRIS: Who else had some stores, some businesses? We had contractors. Mr. Brown, again, you know … you know, Mr. Brown used to paint and …

MRS. HARRIS: I wouldn't know those. In the area where I lived, you know, barbershops.

DR. LEE: Barbershops.

MRS. HARRIS: And restaurants, Ms. Harcum ran one in the area where I lived.

REVEREND HARRIS: My sister ran a restaurant.

DR. LEE: What's her name?

REVEREND HARRIS: Effie.

…

DR. LEE: Where was that located?

REVEREND HARRIS: South B Village. We lived in South B Village, and she had a restaurant downstairs and we lived upstairs.

DR. LEE: What was the name of the restaurant?

REVEREND HARRIS: Lenox Cafe.

      … She had a neon sign on the front of it.

Dr. Lee: Where is that sign now?

Reverend Harris: The store, the building is gone.

Dr. Lee: Anybody save the sign?

Reverend Harris: No. She … when the Army … when Fort Lee came into bloom, she was doing good, and I had to kill all the chickens, and she could cook some chicken.

Dr. Lee: So you have some experience with that?

Mrs. Harris: Did she have to have a license?

Reverend Harris: I think she did. I think she did.

Dr. Lee: And you at one time had a kindergarten program?

Mrs. Harris: Yes.

Dr. Lee: Now, this was after integration?

Mrs. Harris: Yes.

Dr. Lee: All right. What children were coming to daycare … well, the kindergarten?

Mrs. Harris: You mean where were they coming from?

Dr. Lee: Yes.

Mrs. Harris: Well, Chesterfield, all over.

Dr. Lee: Black and white?

Mrs. Harris: Yes.

Dr. Lee: How many children would you say were coming in on average?

Reverend Harris: We had fifty-five at the beginning, and the first year they changed the system so that kindergarten children could go to the public schools, and it almost killed our programs.

Dr. Lee: Okay. But you kept going for … you changed it to a daycare center …

Mrs. Harris: Yes.

Dr. Lee: And had that for twenty-eight years?

Mrs. Harris: Right.

Dr. Lee: And the address of that?

Mrs. Harris: 213 Terminal.

Dr. Lee: So it was just one down from where you had the snack bar?

Mrs. Harris: That's right.

Dr. Lee: And you were working at Allied Chemical?

Reverend Harris: Yes.

DR. LEE: And what capacity?

REVEREND HARRIS: As a janitor.

DR. LEE: And you stayed there how many years?

REVEREND HARRIS: Fifteen years.

DR. LEE: What were some of the things you saw there that led you out of that kind of work?

REVEREND HARRIS: Well, I had to … my boss was a German, and he couldn't speak good English, so when it was time to collect the money for … from all of the janitors, and we had thirty-some janitors all over the plant, and he was the boss, but when it was time to collect the money from the janitors he would give that to me, so me and … I could go all over the plant.

DR. LEE: And you were collecting money for …

REVEREND HARRIS: For Red Cross or whatever the …

DR. LEE: Cause is.

REVEREND HARRIS: Yes. And I had to fight with the black boys from … they didn't want to give up no money, and I had to turn … twist their arms, and so they'd give it up after they get through cussing.

DR. LEE: This is before you were a minister?

REVEREND HARRIS: Well, it started before I was a minister, but it lasted until I left the plant. And when I left the plant, I was already preaching.

DR. LEE: All right. Okay. So you were listening to all this cussing and fussing?

REVEREND HARRIS: Oh, yes. And I wait for … but we had all kind of folks in our gang. We had pictures with all of them sitting with … with the … they used to go in and take all our pictures from time to time, and I got two or three copies of pictures of my gang. And our second boss was white, and the police force, the safety people at the plant …

DR. LEE: At the Allied Chemical plant?

REVEREND HARRIS: … was the boss of the janitors.

DR. LEE: Okay.

REVEREND HARRIS: So the boss with us and the fellow that would walk all around to see if everybody is doing their work, he was … he had to wear a uniform, too. See, both of them wore uniforms, but I outlasted all of them. They had to retire before I did, and … but after fifteen years, and I had been preaching now, and I have … I take some classes at Virginia Union after I was in school before. And so now I am preaching and pastoring, and I took the first church at Bermuda Hundred, and I was a member of this church, Union Baptist.

Dr. Lee: And the Bermuda Hundred was First Baptist?

Reverend Harris: Yes. And then our pastor, Dr. King, got sick and he couldn't function, so I had to take over some of his duties. See, I was only serving at Bermuda Hundred two Sundays a month when I first started. So Dr. King got sick and he died. He never came back to the church. And about … in 1959 … wait a minute … I'm getting a little mixed up. Well, yes. I'm right. It was '60 … 1961, Dr. King died. So this church asked me to be their pastor, Union Baptist. In the meantime, Dr. King had another church down in Ivor, Virginia, and they also wanted me to be their pastor. So I took all three of them churches, and I was working, still working in the plant.

Dr. Lee: And you had children at this time?

Reverend Harris: Yeah. I had four children then.

    … I stayed with First Baptist ten years. I stayed with Gillfield Baptist Church in Ivor thirty-three years while I was still pastoring at Union because they came on about the same time. And now I am forty-five years at Union Baptist.

Courtesy of Carmela Hamm

Dr. Lee: And still active in civic activities, civic (*inaudible*) …

Reverend Harris: Well, I can say that in your presence, but thanks, but here's my right arm. I can't function too much without her. I can't even button up my shirt. But if you put my hand on the altar, I preach you a sermon and that's what I've been doing.

Dr. Lee: What would you say is a scripture passage that has really meant the most to both of you and kept you moving forward and raising your family and being involved in all of these activities?

Mrs. Harris: Well, the 121st Psalm is my favorite, but I have used so many different scriptures with the children, and that they had to commit to memory.

Dr. Lee: Which is the 121st Psalm?

Mrs. Harris: What is it?

Dr. Lee: Yes.

Courtesy of James Willcox

Confrontation at the Municipal Building

Determined to protest a proposed landfill near Rosedale, activists led by Reverend Curtis Harris, faced members of the Ku Klux Klan on August 8, 1966. The news media covered the event as participants and observers witnessed a peaceful, though tense, confrontation as both groups prayed before dispersing.

MRS. HARRIS: I will lift up mine eyes unto the hills. From whence cometh my help, and where it comes from, knowing that it doesn't come from that mountain, it comes from who made the mountain.

DR. LEE: Yes. Yes. And what is the passage that means the most to you?

REVEREND HARRIS: I don't have a special passage. I guess my position is that I am a person who look at life and deal with it on the spot. You know, there's always been something that I have to do to function, and I believe that the Lord helps me to do it.

DR. LEE: Yes.

REVEREND HARRIS: So I may not be able to quote a scripture, but as long as I feel that the Lord is helping me to do it, then I make it happen.

DR. LEE: I understand.

REVEREND HARRIS: So that's all that … you know, when you go to jail thirteen times, when you ain't done nothing, it …

Dr. Lee: (*Inaudible*) comes from.

Reverend Harris: Yes. So I guess her scriptures is okay; it's good for her, it's good for me, but I go way beyond that in terms of my commitment.

Dr. Lee: I understand. And so when he is being jailed, and on the front lines in marches and that kind of thing, your role, what's your role in the relationship?

Mrs. Harris: Well, I was home with the children during that time to take them to their games and whatever activities they were in, you know I had to be there for them and of course getting a bondsman to get him out of jail.

Dr. Lee: Was there a discussion prior to any of the incidents of what you are going to do, like plan of action, this is the bondsman, this is where the money is, if they come during the night, where you go, that kind of thing?

Reverend Harris: What was the concern … what we did is we were … every time I left home there was a possibility of not returning, and I realize it now more than …

Dr. Lee: You can keep going.

Reverend Harris: I realize it more now than at that time that she must have had some sleepless nights while I was in Mississippi, in Georgia, in some parts of Virginia, dealing with civil rights, but you know, when they cut the man's head off not too long ago … do you remember that?

Dr. Lee: Yes.

Reverend Harris: I went to that place. I went, I interviewed the sheriff, I had my way down in that town, and spent the night, had a fellow driving me, so after awhile I had to come back and … so in the meantime she was I guess praying for me and for others. That was a very important factor in my life.

Dr. Lee: That's one reason that I am so glad that I could interview both off together. I just had a feeling that, you know, there was a story there that a lot of people had not heard how you worked together and really built a legacy. And actually, your home is very much like that. This is practically an archive. And that's something that's very special. I surely appreciate all that you have done and are still doing. You inspire me. Look at him crying now. Thank you so very much. I sure appreciate it.

Reverend Harris: Thank you.

Kenneth Charles Harris, July 9, 2005

Courtesy of Carmela Hamm

As the second offspring of Curtis and Ruth Harris, Kenneth Charles Harris recalls what it was like to grow up in Davisville and the son of a civil rights leader. During the 1940s a $330,000 United States Housing Authority project was built to provide shelter for ninety-six African American families. One of the first two men hired was "Claiborne Gholson, colored," reported the *Hopewell News*, on October 20, 1940. Only weeks later, on November 29, the *News* gives us a visual picture of the planned housing development. "Eight long buildings, each containing twelve family living units ranged in size from three rooms to five and a half rooms." Although none of the units had basements they were all several feet up off the ground. The brick-faced, cinderblock-walled homes were sure to be "standing and in good condition in sixty years when the federal loan was due."

The interview took place in the home of Kenneth and Renada Harris on July 9, 2005.

DR. LEE: Your earliest memories of home, what were they?

KENNETH HARRIS: Having a lot of fun playing with all the kids in the neighborhood. It was great. You know, there was subsidized housing, but it didn't matter to me when I was young. I didn't know what subsidized housing was. I was just a kid having a good time playing with my friends in the neighborhood.

DR. LEE: Okay. And so at that time, we're looking at the early 1950s, society was segregated, everything was separate, blacks and whites did not intermingle.

KENNETH HARRIS: I can remember having to get on a different bus or get ... go in a different door when we got on the bus.

DR. LEE: Public?

KENNETH HARRIS: Public transportation.

DR. LEE: And that door was?

KENNETH HARRIS: The back door.

DR. LEE: Okay.

KENNETH HARRIS: I can remember that, and we had to exit that door when the bus stopped and we got off.

DR. LEE: Okay. How old would you say you were at that time?

KENNETH HARRIS: Six or seven.

DR. LEE: What were your feelings at that time? Were you aware of the difference?

KENNETH HARRIS: No. It was just that's the way it was, you know, just some things were a certain way. You had to wear clothes when you went outdoors. There were certain places you couldn't go, and that's just the way it was. I can remember going to a segregated drive-in theater where you had … you went in a different gate and set behind … you know, the section for the black people was behind the white people.

DR. LEE: Do you remember the drive-in theater?

KENNETH HARRIS: Bellwood.

DR. LEE: And so you grew up with this … in this environment where everything was separate. When *Brown versus Board of Education* was handed down, was there talk in your community or church or home about that?

KENNETH HARRIS: Well, I mean you are talking about when I was seven years old. You know, if you want to ask me about some cartoons that were coming on TV when I was seven, I probably was listening to that more than I was listening to what adults were talking about.

DR. LEE: Okay. Which cartoons were you watching?

KENNETH HARRIS: *Popeye*, Mickey Mouse, *Mighty Mouse*, Donald Duck, *Superman*, and programs like *The Three Stooges*, *The Little Rascals*.

DR. LEE: Okay. All right. So in the world of the child all those things were separate, it didn't really seem unusual because that was the way it was for everybody?

KENNETH HARRIS: Yes. Since I was born. You know, like somebody being born with one leg.

DR. LEE: Which school did you attend?

KENNETH HARRIS: Carter G. Woodson School. I had fun. I enjoyed school, being with my friends. Mrs. Gilliam was one of my favorite teachers.

DR. LEE: Joy Gilliam?

KENNETH HARRIS: Yes.

DR. LEE: And what made her one of your favorites?

KENNETH HARRIS: She was … I guess being an eight-year-old, nine-year-old, I think when I was in that class I thought she was nice looking for some reason. I wouldn't tell her that now, but …

DR. LEE: Where was Carter G. Woodson located at that time?

KENNETH HARRIS: Right down the street from my dad's house.

DR. LEE: On Terminal?

KENNETH HARRIS: On Terminal. It's a mattress factory now.

DR. LEE: Yes. Within walking distance from your parents' house, actually?

KENNETH HARRIS: Yes.

DR. LEE: And that went up to what grade, fifth or sixth?

KENNETH HARRIS: Depends on when you are talking about.

DR. LEE: When you were there.

KENNETH HARRIS: When I was there it went from first grade to twelfth grade … to eleventh grade, because they just had eleventh grade at that time.

DR. LEE: When did you go to Hopewell High School?

KENNETH HARRIS: 1963.

DR. LEE: And what grade were you in then?

KENNETH HARRIS: Eleventh.

DR. LEE: Okay. What was that like to go from Carter G. Woodson, an all-black environment, to Hopewell High School? And you were one of five, seven, that went into Hopewell?

KENNETH HARRIS: It was … I thought it was about twenty people that went there. You are talking about '63?

DR. LEE: Uh-huh.

KENNETH HARRIS: The summer of '63 was when my brother and I went to summer school.

DR. LEE: And where did you to summer school?

KENNETH HARRIS: At Hopewell High.

DR. LEE: Okay. And so it was just you and your brother; no other blacks?

KENNETH HARRIS: Right.

DR. LEE: What was that experience like?

KENNETH HARRIS: I didn't want to go. I think my father, you know, he used my brother and I as guinea pigs, you know, because we didn't have any choice. Growing up, I didn't have any choice whether or not I wanted to be in the movement or be a part of it. And I don't think most fifteen-year-olds don't volunteer to go to summer school, the school is not air-conditioned, so I didn't volunteer to go. I didn't want to go, but I didn't have any choice.

DR. LEE: Okay. So there was some resentment there?

KENNETH HARRIS: I didn't want to go.

DR. LEE: We're talking six weeks in summer school?

KENNETH HARRIS: Yes.

DR. LEE: And at that time I don't think too many people were going to summer school, black or white, so you are talking about a small group of people attending summer school?

KENNETH HARRIS: White kids were going to summer school all the time. There wasn't any summer school program for blacks. You know, if you failed, you know, a class, you couldn't make it up during the summer in the black school.

DR. LEE: Okay. (*Inaudible*) Okay, so that first year, you had gone to the summer school prior to going into Hopewell High School the twelfth grade?

KENNETH HARRIS: Eleventh grade.

DR. LEE: Eleventh grade. Okay. What was it like that first day going into the eleventh grade at Hopewell?

KENNETH HARRIS: I never had any problem. To me, everything was fine as far as getting along with the other kids in school. I went to school, did my work, went home. I didn't swap phone … telephone numbers with anybody, or calling my little white buddies after school or anything. None of that.

DR. LEE: Had there been any kind of preparation prior to going into Hopewell from your parents, from civic leaders, church?

KENNETH HARRIS: No.

DR. LEE: So you were just thrust into the situation?

KENNETH HARRIS: Yes. And I don't … I don't know if you know Milton Richardson from Petersburg. He's … I think he's president of the Petersburg Chapter of the SCLC, and he might be a few years older than I, and he talked about how he was inspired by Dr. King at an early age, and how much he was involved in the movement at an early age, but I just … I wasn't I am … I was just a kid wanting to chase girls and play. I wasn't interested in the movement and I didn't want to go picket.

DR. LEE: Your father was already involved …

KENNETH HARRIS: Oh, yes.

DR. LEE: … at the time? And were your other brothers and sisters involved in the movement?

KENNETH HARRIS: Well, I had one brother that's older, he … whether he wanted to go, I don't know. You'll have to ask him, but I didn't want to go. But my father, being the person he is, I didn't have any choice. I had to picket. I had to march.

DR. LEE: Do you remember your first march?

KENNETH HARRIS: No. There were so many of them I couldn't … you know, we would meet at Union Baptist Church right across the street from my father's house, and we would march downtown to some of the stores that were segregated, you know, and sing a few songs, and march back to the church.

DR. LEE: Is there one that stood out in your mind more than others?

KENNETH HARRIS: No.

DR. LEE: The stores that you picketed, had you been in any of those stores?

KENNETH HARRIS: Oh, yes.

DR. LEE: How were you treated?

KENNETH HARRIS: Well, you could go in there and buy anything you wanted to buy but you couldn't set at the lunch counter, like W. T. Grant's and Woolworth's, some of the drugstores, you know, they had lunch counters. And I can remember when we went in Woolworth's, and I am a little guy, this is maybe '61, and I could see underneath the lunch counter, that's how tall I was, and it was chewing gum from one end of the lunch counter to the other and I had never seen anything so filthy in my life, and I said, I don't want to come down here anyway. It's filthy. Why would I want to sit here?

DR. LEE: And so you didn't?

KENNETH HARRIS: No … I did what … you know, I was in the group, what we had … you know, I was doing what we were supposed to do, sit down there and wait until the policeman come, and then the police arrested all of us and marched us across the street to the jail.

DR. LEE: How old were you then?

KENNETH HARRIS: I must have been about twelve, thirteen.

DR. LEE: Okay. And so was that the first time that you were arrested?

KENNETH HARRIS: That was the first and only time.

DR. LEE: Okay. What was that experience like, at the age of twelve?

KENNETH HARRIS: It was ... it was ... to me, it was boring because as a child I wasn't involved in really what was going on. I just was with the group, and the group went down there, and the group got arrested, the group went over to the jail and somebody did paperwork as far as doing our bond so that we could go back home. You know, I was never behind bars. And then after I can recall later on that we went to court, and I don't even remember what happened at court. But I remember that because of that getting arrested, when I was fifteen and wanted to get my driver's license, and it's a place on there that would ask that have you ever been arrested before, so if you checked yes, you needed permission from the judge to get your driver's license. Then I had to take the papers back up to the judge downtown to sign it. And I can remember him looking at me and he asked me am I going to do this anymore. And I said, no. If I said, yes, I wouldn't be able to get my driver's license.

DR. LEE: All right. So at the age of twelve you were first arrested. At fifteen you got your driver's license, sixteen you went into Hopewell High School. And were you involved in athletics, civic organizations in school, any extracurricular activities?

KENNETH HARRIS: First year, the only thing I guess would be considered extra was the marching band, because we did practice before and after school, and went to football games and stuff like that. But that's it, the marching band.

DR. LEE: Marching band. Okay. Had you been involved at Carter G. Woodson in extracurricular activities?

KENNETH HARRIS: Yes.

DR. LEE: In what way was it different at Hopewell?

KENNETH HARRIS: There was more of everything. Just ... that was ... I guess the most overwhelming thing that it was so much more of everything, more people than when I was at Carter Woodson. I mean the whole school there might have been 200 people. When I went to Hopewell High it was 200 people in my class in the eleventh grade. And they had to eat lunch in shifts because there were so many people. And I think what was the most ... you know, the biggest thing, there was so much, so big.

DR. LEE: Okay. Did you notice a difference in quality, books, the equipment, facilities?

KENNETH HARRIS: Well, they had more equipment. You know, they had more things to offer, even though I didn't … wasn't involved in some of them, like the electronic classes and the trade schools and … you know, which wasn't at Carter G. You know, the library, you know, man, there's all these books. Carter G. Woodson's library wasn't like that. And as I say, just being a kid, I don't want things … I wasn't looking for a challenge. You know, I don't want things to be hard. I just want to pass. But I had to worry about, you know, getting a whipping. I wanted to do my …

DR. LEE: Kid stuff?

DR. LEE: … And in the Navy, you went to Gulfport, Mississippi, Corpus Christi, Texas, Long Beach, California, Davisville, Long Island, Vietnam, Rhode Island. In all of those travels, you began to see how different life was in different parts of the country. What struck you most? Compare it with Hopewell.

KENNETH HARRIS: It's just that it was so much out there to do, so many different things, different ways of looking at life and living life.

DR. LEE: Did you see segregation in the Navy? Did you experience racism, discrimination?

KENNETH HARRIS: You mean from Navy people, from my superiors in the Navy?

DR. LEE: Not just superiors, but colleagues, those on the same level, anywhere in the Navy.

KENNETH HARRIS: Well, I guess it was before Vietnam they didn't have many … any blacks in … I went into a part of the Navy called Seabees, construction battalion, and there weren't any blacks … hardly any blacks in that part of the Navy. And I was in a battalion with 800 people, and it wasn't but twenty blacks in the battalion, and that's including the ones that were cooks and barbers and … like skilled tradesmen, so it was … I'm saying for some reason they didn't let blacks or blacks weren't in that part of the Navy.

DR. LEE: Okay.

KENNETH HARRIS: But during Vietnam when they needed …

DR. LEE: Bodies?

KENNETH HARRIS: … bodies, you know, we'll take you now, you know, we'll take anybody. We'll send you to Vietnam.

DR. LEE: All right. And when did you meet Renada?

KENNETH HARRIS: That must have been in the '70s. '75, somewhere around there.

DR. LEE: So this was after your apprenticeship …

KENNETH HARRIS: Yes.

DR. LEE: … that you met her? Here in Hopewell?

KENNETH HARRIS: Yes.

DR. LEE: And I ask because she is Caucasian, how was she accepted … how did you meet her?

KENNETH HARRIS: At a party.

DR. LEE: And you knew right away that this was the person?

KENNETH HARRIS: Oh, no. No. Nothing like that. Just something that grew over a couple years.

DR. LEE: Okay. And when you decided to marry, was there any thought in your mind about race relations?

KENNETH HARRIS: No.

DR. LEE: And when you started your family, Ken Jr. is thirty now, so at that time we're talking 19 … late 1970s, 1980?

KENNETH HARRIS: I am trying to remember when he was born. I think he was born in '71 or '70.

DR. LEE: How had things changed in Hopewell by 1970 from the time you had grown up?

KENNETH HARRIS: Well, things had changed as far as the laws, you know, that it was places you could go now, that we used to couldn't go. You know, they didn't want us to swim together so the city made a tennis court where the swimming pool was. There was a city swimming pool, so they filled it up with dirt and made a tennis court.

DR. LEE: What was the name of that?

KENNETH HARRIS: The name of the pool? I don't remember the pool name.

DR. LEE: So there they filled the swimming pool so that blacks and whites wouldn't swim together and made a tennis court. Did blacks and whites play tennis together?

KENNETH HARRIS: Sometimes. You know, if you went down there and it was some white guys playing, you'd play against each other.

DR. LEE: I know that Lynchburg did the same thing to their swimming pool and Petersburg I believe also rather than to have blacks and whites mingle at the same time, so it seems that Hopewell is following the general pattern regarding race relations.

DR. LEE: But in '71 you do notice a difference, a change from what you experienced prior to that time?

KENNETH HARRIS: Yes.

DR. LEE: You are able to go anywhere you want?

KENNETH HARRIS: I mean and feel welcome. I mean, you wouldn't have to worry about somebody hitting you in the back of the head or something. And in some of the places you went they used to have four bathrooms. They didn't have but two. Well, they wouldn't … before that, you know, I never thought … growing up, I never thought about that we're in different classes as people, you know.

There were some black class structure, you know, that some blacks thought they were better than other blacks. And I didn't realize it was in the white community, too, because it was, like I said, growing up, living in subsidized housing, on Sundays we used to play football against the white guys that lived in subsidized housing and, you know, we used to meet at this field, and just play here in Hopewell on Sundays, and would play football against each other. Sometimes they won, sometimes we won. But I didn't … at that time I didn't think that these were the poor white guys and we were the poor black guys. I mean, we lived in subsidized housing. It wasn't the black guys that had parents that were teachers and wore neckties.

DR. LEE: Okay. So there was not an awareness of class differences at that time?

KENNETH HARRIS: Right.

DR. LEE: When did you begin to notice that difference?

KENNETH HARRIS: I think when I was about forty.

DR. LEE: After you had been away and came back and was able to see differences, would you … some would consider your family uppity; would you consider your family uppity?

KENNETH HARRIS: Yes.

DR. LEE: In what ways?

KENNETH HARRIS: Well, I mean I didn't think that way when I was …

DR. LEE: Growing up?

KENNETH HARRIS: … growing up.

DR. LEE: But looking back now?

KENNETH HARRIS: Looking back now, you know, at one time my family had a restaurant, and for a black to have a restaurant, that was uppity. You know, for blacks to have a nice car or to have their own home, that was considered to be uppity. You know, as I said, at that time I didn't think so. Like I said, I didn't find out until I was forty years old that I came from an uppity family.

DR. LEE: How did you come to that now?

KENNETH HARRIS: You know, talking with my friends that I grew up with now, when I talk to them now, you know, we talk about what we did as kids.

DR. LEE: Okay. What would you hope Hopewell would … how would you hope that Hopewell would benefit from all of the strife that went on, all of the action that took place here?

KENNETH HARRIS: How do I hope that it would help us? Well, I don't … some things in Hopewell haven't changed. Some of those people, those leaders that were a part of the segregation in this country, in this city, they are still here. And some of them, they still want things to be segregated. They don't want black people and white people to be together. They like it like it is. And I think as far as people's minds, I don't think we're going to ever change it. I think it is something that's going to always be. I don't think it's going to ever be a meltdown.

DR. LEE: Now, your marriage with Renada, has that ever been a point of conflict with some of those segregationists here in Hopewell?

KENNETH HARRIS: Other than just the stares, or just looking … the double take. Nothing more than that. I mean, that still goes on. You know, we go stand somewhere in line and everybody look past me, and they ask Renada and they wait on her. That still goes on today.

…

I had a good time growing up in Hopewell.

DR. LEE: What were some of the places you hung out with the boys, just hanging out? The carshed?

KENNETH HARRIS: At the basketball court, places like that. Well, we didn't have any …the community center, you know, used to be segregated. There was a black one in Davisville, you know. Hanging out at the community center. Ida Cook.

DR. LEE: What kind of activities did the Boys Club do?

KENNETH HARRIS: We had a boxing team, basketball team, played softball.

DR. LEE: Do you remember the names of any of the teams?

KENNETH HARRIS: No. The Davis … the flying D's, Davisville.

DR. LEE: Flying D's. Who would you play; other teams from Petersburg?

KENNETH HARRIS: Oh, no. We would play teams from other black sections of Hopewell.

DR. LEE: What were some of those other sections?

KENNETH HARRIS: And that was … and it was a long class structure that I wasn't aware of. It was the part of Hopewell called Dreamland where blacks lived that had nice houses, and school teachers lived there. And there was another section of Hopewell called New Town where you all went down Boston Street that was a different class. That wasn't the same as living … and then certain areas of Arlington Heights, you know, that was where all the uppity black people lived that had individual houses, and some of them even had cars.

DR. LEE: Okay. So we're talking about Davisville, Dreamland, New Town?

KENNETH HARRIS: And South B Village. I mean, that was way down there. I mean that was below subsidized housing. Some of these people had outdoor bathrooms.

DR. LEE: Are all of these areas still around?

KENNETH HARRIS: No. I mean they tore down South B, and now they are called Highland Park.

DR. LEE: Okay. All right. And everybody went to the same school, Carter G. Woodson, all the blacks?

KENNETH HARRIS: Yes. But they had a black elementary school here in Arlington Heights that went from first through the fifth grade. First … yeah, I think it was first to maybe seventh grade. And then one time blacks were in the eighth grade they had … the ones that lived in Arlington Heights had to catch a bus to Davisville to go to high school at Davisville. Carter G. Woodson was an elementary and a high school. It wasn't a whole school within Davisville.

Jeanie Langford, April 6, 2005

Courtesy of Jeanie Langford

Jeanie Langford agreed to meet me in the Appomattox Regional Library in Hopewell on April 6, 2005. Her interview provided information about the early industrial life of Hopewell. She recalled her first memories of Hopewell and also talked about her family life. Her comments about the first days of desegregation in the public school system provide the perspective of a white female growing up in a small town during the 1960s.

JEANIE LANGFORD: My father's name was Fred White LeNoir. My mother's name, Betty Clark LeNoir. And my brother's name, Fred White LeNoir Jr.

…

DR. LEE: … What background?

JEANIE LANGFORD: French. They were French Huguenots. They've been in this country for a long time.

DR. LEE: And when you moved here at the age of three, what neighborhood did you move to?

JEANIE LANGFORD: We moved first over to a little neighborhood off of … they called it I think West Hopewell, it was Lynchburg Street, and that was in 1958. We rented that house, my parents did.

DR. LEE: What are your first memories being in Hopewell?

JEANIE LANGFORD: First memories … first, I was kind of surprised. We came from the mountains and everything seemed kind of clean, and of course I was really little, but you come here and of course the first thing you are confronted with are all these smoking factories, and at first, when you first come to Hopewell, I think most people get the feeling that it's kind of dirty, but it's not, so you kind of get that dirty feeling at first. Smoky, smoggy.

DR. LEE: And so at the age of three or in those formative years your first memory entering Hopewell was one of …

JEANIE LANGFORD: Smoke and smelly things, smelly air.

DR. LEE: I can understand. Where did you go to school?

JEANIE LANGFORD: I went to DuPont Elementary School, which is off of Atlantic Street here in Hopewell. I went then to James E. Mallonee for what they call middle school, that was sixth, seventh and eighth grade. That was what had been the old high school. Then I went to what we called then the new high school for my entire high school years, and then the College of William and Mary.

DR. LEE: Were the schools segregated at that time?

JEANIE LANGFORD: Yes, ma'am, they were.

DR. LEE: Were the neighborhoods segregated?

JEANIE LANGFORD: Yes, ma'am, they were. Even the newspaper was segregated.

DR. LEE: In what ways were the newspapers segregated?

JEANIE LANGFORD: Interestingly enough, when you look at the microfilm from the Petersburg paper or from Richmond, you go through and you will have the Hopewell social section, and then you'll have in the Hopewell papers a section called "Colored News." In the Petersburg paper it's called "Colored Dots" and so that's where the African American obituaries should be, all their little news about their chitterling festivals, or their Tom Thumb weddings, all their little social events would be there. Generally, the only way an African American got on the front page is if they had done something bad, if they'd been arrested or were involved in some type of crime. Otherwise, they were on that page. And occasionally … Carter G. Woodson was the African American high school up until the early … the late … early sixties, I think, and the basketball team was really good, so they would get on the sports page. But other than that, it was confined to that little section called "Colored News."

DR. LEE: Did the athletic teams interact, the black and white athletic teams?

JEANIE LANGFORD: No.

DR. LEE: So was there any black and white interaction in Hopewell?

JEANIE LANGFORD: Honestly, no. When I was real little the only black people that I ever saw anywhere … the first one was Miss Jane Covington, and she came to the house once a week. She was supposed to clean the house and babysit my brother and myself while Momma went grocery shopping. But Miss Jane didn't like to clean much, except for Freddy and I, and she would cornrow our hair, and then she would polish us, she'd bathe us and polish us with baby oil. And my dad would come home from work, and of course there we were, we were really tan, but we had these little cornrows, and be shining and Miss Jane would be very proud. Daddy would be a little upset on occasion, but he got over it.

DR. LEE: Now, what were your parents' occupations?

JEANIE LANGFORD: My father was a chemical engineer, and my mother was a homemaker her entire life. She never worked outside the home except right before she married my father.

DR. LEE: Okay. And Miss Jane Covington came in how often?

JEANIE LANGFORD: Once a week.

DR. LEE: Once a week. And did you call her Miss Jane?

JEANIE LANGFORD: We called her Miss Jane.

DR. LEE: Now, that's unusual, because most people did not refer to African Americans with a courtesy title.

JEANIE LANGFORD: She was Miss Jane.

DR. LEE: Did she request that or was that something that your parents …

JEANIE LANGFORD: That's something our parents taught us, because that was respectful. You did not call an adult by their first, quote, unquote, name. I still sometimes have a problem calling adults by their first name. So the Miss Jane was added, so … and as far as I can remember, she never asked us to do that. That's just what we did, because that's the way we were taught.

DR. LEE: Would you say you learned any values from her? Did she impart any …

JEANIE LANGFORD: She was a very, very good woman, very kind, very protective over my brother and I. She kept us immaculately clean, and she taught us a lot. She taught us … she would sit and read with us and she would do things like that. She played with us out in the yard. She was a wonderful lady.

DR. LEE: Did you visit her neighborhood or community?

JEANIE LANGFORD: No, ma'am. Now, my mother would, when it was time to take her home, my mother took her home to her house, which would have been in the African American section of town, and drop Miss Jane off at her front door. But no, you didn't go and visit back and forth.

DR. LEE: Okay. What were your parents' attitudes regarding race?

JEANIE LANGFORD: In all honesty, my father was a member of the Klan. My mother was probably less racist, if you want to put it that way. She was raised from that very small community. There was only one family of African Americans in that whole county, in all of Giles County, and that was Baby Jack and his family, and they shopped at her parents' store because there was no place else to shop. My father was a little more worldly. He'd been in the Army. He'd been to college. He came from a little bit bigger city. And his attitudes on it, he was raised like most people in his time, separate but equal, you don't really mix. He never really, even though he was in the Klan and he did take us to Klan rallies, he didn't teach us to hate, but separate was just the way it was supposed to be.

Dr. Lee: Okay.

Jeanie Langford: But we were never taught to hate. And I did go to a Klan rally. I can't remember the exact year, but it was up on Darbytown Road in Richmond in a big field, and they had … it was almost like being in a carnival. They had lines and lines and rows and rows of different booths with maybe Abraham Lincoln in them, or this thing in them, and they had records for sale, and the records were racist, but they had records for sale. They did burn a cross, but you never really … I didn't hear a whole lot of hate, hate, hate. A lot of it was just, let's keep it the status can quo, separate and as equal as possible. But that's the way I was raised.

Dr. Lee: How old were you when you attended this rally? Could you …

Jeanie Langford: I would say I was probably nine.

Dr. Lee: Was it daytime?

Jeanie Langford: Nighttime.

Dr. Lee: And most of them would have been at nighttime?

Jeanie Langford: I believe so. Like I said, that was really the … and that was a huge one, like the whole state or something, it was just people everywhere, and state police, and FBI people everywhere, I guess making sure nobody did anything they weren't supposed to. I think … that's the only one that I really know about. Yes, I would say night.

Dr. Lee: Summertime, wintertime?

Jeanie Langford: It was probably fall because it wasn't real hot, so I think it was fall.

Dr. Lee: So we're talking about 1960s?

Jeanie Langford: We were talking probably '65. '64, '65.

Dr. Lee: So we're talking after civil rights?

Jeanie Langford: Oh, yes. Because I did not go to school … the schools for me, in elementary school was all white. In junior high, which would have put me in the sixth grade, twelve to thirteen, so I was born in 1955, so we're talking like '67 is the first time that I went to school with African Americans, and the first time that I had an African American teacher.

Dr. Lee: Do you remember her name?

Jeanie Langford: Her name was Miss Goode. She taught math.

Dr. Lee: Was …

JEANIE LANGFORD: It was a difficult experience, more so I think for the parents because it was also at a time when math was changing, where it was not so important to add two and two and get four. It was more, in a way, important to add to know why you are adding two and two makes four. So the parents got a little excited on occasion because she would be more concerned on the method versus the answer. It was hard for them to understand. It was hard for everybody to understand. And it did cause a few little problems. My daddy made a few visits, but after awhile that kind of mellowed off, too. It was just that kind of … all that initial shock of everything all at one time.

DR. LEE: What was the name of the junior high school?

JEANIE LANGFORD: That was the James E. Mallonee School.

…

DR. LEE: And this was the white school and black kids were bussed in or …

JEANIE LANGFORD: Well, I guess you could say that. In Hopewell basically you could always walk anywhere you wanted to, but yes, that was probably the beginning of bussing here in town. Now, the high school had been integrated a little bit longer. I think along about '62 or '63 the first African Americans went up to the high school. But as far as the elementary school, until they closed Carter G. Woodson, which was the black high school, and then made that middle school, so all the kids in the sixth, seventh and eighth grade in the whole town went to Mallonee. That was the first time I went to school with everybody.

DR. LEE: And what year was that?

JEANIE LANGFORD: '67. Fall of '67.

DR. LEE: And that's when Carter G. Woodson was closed?

JEANIE LANGFORD: Along about that time. Should have been. Now, it's re-opened and Carter G. Woodson is the middle school and Mallonee no longer exists.

DR. LEE: All right. What were your memories, what are your memories of that first year?

JEANIE LANGFORD: At first what they did, and it took me a long time … well, even now to figure out what happened. That first year, even though the black children were there, and they were at the same school with me, I didn't really have them in my classes because, apparently, what they did was they had advanced class, advanced class, and they brought it down to so many different levels, and of course I was up here in the advanced classes, and a lot of the African American children weren't, so that first year or so, even though we were all in the same school, they weren't really in my class. Do you see what I'm saying?

DR. LEE: Had there been testing prior to …

JEANIE LANGFORD: I don't remember. I think we all had to take these little IQ tests, and they were SR. Do you remember those, those little SR reading tests? I don't remember somebody sitting down and saying, okay, this is a test, and if you get X on this test, well, you are going to be in this class, and if you get something on this test, you are going to be … I don't remember that. But that's kind of the way it seemed, thinking back on it, that it turned out.

DR. LEE: Uh-huh. So you were in an integrated school but in segregated classes?

JEANIE LANGFORD: That's kind of the way it worked up until the ninth grade. Now, in the ninth grade everybody kind of got piled in together, but those … we were … everybody was together but we really weren't together. Do you see what I am saying?

DR. LEE: Yes. Yes. Were the athletic departments integrated?

JEANIE LANGFORD: Yes.

DR. LEE: Drama club, newspaper, all of the extracurricular activities?

JEANIE LANGFORD: Not really. Mostly just athletics more than anything. There were a few … the band was. I was in a couple plays in high school. I don't remember any African Americans being in the plays. So it was still kind of separate feeling because the black community, of course, was still … it was still kind of wanting to be segregated, too, so it was having some of its old things left over from Woodson days still contained in its community, like its plays and its different things, so we were still kind of at that …

DR. LEE: Awkward …

JEANIE LANGFORD: … we were together, but it was still … it was awkward, because you didn't know if you were supposed to say … you knew that you probably weren't supposed to say "colored" anymore, and you knew you weren't supposed to say the N word, and you knew you weren't supposed to say probably say Negro, but you weren't sure if black was okay, so it was kind of … you didn't know really what to call each other.

DR. LEE: Would you say it was tense?

JEANIE LANGFORD: Tense, yes, but not overwhelming. It was just this adjustment period. People weren't fighting each other in the schools, and nobody was stabbing each other or anything like that, but you could tell there was a tenseness because we didn't know what to say, and they didn't know what to say, either, so we were still kind of doing this part.

DR. LEE: And your brother also went to school. Older?

JEANIE LANGFORD: Younger.

DR. LEE: Your brother is younger. He went into this integrated situation, also?

JEANIE LANGFORD: At a much earlier stage. He got to run across it in elementary school, because he is three years younger, so he started going to school with black children when he was about in the third grade. So his ... it was more natural for him being as a seven-, eight-, nine-year-old person, versus somebody who is twelve or thirteen, so he just eased right into the whole thing. So from his ... my age group, say people forty-nine to fifty or so and older, it was probably a little more difficult than somebody even that's only three years younger, because it happened at an earlier age, and so he had no problems. He had black friends, he had white friends. He wrestled on the wrestling team with black teammates. He even went to church with some of his teammates, an African American church. He loved it and they loved him, and he just thought that was the best thing in this world. And he went to the black church with his friends, his wrestling teammates for two or three years because he said if I could go to a regular church, and our church, and have that much fun, he said I would go every Sunday. He said, you go to their church, they have a great time. They sing and they dance and everybody sits around and eats chicken. He said and ... he says it is fun to go to church. White people don't know how to go to church.

DR. LEE: How did your father take this?

JEANIE LANGFORD: At first he was a little shocked. And he was not too happy about it, but then I guess he figured it was better to have Freddy going to some church than no church at all.

DR. LEE: Okay.

JEANIE LANGFORD: And if Freddy's teammates came over to the house. By then he had become ... Daddy had become more accepting, and Freddy's teammates would come over to the house, and Mom would always have the ... Mom always had food laid out. She didn't care if you were green. She had food laid out for everybody.

DR. LEE: That's the Southern way.

JEANIE LANGFORD: Well, that was Momma's way. You know, she never met a stranger. But it was easier by then. Now of course that's not to say that Daddy would have really been very happy if Freddy had run out and married a black lady. I think that might have done Daddy in, but as far as having them over to the house, by this time Daddy was okay with it.

DR. LEE: Do you think that gender made a difference, too, that he was a boy?

JEANIE LANGFORD: Yes, the boys ... I don't care, in any endeavor, there is a difference between raising a girl and raising a boy. I would be in college, I'd come home on holiday and my daddy would want me in at 10:00, and my brother who he's three years younger, and he could stay out at night, you know.

DR. LEE: I do.

JEANIE LANGFORD: So there is a difference between the two genders and …

DR. LEE: The age difference?

JEANIE LANGFORD: … and the age difference. And it was only, like I said, a matter of about three years. He's three years younger.

DR. LEE: Now, which church did you all attend?

JEANIE LANGFORD: The Baptist church. Then, of course, now Freddy with his wrestling buddies was going to the black Baptist church down here at City Point.

DR. LEE: Okay. And he did that for about two or three years?

JEANIE LANGFORD: Two or three years, the whole time basically he was on the wrestling team. And they loved having him. They just thought he was great.

DR. LEE: In what ways did segregation impact your life?

JEANIE LANGFORD: Well, I have seen, like I said, the Klan rallies. I saw my father get up and walk out of a restaurant here in Hopewell because Reverend Harris walked in. We left Buckroe Beach one day because we were sitting there at the beach and then all of a sudden, just out of nowhere, black people had decided to come to the beach, so my dad left the beach. Segregation … that was … when I was younger, that was the way it was supposed to be. And at first it was hard. You … sometimes you felt intimidated because you are around this group of people that you didn't know anything about. And some were more … some of us were more vocal and intimidating toward the other, and the same thing rung true from the other side. Some of them would be frightening to you at times. Like the first time I ever saw Michael, Spiderman James, he was 6'9", black as coal and played basketball. And here I am 4'9", nothing, and he walks up to me and says, "Hey, little lady." Well, I was scared to death, because here was this giant black person. I was in the ninth grade. And here he was, just standing there, and I was like scared to death, but eventually, you know, you kind of got over it.

JEANIE LANGFORD: And it was like I was telling you before about Gwen Collum. There was a girl in our school named Gwen Collum. She was a very, very large black girl. And for some reason that I will never understand to this day, she decided that she was my protector, and she would follow me, go behind me in the hall. If anybody bumped into me, if anybody said anything ugly to me, she was right there. She decided … just made herself into my appointed protector, and stayed that way for four years. She would go watch me play field hockey.

She didn't know a thing about it. But she would stand on the sidelines and just look at the other team like, you hurt her, you deal with me. And you know. It was almost like she had decided, and I hate to use this term, but you have all seen *Gone With the Wind*, it is almost like she self decided that she was my mammy, and that was it, and you were not going to mess with me when she was around.

Dr. Lee: Did you both engage in conversation or …

Jeanie Langford: Yes.

Dr. Lee: … or become friends …

Jeanie Langford: No, it was … it was not really friends. It was just she decided that that was her job. I mean, we didn't hang around together. We didn't … she didn't come to my house, anything like that, but she just out of the clear blue just decided that she was my protector, and that I belonged to her, and she was going to take care of me.

Dr. Lee: Have you all ever had a conversation about that time period?

Jeanie Langford: Believe it or not, about two years ago she walked in the door …

Dr. Lee: At the library?

Jeanie Langford: … here at the library, and I haven't seen her since we graduated in '74, and that's the first really more than hello, goodbye, how you doing today, Gwen, because, you know, you're thinking, why is this person taking care of me? That was probably the first real conversation we ever had in our whole life.

Dr. Lee: So she is still in Hopewell?

Jeanie Langford: Uh-huh.

Dr. Lee: That's fascinating, very.

Jeanie Langford: But that's what she determined that she was going to be, my protector.

Dr. Lee: Well, you are petite.

Jeanie Langford: But, see, I was as mean as a snake so I didn't need a protector, but she was my self-appointed protector.

Dr. Lee: That's good.

Jeanie Langford: And it is kind of funny, my brother was a ninety … wrestled … he was a ninety … his first three years in high school he wrestled ninety-eight pounds, and his senior year he wrestled 105 so of course he's the littlest one on the team, but some of the black boys on the team, kind of the same thing developed, this I need to take care, even though Freddy is perfectly capable of taking care … but I need to take care of you. Nobody is going to bully you. Nobody is going to say bad words around you. The same thing.

DR. LEE: So you don't remember any fights or altercations?

JEANIE LANGFORD: They were there, but it was a different time. You fought, you punched somebody in the nose, you fussed at them, you hollered at them, and the next day you are laughing together. You didn't tote a gun to school. If you did have a fight, everybody stood around and watched you fight, and then you got over it. A lot of great friendships ... yes, there were fights, yes, there were some racial clashes over probably now what people would consider silly, a black guy talking to a white girl or something like that, but as far as horrible fights and a whole lot of disrespectful stuff, no.

DR. LEE: Okay.

JEANIE LANGFORD: Everyone was ... I don't know whether it was because it was Hopewell and the town has always been so full of so many different people, Greeks, Czechs, Poles, Armenians, Bohemians, Carolinians, West Virginians, just people from everywhere. I don't know whether it was just because the way Hopewell is made you a little more accepting or maybe really it wasn't as bad as everybody thought. I really don't know. But I don't remember anybody ever threatening me, intimidating me, saying bad things to me. I don't remember me ever saying anything bad or fighting with somebody just because they were black or anything like that. I really don't. But, yes, there were some incidents. The first black kids on the football team, I know they had a hard time because the football team had always been all white. The first white kids that wanted to play basketball when they got the influx of the black players from Woodson, black players, basketball players were better, so the basketball teams became dominated by the black kids when the school integrated. And then, you know, there were these little manly tiffs every now and then, but I really don't think it was as bad here as maybe it was in some other places. It wasn't people out burning crosses on everybody's yard every night, and people weren't running through, shooting at buses, or ... none of that stuff here that I remember.

DR. LEE: Cheerleaders, majorettes, were they ...

JEANIE LANGFORD: Now, all took awhile, too. At first it wasn't.

DR. LEE: Slower than the athletic parts?

JEANIE LANGFORD: Some parts of it were a whole lot slower than other parts.

DR. LEE: When was this?

JEANIE LANGFORD: It was probably along about Freddy's time. Three, four years, probably '76, '77 before you started maybe seeing a black cheerleader on the squad or you started to see a black girl in the Ms. Hopewell High Pageant, this thing that ... some things took more time. It was the athletic teams first, then the other things kind of came after it.

DR. LEE: What recreational facilities did you attend?

JEANIE LANGFORD: Well, I went to dancing school. Of course, that was segregated. That was segregated even … I think that stayed segregated. There were of course little league and pony leagues and baseball teams and they were segregated until late sixties, early seventies. There would have been … there were swimming pools, but now that was another thing, there were some swimming pools here in town, but when the integration started to occur, some of the swimming pools shut down because white people didn't want to swim with black people. That's just honest truth of the matter. They would swim at the pools … like there used to be a pool up at $3^1/2$ Street. They just, rather than let the black people swim in the pool, they filled it up.

DR. LEE: Cement?

JEANIE LANGFORD: They filled it up with dirt. There was a place down on River Road called Crystal Lake, and rather than let the black people come to Crystal Lake, the man that owned it, he just closed it. Yeah, he sure did.

DR. LEE: Did it reopen?

JEANIE LANGFORD: No. Now that's where Mathis Field and all out there, that's where that used to be, but that used to be a lake.

DR. LEE: Restaurants?

JEANIE LANGFORD: Restaurants, so many of them are gone. George's Drug Store was one of the last holdouts not to let African Americans sit at their lunch counter, and those drugstores are gone now. People were still uncomfortable about it.

DR. LEE: Were there sit-ins?

JEANIE LANGFORD: There were sit-ins at George's Drug Store.

DR. LEE: What year was that; do you remember?

JEANIE LANGFORD: I guess '65, '66, because they … George's was bound and determined to keep the lunch counter segregated, and they did come and sit and sat on the porch at George's Drug Store.

DR. LEE: Black and white?

JEANIE LANGFORD: Just, as far as I can remember, it was just blacks who sat out. They were going to sit in that restaurant.

DR. LEE: High school students?

JEANIE LANGFORD: I don't know. I honestly don't know. I think mostly it was some of the older black folks, like Reverend Harris, and I think some of the Gilliam family. I don't … I really honestly don't know about if it was any of the younger people. I really don't.

DR. LEE: Would that have been covered on the front page?

JEANIE LANGFORD: Yes, it would have, and we'll find it, because I found the thing with the Klan rally at the courthouse for you, that that was August the 9th of 1966.

DR. LEE: And Jim Willcox had some pictures of it.

JEANIE LANGFORD: I gave them to him. And so where I've been looking through the papers in the 60s, I think the 60s are where you really need to sit down. That's where it is all going to jump right out at you.

DR. LEE: And so do you remember there always being a strong ethnic community multicultural?

JEANIE LANGFORD: Always. That's ... it was that way the day that Hopewell was founded, because DuPont brought people from all over Eastern Europe, along with people from, of course, Carolina, West Virginia. And they put them in this little, tiny even less than now, it is nine square miles, even this, it was much smaller than that, and you didn't have it divided. Now, you had black and white divided, but you had a Greek living next to a Pole, living next to a Czech, living next to a North Carolinian, and I think they learned to accept and be accepting maybe a little bit better than some other places did because they had to. You didn't have Little Italy, didn't have Little Greece. You had to learn to ... and that maybe is why, at least to me, I don't feel like it was that awful, that it was that violent, that it was that upsetting. It just seemed like, okay, one day we weren't, and the next day we were.

DR. LEE: Would you say that other ethnic groups were more accepted than blacks?

JEANIE LANGFORD: Yes. Of course. This is a Southern town. A lot of these folks after they got here ... and second generation ... of course the first generation of them didn't speak much English, but that second generation does, and so they are learning from these ... the people who have been here before, the true, deep-rooted Southerners, so they are learning, and so they built up not only their own feelings from their own ethnicity, but what they learned from the people who are already here.

DR. LEE: And most of the people worked in the factories. I imagine there were a small group of people who were entrepreneurs?

JEANIE LANGFORD: A few.

DR. LEE: Would that have been all nationalities?

JEANIE LANGFORD: Oh, yes.

DR. LEE: Do you remember any of these businesses?

JEANIE LANGFORD: There was, of course, the Klonis brothers.

… They were Greek. They ran a supermarket.

DR. LEE: Where was that located?

JEANIE LANGFORD: That was located on City Point Road.

DR. LEE: And is it still in business?

JEANIE LANGFORD: No. All three of the brothers are deceased. You would have had, of course, the Adkins Heating and Lighting.

…

JEANIE LANGFORD: …You would have had Cormanys Sporting Goods…. You would have had things like Caudill Heating and Plumbing…. I'm trying to think. Black … you would have had … in the black community you would have had Rainbow Cabs.

DR. LEE: Okay.

JEANIE LANGFORD: I don't know who owned that, but that's been around ever since I can remember. And sometime you might see it, it would be a red cab and it will have a big rainbow painted on the side, and that used to come off of Arlington Road over in the black section. The Dereski family, … they are white, but have always owned a pole and nursery company right over on Arlington Road in the black section of town.

DR. LEE: Speaking of black and white sections of town, if you could discuss a little bit about how it was the town was designed when the factories started coming in, with A Village and B Village.

JEANIE LANGFORD: When DuPont, after they finally figured out after the great fire of 1915 and they figured out that they had built this Wild West, the town from Hell, had 40, 50, 60, 70,000 people in it, but nowhere to live, they decided they had to do something. So they ordered a bunch of houses, and I call them dormitories, from the Aladdin Company. They set up these little houses, and they set up the dormitories, but how they divided it was they had A Village, which is down here in City Point, that was management. They had B Village, of these little tar-paper houses, that was white, which didn't matter if you were Greek, Czech, Pole whatever, that's where you lived, and there was South City, and that was the African American section of town. Davisville was part of that place that they called Georgia Hill. And Death Valley was just a general … there was a place here called Death Valley, and that's where all the lowlife, drifter people lived, and you didn't go there after dark.

Black people did not go out of their village after dark. They went to work, but they not come into the white section of town after dark, and even today the railroad tracks are kind of your dividing line. South of that Norfolk and Western line was completely black section. Some sections that were white over

Downtown Hopewell, back when...

As the chief engineer for building the villages of Hopewell, Frederick W. Foote provided a description of the diverse population. In his Town Site Construction and Cost Estimate for E.I DuPont *(1915–16) he wrote: "The laboring class consisted of Italians, Greeks, Armenians, Serbians and negroes. Carpenters tended to be Brushwood Virginians and North Carolinians. Electricians generally were American men from all sources having some wiring experience." Those painters native to Virginia and Carolina seemed conscientious—though not speedy." Plumbers and pipe fitters from American cities fared well. Those involved in masonry were "a rather difficult class ... on account of their high rate of compensation and close trade organization."*

time turned into black sections, so ... but right out Route 10, headed out 10, that was predominantly African American. At one time a place called Highland Park was all white, now that's a predominantly African American community, but it is kind of like south of the tracks, that's the way it divided.

DR. LEE: Okay. And the ethnic communities, well people were all mixed in, were they mixed into the African American areas?

JEANIE LANGFORD: No.

DR. LEE: Okay.

JEANIE LANGFORD: Not really. It was ... you were either white or you were black.

DR. LEE: Did they maintain their traditions, the ethnic community?

JEANIE LANGFORD: Very much so. And you will find that a lot around town. They had a strong sense ... a lot of them still now will send their grandchildren to take Greek lessons if they are Greek, or they maintain a lot of the Czech and Polish traditions as far as the cooking. They have a big Greek fest here because this is the oldest Greek Orthodox community in the state of Virginia, the church and all that, that was established here in like 1917, and some of these splinters, you will see those Heppa things and the Greek, that's what that's all to do with.

DR. LEE: I don't think many people know that.

JEANIE LANGFORD: That's what that all is. And so they have maintained their tradition.

DR. LEE: That's fascinating. I don't think most people know that this is the oldest Greek community in the state of Virginia.

Jeanie Langford: Uh-huh.

Dr. Lee: Very interesting. Now, after high school, you went to William and Mary?

Jeanie Langford: Uh-huh.

Dr. Lee: Library science?

Jeanie Langford: History.

Dr. Lee: Well, now. Okay. And what prompted you to go into history?

Jeanie Langford: Just a great love of it. My family would all sit around and tell stories and tales, and I'd listened to my grandmother about being raised in Alabama (*inaudible*). I have always loved history.

Dr. Lee: (*Inaudible*) … love of history came from …

Jeanie Langford: Well, my grandparents on my father's side, that's where I get a lot of thrill about the genealogy and all because they would sit and talk about it. Then of course my mother's people are mountain people, and they are great storytellers. And they do a lot of oral tradition, and they are jokesters and pranksters, but they keep up with who they are, where they came from, who was married to who, this, that and the other, and it was instilled into me.

And then of course in the state of Virginia, when I came along you had to take Virginia history twice, once in the fourth grade and again in the seventh grade. So the theory behind I guess that was, if you knew Virginia's history, you knew the entire history of the United States, but you fall in love with it, if it is taught right. If you just teach a bunch of dates, that's one thing, but if you say, okay, this happened, because this happened, because this happened, now how can you not make the same thing happen again? And so being taught that way is why I got such a great love for history.

Dr. Lee: That's fascinating you should say that because I, too, had Virginia history in fourth and seventh grade, and it turned me off because of the way it was taught. I thought, the way it was taught, all black people were slaves, and you know, it was such a shock to me because I didn't know that that's … that was part of my heritage until I heard that. And so it is interesting to see how history affects people. It is not until later that I became very interested.

And so at William and Mary, what focus in history did you concentrate on?

Jeanie Langford: Well, I kind of dabbled like anybody else. I dabbled around with some anthropology, and I dabbled around and thought maybe I'd want to get away and do European history, because I love ancient Egypt, but I got drawn back into Virginia, and ran across some great professors down there who would do like the history of Southampton County or different aspects of Virginia history and just … it was so wonderful the way they taught that you just had to fall back in love, so I got back out of the European history and back out of the anthropology and back into U.S. history.

DR. LEE: Now, would you say Southern history …

JEANIE LANGFORD: Yes.

DR. LEE: … is the area that you are particularly interested in?

DR. LEE: When you finished, what year was that?

JEANIE LANGFORD: 1978.

DR. LEE: 1978. And you came back here or …

JEANIE LANGFORD: I came back here.

DR. LEE: When did you start at the library?

JEANIE LANGFORD: I started at the library in 1996.

DR. LEE: What did you do between '78 and '96?

JEANIE LANGFORD: Well, for awhile there I got a wild hair, and I worked at the Hopewell Moose Lodge as a bartender making the big bucks. And then I got married. And then I stayed at home for awhile. And then I decided, gee, I'd like to come to work again, so I did.

DR. LEE: History called you back?

JEANIE LANGFORD: That, and I want to make a difference. I want Hopewell to see itself for what it really is. There is so much here. It has so much to offer, whether it's from just a pure history standpoint of having been here since the very beginning, whether you want to do industrial history, whether you want to do ethnic history, whether you want to do the history of the city. It is nine square miles, hun, you got it all. And it's beat itself down sometimes and it needs to feel good about itself, so I have kind of made that my mission.

DR. LEE: I see. You are very passionate about it. It is wonderful.

JEANIE LANGFORD: Yes, I am, because I love its history. Some of it is not pretty. We all … I mean, we have lines of bootleggers here, where it is just a family tradition, but hey, you got to do what you got to do.

DR. LEE: There are worse things in life.

JEANIE LANGFORD: That's right.

DR. LEE: Very much so.

JEANIE LANGFORD: And so … but this place is a dream. It is wonderful. And in spite of itself, I love it so much. I wouldn't trade it for anyplace else.

DR. LEE: It shows, very much so.

DR. LEE: Now, are you responsible for building collections?

JEANIE LANGFORD: Yes. As a matter of fact I have some new things coming in tomorrow.

DR. LEE: What's that?

JEANIE LANGFORD: I have some stuff coming in from the Tubize time, from the Dereski family.

DR. LEE: Okay, if you will just give a background of Tubize.

JEANIE LANGFORD: Tubize, after DuPont leaves ...

DR. LEE: In what year?

JEANIE LANGFORD: They close in 1918, five days after the Armistice that ends World War I. Well, they had employed so many people, after they close up, Hopewell almost becomes a ghost town. It almost dies. But the people, the city fathers, they wouldn't let it die, and they promoted themselves, and with a little help from DuPont, because they had all that property to unload, they make what I like to call an early infomercial. They put out pamphlets and they put ads in newspapers saying, Hopewell, the greatest industrial opportunity in the world.

And eventually they get a company out of Belgium that bites, and that company is Tubize, which is T-u-b-i-z-e, and Tubize makes rayon, which they called artificial silk, and they come here and Hopewell snaps right back to life because right behind them comes Solvay, which will become Allied, and the Hopewell China Plant, so Hopewell is just booming again.

DR. LEE: And what time period was that?

JEANIE LANGFORD: That is '21 to '34.

DR. LEE: Okay.

JEANIE LANGFORD: Tubize leaves in '34, so ... but Hopewell made it through the Depression. I even encountered something this morning that Hopewell really didn't suffer much because the industry saved did not suffer from the Depression. And Tubize hired black and white. There are wonderful photographs in there of the workers at Tubize. And in general, I think the relations were pretty good. It was like I was telling you before, it is something you don't think about seeing, but in DuPont's company magazine, the *Splinters* and in Tubize's magazine, the *Spinnerette*, you see pictures of the African Americans and the white workers. And it is great stuff. It really is.

DR. LEE: So you are getting an influx of people in.

JEANIE LANGFORD: You get a whole new influx. You had that first influx from 1915 to 1918. That was the Poles and the Czechs, and the Greeks, but in the '20s you are going to get French-speaking Belgians, a whole new batch of Carolinians and West Virginias, all coming to work at Tubize.

DR. LEE: Men and woman?

JEANIE LANGFORD: Men and woman. Tubize hired many, many women. DuPont did not. Not ... at least not here in Hopewell, but in ... Tubize hired a lot of woman.

DR. LEE: How were they paid? Were they paid less?

Courtesy of Maude Langhorne Nelson Library, Hopewell

JEANIE LANGFORD: These people ... these people, the women were probably paid a little less, but the women ... all of these companies have always paid their people very well and taken really good care of them, in my mind.

DR. LEE: Now, I understand that there were some people who were interested in unionizing.

JEANIE LANGFORD: That occurred in 1934. The big general strike of '34 that was countrywide. And that's when Tubize leaves, in the summer of '34. But there's more to that than meets the eye. Tubize ... the process that Tubize was using to make the rayon was a nitrous cellulose-based process. It is almost identical thing to making gun cotton to use to make rayon. But a new process had come along called viscose. The plant in Rome, Georgia, was using viscose. All the other plants were being converted to viscose, but this plant here in Hopewell was so old they couldn't convert it. So they kind of staged the strike, it seems like to me, and some of the unrest so that they can close this plant, get rid of this rock around their neck, and leave with people still feeling good, because you will never hear anybody, even though Tubize leaves, you will never hear anybody say an ugly word about Tubize, but they needed to get rid of this plant because the process that they were using here, the government was getting ready to outlaw. They couldn't convert the plant to the new process so they needed an easy way out, and a strike … it could have been cajoled a little bit, was the easy way to get out.

DR. LEE: How was it covered in the newspaper?

JEANIE LANGFORD: Oh, of course, it was covered that the workers went on strike. That's the part you heard, but what you didn't hear until later on was Tubize had Pinkertons on the street agitating, they had a fellow named Operative X who smuggled guns into the management, and this thing and that thing, but it is covered so that it looks like it was the people's fault.

DR. LEE: Okay.

JEANIE LANGFORD: Originally.

DR. LEE: Okay. And we are talking 1934?

JEANIE LANGFORD: Uh-huh.

DR. LEE: Until … was it just …

JEANIE LANGFORD: They were … they struck, supposedly, in I believe it was June. September, Tubize closes the plant permanently. That was it. They didn't even let them back in the gate.

DR. LEE: What was the culture like at Tubize?

JEANIE LANGFORD: Oh, gosh. Tubize took what DuPont had and just refined it to the nines. Tubize came over with a philosophy that a good worker is fit, a good worker is well paid, a good worker is busy, so what they did … (*inaudible*). They provided an outlet and if you wanted to shoot skeet, they had the skeet club. If you wanted to act, they had plays. So Tubize provided this. If you wanted to play baseball, they made sure you got to play baseball. Anything to keep them fit, healthy and happy. If they are happy, they are not going to complain. If they are fit, they don't miss as much work. If they are fit, they are healthy, so they are working, and that was their theory on it and it worked for them.

DR. LEE: Now, were these activities integrated?

JEANIE LANGFORD: No.

DR. LEE: So separate but equal?

JEANIE LANGFORD: Separate but pretty equal. They had an African American baseball team. They had an African American quartet. I told you about the Hawaiians but they had an African American quartet that went to the radio shows with the Hawaiians, but probably in separate vehicles. A lot of the African Americans here in Hopewell were chauffeurs for Tubize. Some of them were custodians. Some of them worked in the cafeterias, but a whole lot of them worked as pipe fitters and millwrights, so a lot of them had really good-paying jobs, but we're still separate but pretty equal then.

DR. LEE: And how long did that last?

JEANIE LANGFORD: That would have been the entire time that Tubize was here. That would have been '21 to '34.

DR. LEE: Okay. All right. Now, after Tubize?

JEANIE LANGFORD: After Tubize, you still … you are going to get … Allied Chemical is still going to stay, you are going to have cellanese. You are still going to have a small piece of Tubize, just a small, small plant.

DR. LEE: What percentage (*inaudible*). Wonderful. Better? Okay. I want to pick up with Tubize, the culture of Tubize, musical culture.

JEANIE LANGFORD: Tubize, as I said before, believed in providing outlets and entertainment for their people. One of the things they probably were best at was the musical part. They had an African American quartet. They had what I call a Sunday afternoon concert band. But I guess their best thing, greatest thing was the Tubize Royal Hawaiian Orchestra, and they were a group of gentlemen and some hula girls who performed at company functions, they performed on WRVA, they performed at the Mosque twice before sold-out crowds, there were 5,000 people. They recorded on OK Records in 1929 in New York. And they existed pretty much as long as the plant stayed open until about 1932, '34, or so. They were in the Riggs Music thing, but that was their outlet. That's how they kept their people busy. If they had a need, Tubize tried to fill it. When Mr. Coley, who was the head of the Tubize Royal Hawaiian Orchestra, wanted a new guitar, he was permitted to borrow the money for the guitar from Tubize and pay them back at the amount of three dollars a week. The guitar cost $197 in 1929, and today the guitar is valued at over half a million dollars.

DR. LEE: And where is this guitar?

JEANIE LANGFORD: The guitar is in Florida hanging on a wall right now.

DR. LEE: Private home or …

JEANIE LANGFORD: Private home. That was that big guitar you saw in the showcase, he bought that for $129 a month.

DR. LEE: On installment.

JEANIE LANGFORD: I was given … I was given … I have paystubs and everything that go and that show where each week he paid back for that guitar.

DR. LEE: That's wonderful.

JEANIE LANGFORD: I have all their applause memos, everything.

DR. LEE: What collection is that in?

JEANIE LANGFORD: That's in Jeanie's collection of unfinished stuff that … actually, Greg will tell you the funny part of where Jeanie got that. That came from the city dump. A gentleman found it.

DR. LEE: Oh, my goodness.

JEANIE LANGFORD: And he kept it in a suitcase, and then when I got interested in all this, he brought me what I call the dumpster goods.

DR. LEE: How do you find out about these things? Do people come to you?

JEANIE LANGFORD: People just come to me. I seem to have a magic. They just know that I care and so they just bring me their stuff.

DR. LEE: What do you say is one of your favorite collections here?

JEANIE LANGFORD: My favorite, my favorite era is the '20s. I love the '20s. Then secondly, I love, of course, the DuPont days '15, '16 but the '20s and '30s are my favorite, and of course the Hawaiians are real close to my heart, but in general

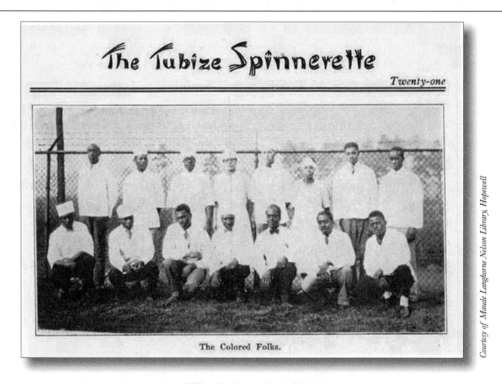

Courtesy of Maude Langhorne Nelson Library, Hopewell

The Colored Folks

The cafeteria seated 500 people and about 16,000 ate there during a week. In a 24-hour period Tubize employees ate 250 pounds of chicken, 125 pounds of sugar, 150 pounds of potatoes, 160 pounds of flour, 450 half-pints of milk, 200 pints of milk, and 41 gallons of coffee. During the lunch hour 1,400 people used 7,000 dishes and 2,800 knives, forks, or spoons.

Tubize Spinnerette, *March v. 2. #10 (pg 21, 24)*

Tubize is very close because so many of the people here worked for Tubize. Their parents worked there, and there's such a good feeling about Tubize, so I think my favorite part is Tubize, probably the *Spinnerette*s are my favorite.

DR. LEE: Now, the *Spinnerette*, what time period are we looking at there?

JEANIE LANGFORD: Well, now, I'm actually … I actually almost have a complete set, which would take me '25 … 1925 to 1932.

DR. LEE: Okay. And we're talking about monthly?

JEANIE LANGFORD: Monthly.

DR. LEE: Okay. What would someone learn from looking at the *Spinnerette*?

JEANIE LANGFORD: You would learn everything that was going on in that plant and outside that plant. It was a plant magazine that taught history.

DR. LEE: And which plant?

JEANIE LANGFORD: Tubize. It taught history. It would tell you … one month give you a history of Appomattox Manor, the next month of the Appomattox River Bridge. Then it would tell you a little bit about the process of making the material at the plant, but then it would tell you what everybody in town was doing, who drove to Petersburg to see what girl, who had a baby, who was secretly dating who, who was doing what. Anything that they were doing, it is in that magazine. All of their little secrets are in that magazine.

DR. LEE: So this was very much a town that was open, I mean not …

JEANIE LANGFORD: Whether they liked it or not …

DR. LEE: Yeah.

JEANIE LANGFORD: … it was in there. They were some nosey folks.

DR. LEE: So people were very aware that their actions were being watched?

JEANIE LANGFORD: They played the part, they knew it later. They knew it the next month when they saw that Billy Bob had been out with Mary Joe.

DR. LEE: Now, *Splinters*, can you talk a little bit about those?

JEANIE LANGFORD: Those are DuPont magazines, and they go from 1917 (*inaudible*). They are a monthly magazine that is centered around Hopewell and the doings during that time, very similar to the *Spinnerette*s. They are kind of gossipy and nosey, but DuPont is kind of doing … has done the same thing, they had the sports team, they had the musical team, they had the orchestra, they had the skeet shooting, but Tubize later just refines it more. But it's … and like I said, it's the same thing, if you did it, it was in that magazine.

DR. LEE: And those also would have been segregated, the news about people?

JEANIE LANGFORD: Yes, but now you will find in both the ... *Splinters* and in the *Spinnerettes* African Americans and white people in the same pictures.

DR. LEE: Okay.

JEANIE LANGFORD: And which I found especially with the *Splinters* and the time period then, I found that extremely interesting.

DR. LEE: Very interesting.

JEANIE LANGFORD: That they would be photographed together.

DR. LEE: Workers?

JEANIE LANGFORD: Uh-huh.

DR. LEE: Performing the same kinds of jobs?

JEANIE LANGFORD: Same kinds of jobs. DuPont was one of the first companies in the United States to pay African Americans and white workers the same pay for the same job.

DR. LEE: Okay. Could you give me a range of how much that would be?

JEANIE LANGFORD: They were making about ten dollars a week at DuPont, give or take a little bit.

DR. LEE: Now, let's put that in perspective.

JEANIE LANGFORD: And that's big money in 1915.

DR. LEE: Put that in context. About how much would rent cost at that time?

JEANIE LANGFORD: Well, they would be able to eat at the cafeteria for about two dollars ... well, for an entire week, for about a dollar and a half. And rent in the little houses would probably be a couple, two, three dollars. And then the rest of the money is yours.

DR. LEE: Did the companies help to fund schools?

JEANIE LANGFORD: Yes. Particularly DuPont. DuPont built a school here called the Village School, so that would have taken care of the village. They also had, I believe, an African American school. I know that they built an African American YMCA. They tried to be as equal as possible, but I'm not sure about the black school.

DR. LEE: Okay.

JEANIE LANGFORD: But they did build schools.

DR. LEE: Okay. The African American community would have been B Village South, right?

JEANIE LANGFORD: South, right.

DR. LEE: Which is different from B Village?

JEANIE LANGFORD: Uh-huh.

DR. LEE: Okay.

JEANIE LANGFORD: And I am not … but I would bet that there is a school that DuPont has provided over there.

DR. LEE: The 1920s, women would have started voting, is there any talk of this in the *Splinters* text or the *Spinnerette*?

JEANIE LANGFORD: Not really. It's like, okay, well, they are voting, so fine. Evidently Tubize was very open on their hiring. If a woman could do the job, she got the job, because a whole lot of women worked at that plant.

DR. LEE: Are we talking about round-the-clock shifts?

JEANIE LANGFORD: Uh-huh. Shift work.

DR. LEE: And there's pay differentials with that, also, at that time?

JEANIE LANGFORD: That, I'm not sure about. My guess would be at that time probably not because you are not dealing with the union yet, probably not a shift differential yet.

DR. LEE: How would you say that Hopewell has changed within the last thirty years? So we're looking at '75 to … well, since '75, because you graduated in '74?

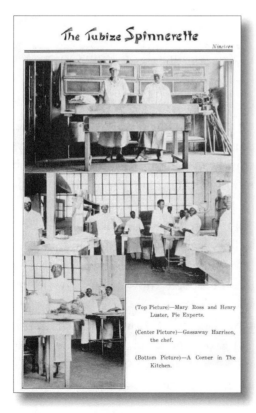

The Tubize Spinnerette

Nineteen

(Top Picture)—Mary Ross and Henry Luster, Pie Experts.

(Center Picture)—Gassaway Harrison, the chef.

(Bottom Picture)—A Corner in The Kitchen.

Kitchen Workers

Top left: "Gassaway Harrison, the Chef"
Left: "A Corner in the Kitchen"
Each kitchen worker was known for his or her specialty. Mary Ross trained Henry Luster to make pies; he also became her chief right-hand man. Gassaway Harrison was the chef; Andrew Joyner was responsible for making coffee; Weaver Shepperson made "good hot biscuits" for breakfast; William Pernell made at least 1,500 cornmeal muffins daily; Richard Morris, Joe Colbert, Pearl Luster, and Mary Ross served behind the counter every day at noon. Merlin Jenkins, James White, and Artice Wilson manned the dishwashing machine from 10 a. m. until 2 p.m.; in that time they cleaned 11,200 pieces.

Tubize Spinnerette *March 1927, v.2 #10 (pg. 21)*

Courtesy of Maude Langhorne Nelson Library, Hopewell

Members of "Doc" Rainey's Filter Recovery crew

Shown are (l-r): Hanpar Vartan, Jake Teachey, J. I. Maile, Jack Dowdy, "Doc" Rainey, Michael L. Shirian, Jerry Simpson, George Gilliam, William Hamilton, Jesse Jones, and Robert Scott. At the time this photo was taken, Simpson and Scott had been employed in the department for more than five years and had commendable work records.

Tubize Spinnerette, *July 1928, v. 4 #2*

Courtesy of Maude Langhorne Nelson Library, Hopewell

JEANIE LANGFORD: In '74. It's different. I see … I think it's because I see a whole lot more crime.

DR. LEE: More crime?

JEANIE LANGFORD: I see a whole lot more children who need something to do. We need something for these kids to do.

DR. LEE: And that's all children, irregardless?

JEANIE LANGFORD: All children. It doesn't matter. It's … they need something to do, whether it's going outside and playing baseball, whether it's sitting at a boys and girls club, the children need something to do besides either run around on the street or sit and look at that computer all day. They need some type of … we need some type of recreational program here. I have seen … right now Hopewell has been in kind of one of its … it's a roller coaster here all the time. You follow the industry. I have seen it decline. I have seen pretty, old buildings torn down for urban renewal. They tore down the whole downtown. They had some gorgeous buildings. I have seen a lot of people move away. They don't want to stay here anymore, because they think there's nothing here, so right now, for the last thirty years or so, Hopewell has been down on itself, and it needs to pick its head up, look around, get the downtown plan, get some people in here who know how to handle children, what to do with these kids, get some programs started, and Hopewell needs to get some pride back in itself. That's what I have seen the most is the loss of a lot of pride in itself. And that and the crime I think are the two biggest changes that I have seen.

Dr. Lee: How would you say the ward system has changed Hopewell?

Jeanie Langford: I don't honestly know if it has changed it for the good or for the better. It gave, when they did it, it gave the African American sections a voice. Now, whether I think they were in some cases the right voice or not, I'm not going to say, but its intentions were good, but sometimes, like anything else, it doesn't quite work the way it was intended to work.

Dr. Lee: How is voter turnout?

Jeanie Langford: It varies. Sometimes it's very, very poor. I honestly believe that the entire state of Virginia should have their council elections instead of in May, when nobody really cares, all anybody wants to do is be outside, have them in November when you are electing something else. But voter turnout is sometimes good and sometimes it is next to do nothing. It depends on the issues.

Dr. Lee: Do you think that would make a difference as to what's done with the young people here?

Jeanie Langford: We need something to fire people up and to wake them up. What it is, I haven't quite decided yet (inaudible) it will come and they will fight for it and they will vote for it, but we have to figure out what we need first, and not have it be something that you say, okay, we need this, and then ten years down the road they finally do it, because we have a little bit of habit of doing that, of saying, gee, we're going to do this, and then ten years later you still haven't done it, but if you find a way to fix the problem, do it now, not later.

Dr. Lee: Jeanie, have you got any political aspirations?

Jeanie Langford: Who, me? Sure. You know, I believe I could be a good politician and I think I am a politician, but I am too temperamental, and my dreams and my aspirations take a little different direction. I know what I want, and I hope that I will get what I want, and I will fight for what I want, but I'm not going to sit on city council and …

Dr. Lee: So you are not interested in being a part of that machine?

Jeanie Langford: No. I kind of would rather for it to operate independently.

Dr. Lee: And what do you want?

Jeanie Langford: I want the new library, of course, and I want Hopewell to be proud of what it is. I want a place where they can come, they have their archival material right there. It is not a case where they can't … I want them to be able to touch it. I want them to be able to feel it. And I kind of want them to be proud and in a way feel what I feel, I mean, hear what I hear and see what I see and then make their own decisions. That's what I would like to see, because there is so much here.

DR. LEE: You are definitely an ambassador ...

JEANIE LANGFORD: Thank you.

DR. LEE: ... certainly. Do you have many young people come to the library and interested in knowing more about Hopewell?

JEANIE LANGFORD: Once they find out what I'm doing, especially when I put things in the display case, they get very curious, and that's why I try to go out and speak as much as I can and get to them, because they are curious, they just think ... some of will just think well, gee, it just sprang up out of the ground, or either they will say it has always been here, but it hadn't always been here, and no, it didn't spring out of the ground. And so once you get them a little bit interested and they find out a little bit ... but it's like anything else, it is a struggle sometimes.

DR. LEE: Uh-huh.

JEANIE LANGFORD: But they ... if you can approach them in the right way, and not bore them with dates and ... but if you can give them an idea to build on, a lot of times they'll respond to it, something that's concrete that they can touch, so that's why I like a lot of my stuff. If I can't get it to a point where they can put their hand on it, then I keep it away from them. You know, because if ... I feel that if you can touch something, it gives you a greater sense of its power and worth than something that's sitting up there that something is going, no, don't touch that, don't touch that, don't touch that. I mean, I could very well take the *Splinters* and the *Spinnerette* and put them away, just for me, but, no, they need to be out there where they can be used and handled and touched, and I try to keep things in a condition to where they can be.

DR. LEE: Good for you. Good for you.

JEANIE LANGFORD: Because that's important.

DR. LEE: It is very important. Very important. After high school, do most of the young people leave or are they staying here?

JEANIE LANGFORD: It depends. Some will go away to college and swear up and down that they are never coming back, but they do. And then you have some that never go to college, but they still stay, and then a few ... you do have some, they won't stay necessarily in Hopewell proper, but they'll stay right over there on ... hiding a little bit ... they'll stay in Prince George, or they'll stay over in Dinwiddie, but in general they don't drift too far.

DR. LEE: I guess Hopewell or this area draws them back, pulls them back in.

JEANIE LANGFORD: There's something here.

DR. LEE: Yes.

JEANIE LANGFORD: There's something special. We just haven't quite figured out what it is yet.

DR. LEE: Well, it's a unique place.

JEANIE LANGFORD: It is.

DR. LEE: Very much. To have so many nationalities in such a small, compact area.

JEANIE LANGFORD: It's actually … I can't think of anywhere else in the … at least in this country where you have something like what you have right here, because a lot of … there were a lot of boom towns that came out of that era of '14, '15, '16, but they either died or they were … it was one town in North Carolina that was involved with a damn, and the workers for that project were all French Canadians, so that whole, little community was just nothing but French Canadians, and it managed to survive, but they just had that one group. Here, you had them all. And I can't think of any … really too many places that are quite that unique like that.

Florine Jones Martin, September 3, 2005

I interviewed Florine Jones Martin on September 3, 2005, in her home. "I'm always going to a meeting to see what's going on." Florine Jones Martin is not just going to a meeting; she finds needs and fills them. She is a volunteer at John Randolph Hospital, the Red Cross, the Food Pantry, the Senior Citizens Advisory Committee, and an active member at Friendship Baptist Church. When her daughter faced discrimination and was denied an opportunity to become a Candy Striper because "they told me they don't take black candy stripers" she saw to it that her daughter received training elsewhere. Later, Mrs. Martin herself became the first black volunteer at John Randolph Hospital. She is proud of her successes in breaking down discrimination. "One person asked me, 'How in the world did you get in here?' I said, 'Well, sometimes you have to open your mouth.' "

Courtesy of the author

DR. LEE: We are in the home of Mrs. Florine Jones Martin, 1603 Stuart Avenue, Hopewell, Virginia. This is for the Hopewell African American Oral History Project that's been funded by the city council of Hopewell and we'd like to talk with you today about your memories growing up here in Hopewell, going to school, the church at Friendship, some of the changes that you've seen, and see what are your hopes and dreams for the future of Hopewell.

FLORINE MARTIN: Well, I was raised right around in this community. In this community.

DR. LEE: This is called?

FLORINE MARTIN: This is called Arlington Heights.

DR. LEE: Okay.

FLORINE MARTIN: Yes. But it was just further down the street.

DR. LEE: Okay.

FLORINE MARTIN: That street at that time was called Sycamore Street.

DR. LEE: All right. And where did you go to school?

FLORINE MARTIN: Well, it's a long story. At the beginning I went to school in Roscoe, Pennsylvania. My parents lived here for a short time, and when I left here when I was a baby in their arms, and I was the only child that they had, and I thought I was born in Roscoe, Pennsylvania.

...

FLORINE MARTIN: ... It's just a small coal-mining town.

DR. LEE: Okay.

FLORINE MARTIN: And at that time everybody went to the same school. There was no segregation there. Everybody went to the same school.

DR. LEE: Blacks and whites?

FLORINE MARTIN: Yes. And my father was a coal miner. And of course, everybody, it was black and white in the area. We lived next door to white people. And I remember my father when I was smaller one morning getting up, and he said to my mother ... he called my mother Ms. Sarah ... he said, Ms. Sarah, he said, tell Florine to get up and put the hoe out for me so that I can work in the garden. And I was awake. I heard him when he told her that. And so, you see there, it wasn't a lot of space. People just had a small space for a garden, and most people had that. But originally he was from South Carolina, so we always had a lot because my father's brother would always send him food in a barrel. And of course we had to share. You'd share with everybody on the street, you know. And so this ... that evening there was a coal mine accident, and my father was killed. The mine caved in. And there ... it had posts that held the coal up, you know, as they went down, they went down in something like an elevator, and all of the men down there would have on their goggles and their hats and whatever dressed up like they should be as going down. But my father died that day. This post, this telegram post fell on his neck, and so he died instantly, I understand. And of course they finally brought him up, and of course I heard my mother screaming and carrying on, a lot of motions going on, and people in the house, and I didn't realize exactly what had happened. Finally, somebody told me. Well, I was crying because my mother was crying and other people were crying. However, when my father was here, they belonged to a church that was pastored by the man by the name of Sandy Turner.

And he ... that church was down the street there, below Friendship, further down on Arlington Road. And so since he was her pastor ... or his pastor, too, my mother sent for him to come and preach my father's funeral. My father was a deacon at this church. And so Reverend Turner came. And he had never been north, and he ... no one knew him. So that night the police driving around looking, you know, and he saw him. And he asked him where was he going. And he told him that he was going to the home of Hardy Benjamin Brown. He said he had to preach his funeral, say he is a deacon and he was one of my members in Virginia.

And of course they didn't know him, and so they, for safety reasons, they put him in jail that night. And that morning they released him and brought him to my mother's home. And of course, that was one of the things they did ... was done that way, you know, at that time. And so my mother had been sick. One of my brothers was maybe about ... just a few months old. So they had the funeral at home, at my house. I remember.

Dr. Lee: How old were you at that time?

Florine Martin: I was about six, six or seven, uh-huh, something like that. And so we lived there for awhile, lived there, and the children got a little older. And I was in school. And I was promoted to go to the fourth grade. Well, when I went to the fourth grade I had to go upstairs rather than downstairs. All of my friends were downstairs. And I thought that was something going upstairs, you know. I said, bye. And they wave at me, you know. That's all right, I'll be there next year. And so eventually my mother decided that she would move back to Virginia because she had her own home there. Had a little house that was ... I think it had two rooms. And see, a lot of people didn't have no home, you know, so anyway.

Dr. Lee: How could she have a home?

Florine Martin: This was their home before they left Virginia.

Dr. Lee: Okay.

Florine Martin: Yes. And so my mother came back home, down to ... the street's name was Sycamore Street. And now they call it Boston Street.

Dr. Lee: Okay.

Florine Martin: Uh-huh. And so my mother, of course, got ... received compensation from my father's death. Well, everybody thought my mother was a millionaire, and I think about it now, you know, we did live good.

Dr. Lee: Well ...

Florine Martin: Well, and my mother didn't have to work. She took care of us. And what happened, the older men who were in charge of my mother, my mother had ... whatever she was doing there in Pennsylvania, and our children ... the children, they would have to come and check on my mother to see if she had remarried, or if everything was going on well with the children. My mother had to call ... she always kept us with her, but sometimes we'd be out in the yard playing or at somebody's house next door, or something like that. Well, she had to get every one of us so that they could see, and they'd call us by name.

And then after we lived there awhile, Momma had to get a lawyer to work with her. That was Judge Binford, who lived out in Prince George. He was our guardian, that's what you call him, guardian. And so all of the checks would go to him and he would mail them to my mother. That's the way it happened. But we got along fine.

Well, my mother, she built another house, and they added more to the two … to those two rooms. So we had another house and four rooms, you know, so we were doing well, you know. We had a lot of land in the back.

DR. LEE: This is still in Arlington Heights?

FLORINE MARTIN: No. The house is down in … some little lots. Uh-huh. Yeah.

DR. LEE: When it was built, it was built in Arlington Heights?

FLORINE MARTIN: Oh, yes. Yes. Down the street there.

DR. LEE: Okay.

FLORINE MARTIN: And so when I came here, when we moved here, my mother used to pay our way to ride the streetcar to school, Carter Woodson School. Well, Carter Woodson School was not where it is now located, integrated. See, Carter Woodson School was over behind the fire department, where the fire department is now. Behind that was … and I think there's … they have ambulances back there now, but anyway, that's where we went to school. It was … oh, we thought we were in heaven going there, this big, old school. But my mother didn't … she thought we didn't … we couldn't walk. We wasn't used to walking to school. We always ride. That was too far for us to walk. And so we ride the streetcar. Get off up there where the railroad track now, and walk. And the children … it was fun for them, because they would walk, by the time we got off the streetcar, they would have walked, you know. And they laugh, oh, you don't have to ride. I say, no, my mother wants us to ride. Well, there is something like a bus station down there in Hopewell now, but we never did go in there to eat because the black was eating on one side and the white was on the other. So my mother said, don't go in there to eat. Well, at that time you did what your parents told you to do.

So I didn't go in there. I didn't go in there. And so we didn't eat in there.

DR. LEE: Could you sit anywhere you want on a streetcar or was it (*inaudible*) …

FLORINE MARTIN: No. No. Yeah.

DR. LEE: Okay.

FLORINE MARTIN: And we didn't understand that, either. But we finally got so that we understood that that was what it was, what was going on here in Hopewell. So …

DR. LEE: Is this your … how many brothers and sisters did you have?

FLORINE MARTIN: I had one sister and two brothers.

DR. LEE: And so the four of you …

FLORINE MARTIN: Grew up together, yes.

DR. LEE: … would take the streetcar?

FLORINE MARTIN: Yes. Yes. Now, one of my brothers died. He died in Connecticut in a nursing home. But I did have his body brought back here because he graduated from Carter G. Woodson School. And so I got his class, I think this gentleman next door was in his class, and several of his classmates got together, and they had somebody to speak at the graveside celebration. I call it a celebration, because we do celebrate things.

DR. LEE: Home going.

FLORINE MARTIN: Home going now. They say home going, don't they? Yes. And so he had a nice home going. And down, further down the … maybe about three miles out there in Prince George. Now, my other brother is in the nursing home down there in Waverly. And I go there regular from time to time. Not as often as I would like to go, but I do call and keep in touch with him. I talk to the supervisors and the nurses, and they'll tell me how he's doing. Even if he breaks a fingernail or they got to give him a shot, anything, they are going to call me and tell me. I'm hoping that I can go maybe in the next two weeks to see him.

FLORINE MARTIN: Well, my mother, we lived there on Sycamore Street, as I said, and my sister, Ethel Brown, she … Ethel Brown Reeves was very talented. She could sing and tear the piano up. So I do have a daughter who is just like her. She's just like her. So this lady was a minister, Mrs. Virginia Weatherspoon, she was a minister.

DR. LEE: Here in Hopewell?

FLORINE MARTIN: She lived in Petersburg, but she had a little church. You know how they had little rooms, you know. And she had a little church down there on Sycamore Street. And she would come down. And she was a good speaker. And she saw my daughter, and she asked my mother would she let her come and stay with her. So my mother did. Ethel wanted to go. She could play the piano, you know. And she bought a piano for her in Petersburg over on Byrne Street I think it was. And so Ethel started to playing. And all of the prominent people who sang would come and they would stay at her house.

DR. LEE: Ms. Weatherspoon?

FLORINE MARTIN: Yes, Weatherspoon. And the community center was right across the street and that's where they had the … all the activities for all of the black people.

DR. LEE: Is this Petersburg or Hopewell?

FLORINE MARTIN: In Petersburg. Now, this is in Petersburg.

DR. LEE: Do you remember the name of her church?

FLORINE MARTIN: I certainty don't. I certainly don't. Well, Mrs. Weatherspoon would have her church in her home. You know, that's where they … you know, they start at, you know, have it in her home. She could preach and she would sing after she went back to Petersburg. She had one down here, but when she went there, she went to her home because there was a church across the street, and that was a Holiness Church, too, so she didn't go there, you know. She wanted her own, you know.

Well, there was … let me see … who was that dude? Back there, played the guitar. This lady. Lady get the … one of these mornings, one as I'm going … going back to … going to heaven to get my crown and somebody had … was Knight … I think her last name of her was Knight, and that lady could sing. And she got so popular until … she did sing at the … in Richmond at the Coliseum. She sang there and that was packed, people from everywhere was there to hear her. And in fact, everything that went on, they had a big activity, it would be in Richmond.

DR. LEE: Was there anyplace here in Hopewell that people could gather?

FLORINE MARTIN: Together? I'll tell you, they would gather … we had that big affair at our church, at Friendship. I tell you, I would have some programs there, and that church would be packed.

DR. LEE: Has it always been located where it is?

FLORINE MARTIN: Not on Arlington Road. The first church was further down, but it was not a Baptist church. It was Methodist church. That's where now Reverend Turner was there and this man, another man by the name of Reverend Davis. Well, I didn't know him. When we came, Reverend Turner had a house. He was in a home. Uh-huh. And that's where my father would go, because he was Baptist. But this Reverend Davis was Methodist and a lot of people went there, but I didn't go to the Methodist church. When we came here, Friendship was … it was in a … it was a home, it was … the old Perry House. That's what they called it. The old Perry House.

…

FLORINE MARTIN: And they moved out of that house and went to Fort Lee to live. And so this church became the Friendship Baptist Church.

DR. LEE: Okay.

FLORINE MARTIN: First pastor's name was Reverend Skinner …. And he was a good pastor. He pastored there for a while. And then Reverend L. W. Jacobs …

DR. LEE: Okay.

FLORINE MARTIN: … became …

DR. LEE: What time period are we talking about …

FLORINE MARTIN: Reverend …

DR. LEE: … when Reverend Skinner first pastored?

FLORINE MARTIN: That was about 1926.

DR. LEE: Okay.

FLORINE MARTIN: And then after he went off the scene, Reverend L. W. Jacobs became the pastor. And Reverend Jacobs was pastor of our church for over fifty years. And he was a preaching man, could sing, too. Oh, yes. And he … Reverend Jacobs had five churches one time. Five.

DR. LEE: In Hopewell or Prince George?

FLORINE MARTIN: No. Prince George and everywhere, all up in … near … let me see. What do you call it … Reverend Jacobs had churches up in Dinwiddie. He had the First Baptist, and then he had another church further down. He had two churches up in … close in the same area. And then … he could really preach. Then he had a church right up the street here, Mt. Calvary Baptist Church, and he … and he had Friendship. He had five at one time.

DR. LEE: Was he young?

FLORINE MARTIN: At that time Reverend Jacobs was young, yes, yes, yes, young. We have a lot of pictures at our church now of the old members and when the church … we walked … went into the new church.

But when he became a member of Friendship, a pastor, there came a time when they asked Reverend Jacobs would he give up his other churches and just be a member at … a pastor at Friendship Baptist. So I think he agreed, but he never … he never did really give them … he gave up the ones that were further away. He gave those churches up, but he kept Mt. Calvary for a while, and then he had a church down in Disputanta.

Now, Disputanta is further out in the county, and he stayed there a long time. In fact, he and his wife both are buried there at that church, because he loved Disputanta, and he loved Friendship, but he finally had to give up Friendship.

DR. LEE: What are your fondest memories of Friendship?

FLORINE MARTIN: Of Friendship? Oh, my fondest memory is … well, when I first came out, I was in that class, and I went on, I am still going to school, see, and I graduated from Carter G. Woodson.

DR. LEE: What year was that?

FLORINE MARTIN: In '38.

DR. LEE: Okay.

FLORINE MARTIN: 1938.

DR. LEE: Was it still over …

FLORINE MARTIN: It … no. No. No. We still over there behind the fire station.

DR. LEE: Okay.

FLORINE MARTIN: Uh-huh. Segregated. And Reverend Harry E. James was our principal, and he was a very smart man. He was a minister.

DR. LEE: Where was his church; do you remember?

FLORINE MARTIN: Reverend James, he pastored over at a church, but it wasn't in this area. It was out in another area. Never did go to his church, but Reverend James was very smart. And he was a real fat man, real fat, and he could outrun any of the boys, you know. If they didn't come to school, he would go and get them and bring them back, bring them on back to school. And we had a young man, they called him Bossy Simmons, and he would go across that railroad track and get him and bring him back. And he did graduate. He graduated. I think he was one of the … in the one of the first classes.

DR. LEE: And so after you graduated in '38, what did you do then?

FLORINE MARTIN: Well, in '38, the first thing I did … oh, my sister was working at the … at the factory, and she got me a job at the factory.

DR. LEE: Which one?

FLORINE MARTIN: Cigarette factory. Brown & Williamson.

DR. LEE: In Richmond?

FLORINE MARTIN: No, no. Brown & Williamson in Petersburg.

DR. LEE: Okay.

FLORINE MARTIN: Yeah. And I worked there for maybe about six years. And I … let me see … after those six years I got married. I got married, and we moved to Davisville, Davisville, where Reverend Curtis Harris is pastor. He has his church there. And so I lived on the … I think it was 600 block, and Davisville was a beautiful place, beautiful place at that time, and everybody doing well, you know. I think I had … Sarah Marie was born over here … yeah. I have two that were born over in this area, and then two children that were born in Davisville.

DR. LEE: Okay.

FLORINE MARTIN: Uh-huh. So they used to have a little meeting, kind of business meetings of all the people who lived in the project, so I went to that meeting and there was a man that came from Virginia State to talk to us, and he showed a film, and he said there was a particular word in that film, and I am going to ask any of you, any one of you in this group to tell me what that word is that touched you.

And so the word was "educate." That was the word. Well, you see, I had been planning that I was going to college. That's what I said. I said, oh, I say I think I could go to college. And so my ... I told my husband I wanted to go to college. Well, in the meantime we were still living in Davisville. Well, I found out about these houses being built over here, and so I told him about it, about these houses.

DR. LEE: In Arlington?

FLORINE MARTIN: In Arlington. This was a new section. I said, you know, I said, I ... there's a man that lives down the street who is an agent for selling houses over there in Davis ... in Arlington. He said, how do you know? I said, I heard him telling somebody. So he said, well, said, you go and see if you can contact him and have him to come here. That's when we were living in Davisville. So he did. I did. I did what he told me to do and the man came to our house, he and his wife. And so we bought this house. It was just four rooms at that time.

DR. LEE: What year was that?

FLORINE MARTIN: Oh, let me see. Lord have mercy. That ... I had ... let me see he ... wasn't too far ... too long. Let me see. '38. Maybe in the '50s.

DR. LEE: Okay.

FLORINE MARTIN: Uh-huh.

DR. LEE: So it was undeveloped?

FLORINE MARTIN: Yeah, this area. It was one row of houses in front of us, and then this row.

DR. LEE: Okay.

FLORINE MARTIN: So we were the first ones that moved on this row and the fellow next door, both of us moved in at the same time.

DR. LEE: And this was in the '50s?

FLORINE MARTIN: I think it was in the '50s.

DR. LEE: Okay.

FLORINE MARTIN: And anyway, we ... my husband died, passed away.

DR. LEE: And what was his name?

FLORINE MARTIN: William A. Jones.

DR. LEE: Okay.

FLORINE MARTIN: Yeah. He passed away. And I had two children in elementary school.

DR. LEE: What are their names?

FLORINE MARTIN: Sarah.

DR. LEE: After your mother?

FLORINE MARTIN: Yes. Sarah Marie Jones. And Sylvia, Ebolene Jones. And then my youngest daughter is Floresta Jones. And I had a son, William Jones, Jr. And so they

Courtesy of the author

… well, I didn't know to keep them home, you know. I thought maybe if he died they'd go on to school and lose a day, you know, but Sarah, Sylvia, they … I'm trying to think, did they … yes, they were here. They stayed here. So one of my mother's friends told me, said, now don't let them go back to school. You don't let them go to school, you know.

I said, oh. All right, then. You know. So anyway, I kept them home. And so we … they had the funeral. I had the pictures and everything. I think Sarah has my pictures because when I am looking for anything she got … keeps them. She's got a book of them. Yeah, I know that's where they are.

DR. LEE: They are probably in good hands.

FLORINE MARTIN: Yeah. Yeah. But anyway, Sarah graduated from high school.

DR. LEE: Which high school did she go to?

FLORINE MARTIN: Carter Woodson. Carter Woodson.

DR. LEE: Okay.

FLORINE MARTIN: But this Carter … it was over there in Davisville, uh-huh. Still segregated, now, see. That's where she was the valedictorian.

DR. LEE: You don't remember what year?

FLORINE MARTIN: No, I don't remember the year now. I don't remember the year then. But …

DR. LEE: So she went … she graduated from Carter G. Woodson when it was in Davisville?

FLORINE MARTIN: Yes.

DR. LEE: And Sylvia?

FLORINE MARTIN: Sylvia, uh-huh, she graduated from Carter G. Woodson in Davisville. Then Floresta, yeah, she finally went to Davisville, but when she got ready to go to high school it was integrated. … And she graduated … yeah, she went to Hopewell High.

DR. LEE: Okay.

FLORINE MARTIN: Floresta did. And so one of … let me see … one of my … one of the teachers of Carter Woodson came to talk to me about Sarah going to college. I said, going to college? Said, yeah. I said, well, I want her to go to college. He said, well … he asked me about the money or whatever. I said, I don't know. I said … I was thinking about it, you know. I didn't have enough money. So he helped me. I did get her into Virginia State. And she was in biology. She was a biology major. And she did very well and got a little job on campus, you know.

And of course, Sylvia, when she graduated, she's valedictorian, too, and all, they all very smart. And so I told you she played beautiful, one time they didn't have nobody at Woodson to play, so Sylvia did the playing for whatever they asked. And so she went to Virginia State, too. And so I had two students at Virginia State at the same time. But the Lord works in mysterious ways.

Sylvia didn't want to go to school. She says, Momma, I want to get me a job at Fort Lee. I say, Fort Lee? Yes, ma'am. I said, well, you not going to get no job at Fort Lee. I said, you going to college. Well, I don't want to go to college. Suzie and Mary and this one got jobs up at Fort … I say, I don't care who is going to Fort Lee. You are not going. So anyway, Sylvia always was spoiled for some reason, and she didn't want to go, sure enough, but I sent her on. And Sarah would take her hand, by the hand, and I always made them respect Sarah because she was the oldest one. If I found out that they were arguing or anything, I said, I'm not going to have it. I said, Sarah, is the oldest, and I expect for you to respect her. And so they got so they would do that, you know.

FLORINE MARTIN: Well, Sarah was a mother to Floresta. Wherever she went, they would take Floresta with her. And because Floresta was like her daddy, she was one who could take care of all herself, you know, didn't have to worry about her. And she's very, very smart. She was … she got all kind of scholarships.

DR. LEE: Did she go to college, also?

FLORINE MARTIN: Oh, yes. Yes. Yes.… She's … I called her my professor. She's teaching at a private school in New Jersey, Spotswood.

DR. LEE: Did she go to Virginia State?

FLORINE MARTIN: She went to Barry College. She got a scholarship to go to Barry College in Georgia. And I didn't want her … this was a scholarship, and it was thirteen children who went to Barry College, and Floresta had the highest rating of those thirteen.

DR. LEE: And were they from Hopewell?

FLORINE MARTIN: Oh, Hopewell … came from Hopewell, Hopewell High, but Floresta had the highest ratings. And so she played the trumpet in the band, and sang in the choir, and she got the scholarship to go to Barry College, and so she got the money to go there. And so I said, after she finished Barry College, then she wanted to go to Michigan State. I said, Michigan State? Yeah. She wanted to get her master's.

So I said, well, Floresta, I said, your godmother lives in Lansing, Michigan. I said, my classmate lives in Lansing, Michigan. And I said, I think I'll call her. I said, she may be through here to see me. You think so, Momma? I said, yeah. So sure enough, one night the doorbell rang about 2:00 o'clock, and I went to the door, and it was Ruth, Ruth Powell Miness. And I opened the door, and it was her, she and her daughter came in. And I said, oh, oh, we just hug and cried and carrying. And she said, you know, I went up the street there and they told me you had lost your husband. I said, yes, I have. She said, well, why didn't you tell me? I said, I don't know, Ruth. I don't know why I didn't tell you. I said, do you know I have a daughter who wants to go to Michigan State? She said, what? I said, yeah. She said, well, I'm right around the corner at … from Michigan State. So Ruth told me to just put her on the plane and we'll meet her. And I said, well, she's got her trunk and everything.

She said, well, just ship it, and we'll take care of it. So that's what she … how she ended up going to Michigan State. Well, Floresta was here about two weeks ago, and she told me that she always wanted to go to … there's another college in, and it wasn't Michigan … it's another college. She said, that was the one I wanted to go to, Momma. I said, sure enough you didn't say it.

She said, I never told you, because things came up like that. And so she went on with Ruth. She's her godmother. And so they went … she went there.

DR. LEE: Had Ruth gone to Carter G. Woodson with you?

FLORINE MARTIN: Oh, yes, yes, yes.

DR. LEE: Did she leave after high school?

FLORINE MARTIN: Yes. Not immediately.

DR. LEE: Okay.

FLORINE MARTIN: She stayed … well, what happened, Ruth … her mother left. Seemed like her mother and father separated. … And so mother had a sister living in Brooklyn, New York. So she went to the sister. We didn't know all of that, you know.

DR. LEE: Right.

FLORINE MARTIN: She went to her sister and they never came back.

DR. LEE: Okay.

FLORINE MARTIN: But they did have this beautiful home down in City Point, down near the waterfront. And so Ruth was a beautician, and she kept the house. Her father was there. And she ran a beauty parlor.

DR. LEE: In?

FLORINE MARTIN: In ... down City Point.

DR. LEE: Okay. Do you remember the name of the beauty parlor?

FLORINE MARTIN: No. Just Ruth's Beauty Parlor. That's all. That's all.

DR. LEE: Okay.

FLORINE MARTIN: And so, anyway, her father had peculiar speech, something like a foreigner, and I used to always like to hear him talk. It was two girls and two boys. Uh-huh. And so Ruth said to me one day, this has been about maybe three or four years ago, she said, guess what?

I said, what? She said, you know, I almost became a millionaire.

I said, well, why didn't you, so you can share the money with me?

She said, you know, a man came here, had the address, had the name and everything, and it was some money that was distributed to ... with this family, and this brother, they was going to give to him the money, that was her father, but her father was black and the others were white. He had that speech. And so Ruth said that's the only reason I didn't get the money. I said, well, I declare, we missed out on that. But he worked on the boat down there at City Point. If you remember here some weeks ago there was ... what was that ... something leaking from this chemical spill at City Point. Well, that's where her father worked, and he was the only black man that was working.

DR. LEE: And what was his name?

FLORINE MARTIN: His name was ...

DR. LEE: Miness was the last name, or was that her married name?

FLORINE MARTIN: Who?

DR. LEE: Ruth's father?

FLORINE MARTIN: Ruth's father? No. Miness was her married name.

DR. LEE: Oh, okay.

FLORINE MARTIN: Her name was Ruth Powell. Miness is after she got married.

DR. LEE: Okay. His name then was Powell?

FLORINE MARTIN: Was Willie Powell. Yes, Willie Powell.

DR. LEE: He was the only black person ...

FLORINE MARTIN: The only black person that had that job, you know, and so they accumulated right much because they built this home, and he did a whole lot of things, you know. And … so he worked on that barge. And after a while, after his wife left, he … they moved to Brooklyn, they moved to Brooklyn, and he married the lady next door. He married the lady next door.

DR. LEE: (*Inaudible.*)

FLORINE MARTIN: Yes. And they moved to Detroit. So when Floresta finished Michigan State, she got a job in Detroit with the *Detroit Free Press* news.

   … And she worked there for awhile. And then she told me that she was going to go to … going to New Jersey, Jackson, New Jersey, with a friend that she had met while she was at Virginia State. And this girl had … her husband lived up in some parts of Virginia, and not too far from here. Up in Cumberland County I think it was. But anyway, she had a beautiful home over there, and she … this man … some way or another they separated, but she went to Jackson, New Jersey, and Floresta went because she had … her mother was up there, and then she had some more sisters up there. So she bought this beautiful home up there, and Floresta lived with her for a long time. And then she decided to go out on her own, and that's what she's doing in Spotswood, New Jersey.

   … She got a job at a private college. So now she is a doctorate … in the doctoral program, and she just returned from Africa. Uh-huh.

DR. LEE: So how many children do you have living here in Hopewell?

FLORINE MARTIN: Well, not any living here in Hopewell. They are in Petersburg.

DR. LEE: Okay. Except Floresta?

FLORINE MARTIN: Except Floresta, now, uh-huh. Sarah is … she was a biology major, but now she's a guidance counselor.

DR. LEE: Where is she?

FLORINE MARTIN: In Hopewell High.

DR. LEE: Okay, at Hopewell.

FLORINE MARTIN: At Hopewell High.

DR. LEE: Where she graduated from?

FLORINE MARTIN: Yes … no. Sarah graduated from Carter Woodson. Yeah, the oldest one. But she taught biology for a while, then she went into guidance, so now she is … they asked her to be principal.

DR. LEE: At Hopewell High?

FLORINE MARTIN: At Carter G. Woodson.

DR. LEE: At Carter G. Woodson?

FLORINE MARTIN: Yeah

DR. LEE: Is this just recently that they asked her?

FLORINE MARTIN: Oh, yeah. They asked her that about three years ago, three or four years ago, yeah, they want her to be … but Sarah is … she's very smart. She's a good teacher. She knows the children. And she said that she thinks she can help those children more if she's there because, believe it or not, people [are] just as racist as they can be. People may not say it, but it's true. So she stays there to help our black children get out of there.

Yeah, from Carter … from Hopewell High.

DR. LEE: Okay. As a guidance counselor?

FLORINE MARTIN: As a guidance counselor. And so I think she's done very well. A lot of things you have to go and get, spend money getting the robes or the caps and gowns, or if they don't have the clothes, pay for them, you know. All those things. She has access to all the money, you know, and to get the money coming in. And the people know her. She can get on the telephone and tell them, well, we need a thousand dollars, or the … I need this and know who to call, and they'll come with that money. And then she will tell them this money is going towards so and so and so. See, a lot of people don't have good connections like that.

DR. LEE: Right.

FLORINE MARTIN: Uh-huh. And so, say, even sometimes she works with me at church with different things that I have to do, and especially during the holidays when we [are] sending out food, or somebody needs this or needs the other. You don't tell her everything. If you have something to do, you go on and do it, and that's the end of it. We … it's something between the pastor, the person who is the head of it, usually I am, with the … at Christmastime we go and buy, and then we have certain people who work with us, and that's it. I have one lady … I did get up one Sunday morning and I asked … I said, we need more help. I said, we need some younger men to come in and help us because there are some things that need to be done that we need some men. So one of the young men that came to me was one of our younger deacons, and he came down and told me that I'll work with you. And it came to me that he worked at Fort Lee. He works at Fort Lee in produce. So you see, he could help when we go to buy things, you know.

DR. LEE: Right.

FLORINE MARTIN: And so one of the deacons, Deacon Aikens, said he would work with me. And it's good contact you see here.

DR. LEE: Yes.

FLORINE MARTIN: Uh-huh. And of course we have some other deacons that work with us, too.

DR. LEE: What are some of the organizations that you were involved in?

FLORINE MARTIN: Involved in?

DR. LEE: You did a lot of volunteer work.

FLORINE MARTIN: Oh, yes. I volunteered at the information desk at John Randolph.

DR. LEE: The hospital?

FLORINE MARTIN: The hospital. The Red Cross. The Food Pantry on Fridays. And I am on the Senior Citizens Advisory Commission. That means that we … anything of interest to the seniors, that's what we do. Right now, we're getting the therapeutic pool. We have gone to the city council and asked for money. That's going to be $50,000 for all of that. And they are … we had to go and ask for it. Well, John Randolph Hospital Medical Center have donated money toward our cause, and we just everywhere, I'll tell you.

DR. LEE: Yeah. So many people could just decide to enjoy theirself at home.

FLORINE MARTIN: Huh-uh, no.

DR. LEE: What keeps you so involved? What makes you keep going?

FLORINE MARTIN: Because I just enjoy what I'm doing. I enjoy what I am doing. And when you meet other people and you see the condition that they are in, you say, thank you, Lord, but for the grace of God would be me. One lady came in there last week and I asked her, I said, I am at the information desk now, but I have started from the back putting … packing the bags and all of that, but I've been there the longest and so I am on … at that information desk. And this lady came in and of course we got records that we have to keep. And I said, have you been here before? She said, it's been a long time. And she said, but, said, I haven't had anything to eat in two days, like that. I said, what? And she's crying, and I went to crying. I said, well, this is the Food Pantry. I said, and that's what we are about. I said, my church sends money down here. They support the Food Pantry. Friendship was one of the first … was one of the first black churches that joined that … that, you know, that …

DR. LEE: Food …

FLORINE MARTIN: Food.

DR. LEE: … Bank?

FLORINE MARTIN: Yes. We were the first one. When they were organized it was no … in the paper.

DR. LEE: Do you remember the year?

FLORINE MARTIN: No. I sure don't. Well, it was about over thirty years.

DR. LEE: Okay.

FLORINE MARTIN: Uh-huh. I went to the meeting … I'm always going to a meeting to see what's going on. So I was there at this meeting, and another lady, her name is Lavinia Nicholas, we went together, and so my husband carried me down there, so I think I got a ride back with her, but that organization was … it was organized by the ministers of Hopewell. So I came back and brought the news, you know, and I said, I think we ought to join that, you know. And so they did, but they sent … they send the check …

DR. LEE: Okay.

FLORINE MARTIN: … each month, you know, to support it. And then we have … there is another place down the street that pays the rent, because they sell clothes, you know, and that's something that a lot of people go in and buy things and they pay the rent on the building where this food pantry is. And there's a lot of food that goes in there from donations, mail carriers, there's Boy Scouts and different organizations give money. Some classes at the high school will have a drive, and they bring in the food. We just have so much food.

　　And then the stores, they do, they contribute; dessert, breads. And some, the pizza places, they give pizzas. And then they have money that they can go and buy at the Food Bank in Richmond. We have already … we have … I've been over there to see what's done. I want to see what's going on, you know.

DR. LEE: Right.

FLORINE MARTIN: But we don't have to go there now. The men do that, on Tuesday, the food bank is … the Food Pantry is closed. So on Tuesdays, we don't go. We're open from Monday, Wednesday, and Friday.

DR. LEE: Which organization have you worked the longest for?

FLORINE MARTIN: The longest one? Well, I think it's the hospital, because believe it or not, my daughter wanted to be a nurse, she was saying.

DR. LEE: Which one?

FLORINE MARTIN: This is Floresta, when she was fourteen. So I called down there and told them that I wanted … my daughter wanted to be a Candy Striper. So they told me that they don't take black Candy Stripers. I said, I beg your pardon. No. We don't take black Candy Stripers. I said, well, thank you. So I called Petersburg. And the lady said, well, they have a Candy Stripe group at John Randolph. I said, well, they told me that they don't take black Candy Stripers.

　　They told you that?

　　I said, exactly. They said, well, what's her name? I said, Florine Martin. Well, Mrs. Martin, we'll be glad to take her. And so I said, thank you. What time do you want me to bring her? Told me to bring her the next day. So Floresta and I went on over there, got on the bus and went on.

Dr. Lee: What is this, the '70s?

Florine Martin: This is … uh-huh … this is Floresta …

Dr. Lee: 1970s?

Florine Martin: Yeah, something like that.

Dr. Lee: Okay.

Florine Martin: And Floresta, we went, and her first patient was a former … what was it … somebody from Virginia State College. And she worked with him. He was sick. And the nurse was with her and helped her, teach her, telling her what to do. And she did that for two or three years, and she had to leave, going to college, you know. But that's what they told her. I never kept … got that out of my head that they had told me that. So I called up and I said, my name is Florine Martin, and I'm calling because I would like to be a volunteer down at the hospital. And they said, well, why do you want to be a volunteer? I didn't get smart. I said, well, I'll tell you. I … a lot of my memories come in and out here, and patients

Courtesy of the author

… I said, but I have never seen a black volunteer, I said, so I thought I would like to be one. Do you know they got that letter to me that day. Yes. And I went down there and I signed up, and I was the first black one that went down there. And so I didn't keep it … I kept that in my head. And the first place that I was assigned to go to was the gift shop, to work in the gift shop. And this lady, I worked with her, Cora Jefferson, and I knew her because she worked at Rucker Rosenstock when they were here in Hopewell.

Dr. Lee: What is the name of that?

Florine Martin: Rucker Rosenstock Department Store.

Dr. Lee: Okay.

Florine Martin: And Ms. Cora Chester, I knew her because that was the store that we went in all the time to buy things, you know. And she told me, she said, well, I'm glad to have you. Come on in. And I went on in that gift shop, and I was selling things in there, and the news got all over the hospital. Child, we got a black person in that gift shop. Say, well, who is it? It's Florine. Because, see, everybody knew me. Say, who? Said, Florine. You mean, in the gift shop? Say, yeah. So everybody from the kitchen all that knew me was coming in there to see me. And finally, one person asked me, said, look a here, say, how in the world did you get in here?

I said, well, sometimes you have to open your mouth. I said, and I opened my mouth. And so they told me to come on and I'm here. Well, Ms. Cora … I worked in there about three or four days, she said, well, Florine, I'm going on home. She lived down there near the bridge. And it's a beautiful house, sit up on the hill. It is sold now. But anyway, that's where she lived. And she said, well if you have any problems, call me.

I didn't have no problems because all I had to do was get the sales and have it straight. And I had … knew where to put the money and leave. And they couldn't believe it.

Well, they had a little banquet, and so they were asking the questions about how did you become a volunteer and why. And I let it loose. I did. I told them how I became a volunteer, because I hadn't ever seen a black volunteer, so I asked, could I become a volunteer, I said, because my daughter, when she was fourteen and wanted to become a Candy Striper, they told me that they didn't take black ones, and I'm smiling and, you know, looking just like I was … just like I knew each one of them. Some of them got red in the face, but they … I said it. And you know, that cleared the air. Even our director, her name is Beverly Epps, she does a splendid job, and …

DR. LEE: Is she black or white?

FLORINE MARTIN: She's black. She's black, yeah.

DR. LEE: She's director of …

FLORINE MARTIN: She's director of the volunteers.

DR. LEE: Okay.

FLORINE MARTIN: That's what she is. And she's the first black one that we had.

DR. LEE: How long has she been there?

FLORINE MARTIN: I think she's been there about … I think she's been there maybe about near ten years, eleven years, something like that. She's doing real good.

DR. LEE: Are there any black Candy Stripers?

FLORINE MARTIN: Oh, yes. Yes. They got plenty of black ones now. Oh, they are everywhere.

DR. LEE: You opened the door.

FLORINE MARTIN: I opened the door, yes. Uh-huh. Yeah.

DR. LEE: What are your hopes for Hopewell? What do you ... do you see Hopewell as a place that people can have the American dream, can own a home and a good education for their children and to be able to get a job?

FLORINE MARTIN: Yes. Yes. Yes. Yes.

DR. LEE: But it's different?

FLORINE MARTIN: Yeah, it's different. It's different. It's different. Down on Broadway now we have ... well, I don't particularly care about the stores, you know, but there are stores that people go into, and they got a lot of secondhand things, you know, selling them. But we do have black people who have businesses down there, too, and they do good. Uh-huh. And we have ... I think somebody just opened up a sub place, they tell me. I have not been to it, but I said I'm going, I'm going. It's been about a couple of weeks now. Uh-huh.

And then they have a little place where you can go and get ... it's opened about until 1:00, get breakfast and coffee or donuts or whatever you want, sandwich, breakfast, you know, you can go there. So there are a lot of things going on in Hopewell.

You can live anywhere you want to live, and the people are living, I tell you. People have nice homes, and they can go and ... in the area.

And I just hope everybody would behave themselves. Sometimes you change, tear up things, you know, and it's terrible, isn't it? It is sad, I think. But we do ... this is a new section, very quiet.

DR. LEE: This is still Arlington Heights?

FLORINE MARTIN: This is still Arlington Heights, uh-huh. And we got a beautiful playground up there.

DR. LEE: What's the name of it?

FLORINE MARTIN: It's just Arlington Playground.

DR. LEE: Okay.

FLORINE MARTIN: Uh-huh. And that was the Harry E. James School used to be there.

DR. LEE: Okay.

FLORINE MARTIN: Uh-huh. Up on that hill. But they rebuilt the school, and it's down there ... down that highway there. And so I came up with the idea that we ought to use Harry E. James, since he was our first black principal, that we ought to have a school named after him. And I called ...

DR. LEE: Oh, you came up with the idea?

FLORINE MARTIN: Oh, yes, I did. Uh-huh. I called Reverend Harris, Curtis Harris. He's in charge … he does a lot of things with civil rights, you know, been all down there with Martin Luther King and all that kind of stuff, you know. And so I called him one day and I said, you know, I say, I think all the schools have white names. I think we ought to have somebody … by Harry E. James.

He said you are right … you are on the right alley, going down the right alley, he said. He said, but you know what I want you to do? I said, what? I want you to go around here and see how many names you can get for people who will agree to that. I say, okay. He brought me the book, and I went around and I got a lot of names. And down at the end of the street is a person who lived there, Wynn, that's his name, Wynn, and when I went there he signed it. He signed it, all the people around here signed, you know, because they knew Reverend James. And I took up, I said we … Juanita Chambers, she's a teacher, and she's a principal of one of the schools, and so she told me, said, well, we need to get something that maybe put a little plate or something down with his name on it. I said, well … she said, I'll give you something. I think we put five dollars or something, you know, like that. And I don't know, I had got fifty, sixty some dollars like that, uh-huh. So anyway, it passed, and of course some people didn't like it, you know, so they claim, because what they didn't like because they wanted their name, but there's time. We wanted that for Reverend James.

DR. LEE: How long ago was that?

FLORINE MARTIN: That's been … let me see how old that school is. The school is about …that school['s] been there about thirteen years now. So now they give a scholarship for any student that has been through Harry E. James, and go through the middle school, Carter Woodson, and finish Hopewell High, they will give a scholarship. I think its a thousand dollars that they give every year. Uh-huh. Yeah. And so anyway that went off. And we …

DR. LEE: Well done. …   You are making this the American dream in your own way.

FLORINE MARTIN: Yeah, uh-huh. I'm not afraid to approach people, you know, when something …

DR. LEE: It's the way that it is done.

FLORINE MARTIN: Yeah, uh-huh. So I just enjoy doing what I'm doing.

James "Jim" Willcox, July 19, 2005

James "Jim" Willcox, barely twenty-two years old and a newly minted Clemson College graduate, came to Hopewell as a young chemical engineer in 1962. The young, white, Darlington, South Carolina, native had worked for Hercules in Savannah for three months prior to relocating to Hopewell. I interviewed Jim on July 19, 2005, in his home in the Westover area of Hopewell.

Courtesy of Carmela Hamm

JIM WILLCOX: Well, I know a lot about the work environment because I worked for Hercules … years. And a lot of the, let's say, distribution of Afro American people in the workforce was predicated on seniority there, so it takes a while for changes to occur. Now, when I came here I would say that most of the African Americans were working in warehousing, raw materials storage, which one was a particularly, you know, arduous situation.

I obviously liked Hopewell or I wouldn't have stayed here after I retired. I did leave here for two years and worked in Wilmington, Delaware, and then came back to Hopewell, all with Hercules, so I only had one employer.

And you know, there's not a lot going on in Hopewell, but the people are nice. And I'm close enough to Richmond and so that's one reason I chose to stay here; I can be in Richmond in a half hour, so it's no problem.

DR. LEE: How was it different from South Carolina? Darlington?

JIM WILLCOX: Darlington. Do you know where Florence is? Right on [I-]95.

Well, Darlington is ten miles west of Florence, just in the greater Peedee Valley there. Well, obviously, this is much more industrial. Darlington was much more agrarian. There was some industry there, but the cotton mill closed when I was in high school. There was a Dixie Cup plant there, but those were the two main industries in the town. Lots of tobacco. Tobacco market. Lots of cotton and things like that. So being an industrial town, which Hopewell was even more of a chemical capital in 1962 than it is now because all the plants employed many more people than they do now. Hercules, for example, somewhere in the mid-sixties employed about 1,500 people and today they probably employ less than 300.

And you know, one industry is closed, and the other one has, you know, cut employment. So it's not near as much a chemical industry town as it was then. We made derivatives of cellulose that are used as thickeners. Most of them are water-soluble products, and they thicken foods, and cosmetics, and toothpaste, and paint and oil-well muds. Most of the toothpaste was thickened by our product. The gravy in Gaines Gravy Train dog food was our product dusted on the kibbles. The lite syrups that when you take the sugar out, you have to have something to make them thick. Our product made them thick. It was made out of either wood pulp or cotton. The real short fuzz of the cotton off the cotton seed.

DR. LEE: Were you aware of race relations nationally, what was going on or …

JIM WILLCOX: I never saw any problems between them. As I was saying earlier, most of the blacks that worked at the plant were either in warehousing or some of those things. They hadn't really started to move up in the structure of the plant that much. Once the people got in the system then, you know, advancement in a union shop is all predicated on seniority, and all the wage roll people were union members.

DR. LEE: Did education play a part in that decision?

JIM WILLCOX: I'm sure it did.

DR. LEE: What about residential segregation, was that something you were aware of?

JIM WILLCOX: Well, I knew there were … Arlington and that area, the black areas, and there wasn't … but I was aware of it, yes. It wasn't that different from what it was in South Carolina.

DR. LEE: Okay. Was there any interactions, because I know many of the plants had baseball teams and musical groups and that kind of thing. Was any of that going on at Hercules?

JIM WILLCOX: There were some ball teams, but I was never involved in them so I don't know that much about them. There were no musical groups at Hercules. That was maybe Tubize.

DR. LEE: So was it totally separate …

JIM WILLCOX: Yeah.

DR. LEE: … black and white, really no interaction?

JIM WILLCOX: I would say there was very little.

DR. LEE: Okay. So the first time that you saw or heard of the Ku Klux Klan?

JIM WILLCOX: The first time I ever … and only time I've ever seen it was here in Hopewell in '66. I never saw it in South Carolina.

DR. LEE: And what was your feeling at that time?

JIM WILLCOX: I'm not sure that I remember that much about it.

DR. LEE: Where did you see them first? Let's set the scene.

JIM WILLCOX: Down at the Municipal Building in downtown Hopewell. And the Reverend Curtis Harris had a group that marched from one direction and the Klan in their robes marched from the other direction. And I think Curtis Harris's group went up on the top of the Municipal steps, Municipal Building steps. Then there was a row of police and then there were the Klan and the mob. And both groups were very orderly. Both made a few comments. Both had a prayer. And then they dispersed and went in opposite directions.

DR. LEE: I read the newspaper accounts of it. And from the photographs it seems like everyone was on their best behavior.

JIM WILLCOX: They were.

DR. LEE: Did you get that sense when you …

JIM WILLCOX: I did, indeed. I was very proud of everybody that they behaved.

DR. LEE: Now, 1966, and Hopewell was in the national news because of the meeting on the Municipal steps, how did things change after that, or did they?

JIM WILLCOX: I don't think they necessarily changed that much after that. I don't know that the event had a big impact one way or another. It mainly, I think, gave the two parties a means of expressing their opinion a little bit and then they went off.

DR. LEE: Were there changes in Hercules at that time, after that time?

JIM WILLCOX: I guess they gradually began to occur after that.

DR. LEE: But not before?

Courtesy of James Willcox

JIM WILLCOX: Not much before, no. I don't think that was a pivotal event. I think it was just a nationwide trend.

DR. LEE: What changes did you notice at Hercules?

JIM WILLCOX: Well, ultimately you had more and more of the operators moving up in the system as seniority allowed. By the time I was running some of the operations, about half of my top operators were black.

DR. LEE: And how many would be in your division or ...

JIM WILLCOX: My department? At one time I must have had thirty-five or forty people.

DR. LEE: And so about half of them ...

JIM WILLCOX: I would say 40 to 50 percent were. Something in that range.

DR. LEE: Mostly men? Or all men?

JIM WILLCOX: I don't believe I ever had any black women working for me. A lot of the jobs, the entry-level jobs over there were pretty strenuous, and you had to come through those to work up into the operator jobs and the better jobs, and not many women were willing to do ... you know, lifting fifty-pound bags and things like that, which is what the entry-level jobs were. And I think this was probably before or just as the women's liberation movement was beginning so a lot of women probably would not have pushed for that.

[*When asked if women performed the same jobs as men, he said,*] No, and you know, physically, a lot of them couldn't do it. There were some that can, and some women did. I had a couple of women working for me. But the evolution of the movement of black males occurred much more rapidly than the movement of total females into the workforce.

DR. LEE: Now, as this occurred, more black males moving into the upper ranks, did you see changes in the larger community or did things seem to remain the same?

JIM WILLCOX: Well, I think you had more blacks on, gradually, on boards and commissions and things like that involving the city.

[*When asked about public spaces such as churches, he said,*] Well, at some point in the sixties I got aggravated with the church, and I didn't go back to the church until the, I guess, early '90, but I think that any of the churches I went to were pretty much fully segregated. Most of them still are.

DR. LEE: Oh, yeah. Yeah. Okay. Now, Curtis Harris was very involved in pushing for change.

JIM WILLCOX: Yes.

DR. LEE: What was the general feeling about his actions?

JIM WILLCOX: Well, I think Curtis was considered more responsible, more moderate than a lot of people, particularly on the national level.

He was pushing for change, but he understood I think that change took time, that things weren't going to change instantly. At least that was my impression. I didn't know Curtis personally at that point. I still don't know him well, but that would be my feeling.

DR. LEE: What's the biggest change you would say that has occurred in Hopewell since the '60s, and particularly since that 1966 incident with the …

JIM WILLCOX: Well, like I say, I don't think the incident had very much to do with the change. I think that was just an … event that each side needed to vent their feelings, and thank heavens it was peaceful.

DR. LEE: 1963 was when we had the march on Washington. You had just …

JIM WILLCOX: Just come here.

DR. LEE: Yeah. Did you sense a change nationally? I know you couldn't tell what was happening here because you had just gotten here, but nationally, did there seem to be an attitudinal change?

JIM WILLCOX: Well, I think it all occurred so gradually, I don't think … it was something you almost didn't see unless you looked back on it because … and I forget when the schools … I remember when the schools were going into integration here in Hopewell. I don't remember the dates, but … 1968 maybe.

[*When asked about the Kepone scare, he said,*] Yeah. And Richmond will never let us forget it. If they run our news in Richmond, they dig up Kepone because it takes the spotlight off of them. But interestingly, I don't think anybody died from Kepone. Most people recovered from the problems that they had with Kepone.

DR. LEE: I remember when I interviewed Jeanie, she said when she and her first family … when she and her first family first moved here, her mother and father, she just remembers the air being yellow. Did you have that experience? I know that was earlier than the '60s, though.

JIM WILLCOX: Well, there were lots of yellow fumes coming out of the Allied plant. Probably still are. Not as many. They used to release … they had a big ammonia plant over there, and I lived down in City Point, the old section when I first came here, and you could get very strong whiffs of ammonia down there.

So you know, the chemical industry has cleaned up a lot. See, back then, too, there was no waste treatment, big waste treatment plant when I came here. And Hercules had a small one. Then they built the big regional plant that still operates. It is operated by the city, but it was funded by the industry and the federal government, because it handles Fort Lee, city of Hopewell waste and it's ... if you go east from downtown, it's on the left, just before you cross the Bailey's Creek Bridge, but it was sort of a showcase, first of its kind when you had this federal/city/state working together to resolve this with a big waste treatment plant.

It was very important because Bailey's Creek used to be the most God-awful-looking thing. Never froze, never got any ice on it. Now people fish in it.

DR. LEE: What was the best thing about working for Hercules?

JIM WILLCOX: Hercules was a very fine company at that time. I wouldn't say they are as good a company now as they were then. They were much more family oriented and people oriented, and I think that's happened with most industry. It's become much less personal.

DR. LEE: So the fact that it was family oriented is what ...

JIM WILLCOX: Well, I ... no. I liked it. I liked the location. I liked what I was doing, because I worked in all facets of it. I worked in development, process development, product development, small-scale production, large-scale production. I worked in sales service, customer service. I worked in all ... pretty much all the aspects of it. I got as high as being ... I was department head twice, two different departments.

DR. LEE: What did you like least about it, working at Hercules?

JIM WILLCOX: I guess I liked least toward the end as the company was becoming much less personal, they seemed to care less about what quality they produced as long as ... they were too much bottom-line oriented, I think.

DR. LEE: Crunching the numbers?

JIM WILLCOX: Yeah. The bean-counters were running the organization.

DR. LEE: Did you see a difference in the quality of work that was put out by individuals?

JIM WILLCOX: I think it ultimately suffered even more after I left in '95.

DR. LEE: So what are your hopes for Hopewell?

JIM WILLCOX: Well, I think my hopes are less ambitious than city council's hopes. I think we'll never have a downtown section that amounts to anything again. We probably won't have a decent shopping center. I think we'll become a bedroom community for Richmond and Chesterfield.

DR. LEE: And why do you feel that way?

JIM WILLCOX: I don't think … well, the people in Hopewell are predominantly blue-collar. There's a lot of moderate white-collar, but they are predominantly blue-collar, and they are just not going to support the type of things that there's hope for downtown, I don't think. And people who live in Chesterfield, which you grew up in, and particularly Petersburg, feel that there's a stigma against Hopewell. It was a chemical capital. Petersburg people think they are much grander than Hopewellians. They like to look down their nose at us. So I don't think people from outside the community are going to come in to support the efforts …

DR. LEE: Of downtown …

JIM WILLCOX: … of downtown.

DR. LEE: … revitalization?

JIM WILLCOX: No. I don't think. That's my feeling. I tell my councilman that quite often, but …

DR. LEE: What areas do you see need the greatest change?

JIM WILLCOX: There's not much room for growth in Hopewell. Hopewell is land bound, and they can't annex from Prince George. That's a state law. And they obviously can't go across the river and grab Chesterfield, part of Chesterfield. And so the town is sort of strangled. They are doing a lot of infilling and little lots, but that's not going to be growth for Hopewell. And younger people tend to move out when that occurs. And your population gets older, and an older blue-collar community is not going to support the type of things they are interested in, I don't think.

DR. LEE: And what areas do you think have remained the same?

JIM WILLCOX: I don't know that any of them have really remained the same.

DR. LEE: There's a change in every one?

JIM WILLCOX: I think in all the residential areas. Well, I think when I came here there were certain elitist areas. And now a lot of blue-collar people are making as much as the white-collar or above people, and, you know, the mix has become quite different.

DR. LEE: Which would be the elitist areas when you …

JIM WILLCOX: Mansion Hills was one of them. This section back here and on back to the river.

DR. LEE: And so that's changed?

JIM WILLCOX: Yeah, uh-huh. And I think we've gotten some people in there we just as soon not have in there, that we gain more vandalism and that sort of thing.

DR. LEE: Would you say Hopewellians adapt to change well?

JIM WILLCOX: I think they have adapted pretty well. I don't think there's been a lot of problems in Hopewell. I think there were a lot of problems, race problems and all in the early parts of Hopewell, in Hopewell's early history.

DR. LEE: And so you are looking at the teens?

JIM WILLCOX: The DuPont days and that period. Have you done any work on that?

DR. LEE: Yes. I have looked at newspapers of the day. What would you say were the causes of those conflicts?

JIM WILLCOX: Well, I think you had a great mixing of people that weren't accustomed to being mixed together. I mean you mentioned earlier twenty-nine languages spoken. Well, a lot of those people had come from areas ... a lot of them from Central Europe, and I think probably the racial tension was pretty high because they weren't associated ... accustomed to associating with blacks. I think that was probably a big adjustment for a lot of them.

DR. LEE: Do you think ... Hopewell is called the Wonder City. Do you think that's ...

JIM WILLCOX: That was back when it was a chemical capital. It was also called the Chemical Capital, which I don't think is appropriate anymore because the chemical industry has gotten much smaller, and I don't know who came up with the Wonder City, whether that was the chamber of commence or who. I guess it's a wonder the way it grew up overnight.

DR. LEE: Yes, it did.

JIM WILLCOX: It did. Yeah. And you know, all of the smaller housing down 6th Street, all down in there, which is gradually disappearing, all of that was prefab in addition [to] the Sears housing. That was done by the DuPont Company. They could put up a block of houses a week. They all came in on the train. And they had dirt streets and dirt sidewalks and tarpaper houses. And the DuPont Company had worked out the figures that they could recover their investment by renting them at a certain price for three and a half years.

DR. LEE: Now, I was trying to think, would it have taken about three and a half years for a person to move up the ladder in DuPont, say?

JIM WILLCOX: Well, I think it was extremely segregated, probably. I don't know that for a fact, but I know they had four classifications of labor, not three, but four. They had black, Greek and Italian, blue-collar, and white-collar.

DR. LEE: Black, Greek ...

JIM WILLCOX: And Italian, blue-collar, and white-collar. So the Greek and Italian couldn't become electricians and carpenters and things like that ... I actually saw this in a copy of a DuPont project where they had the four divisions of laborers, which I'd never seen anywhere else.

DR. LEE: What year?

JIM WILLCOX: That would have been in teens when the big plant was here.

DR. LEE: A very hierarchical structure?

JIM WILLCOX: Right. Then you would have had management on top of that.

DR. LEE: Okay. How long do you think that hierarchy lasted?

JIM WILLCOX: Well, I think that type of hierarchy, probably taking out the Greek and Italians, lasted until the '60s.

DR. LEE: Other than the plants, what did people do as far as work?

JIM WILLCOX: Well, there were the various stores and city functions and things like that.

DR. LEE: And there's a Greek restaurant …

JIM WILLCOX: A lot of the buildings downtown are owned by Greeks that were restaurants.

DR. LEE: Were there other ethnic groups that were entrepreneurial?

JIM WILLCOX: Probably had more Greek than anything that stood out, although there are a number of Italian families here in town.

DR. LEE: I know the Greek Orthodox have their own church.

JIM WILLCOX: Yes. And that was the first Greek Orthodox Church in the commonwealth of Virginia, which is amazing.

DR. LEE: Because one wouldn't think it would be here in Hopewell.

JIM WILLCOX: No. It was built before the cathedral in Richmond.

DR. LEE: And in that way I think of it as the Wonder City … that you would have so many nationalities living in …

JIM WILLCOX: Now, see the Czech group lived in Prince George. You didn't get many of the Czechs and the Slovaks in Hopewell, but they were down around New Bohemia, the Church of the Sacred Heart there at [Route] 460 and [I-]295, that's basically the Czech, Catholic Church.

DR. LEE: And why were they there as opposed to being …

JIM WILLCOX: There was land available, and a lot of them came in as farmers down there.

DR. LEE: Okay. And has that changed?

JIM WILLCOX: There is still a lot of them down there, and a lot of them worked at Hercules ultimately.

DR. LEE: So many of your workforce under you were Czech …

JIM WILLCOX: Some of them were, yes.

DR. LEE: What would be the largest nationality percentage that you worked with?

JIM WILLCOX: Probably almost West Virginians. An awful lot of people have come down here to work in the plants from West Virginia. Was a lot of them came up from North Carolina. I mean there was employment here in the … the plant … DuPont closed its doors on Armistice Day because there were going to be no more wars, according to Wilson, and by the mid-twenties parts of the old DuPont plant begin springing up as other chemical plants, Stamscott Sailers started in '26, and became Virginia Sailers and by about '28, I think it was Hercules Pilot [who] had bought it. Solvay, who was making ammonia here in the mid-twenties, became Allied, became Honeywell.

Celanese, which was making synthetic rayon, which you know about the Celenese plant, they became … no … they were Tubize originally, then they became Celanese, then they became Firestone. So you had the evolution starting in the '20s with the chemical industry peaking probably in the '60s with employment.

DR. LEE: And so most people who graduated from high school would stay here, work in the plants?

JIM WILLCOX: A lot of them stayed here and worked in the plants, yes. Now, most of your engineers would come in from other places, as I did.

[*When asked about intergration, he said,*] and about the time I get here, then the schools integrate and gradually other things.

DR. LEE: So it feels like change is happening? I mean …

JIM WILLCOX: Change has happened, but, you know, I'm not sure that you really notice it when it is happening.

DR. LEE: Like life itself.

JIM WILLCOX: Yeah.

Maza Wilson, August 20, 2006

Courtesy of Carmela Hamm

"I'm out here for the kids," Maza Wilson says with assurance. The petite grandmother is retired from her position as head cashier at Fort Lee, where she was affectionately known as "Little Bit." As an active citizen she assists the current recreational staff, offering guidance, a soft word, and a warm heart. Her dreams for Hopewell include getting the kids off the street. "We just need more people to get involved in helping these kids around here." Despite her petite frame the lady packs a powerful punch. To the kids she is known as Mrs. Wilson.

In 1936 Hopewell citizens formed the Recreation Association. Along with the Works Progress Administration they built Hopewell's first playground and appointed a Recreation Commission in 1938. The summer program opened with three new centers: Carter G. Woodson, Highland Park, and Patrick Copeland High School.

DR. LEE: You are on the commission?

MAZA WILSON: I am the commissioner. At the Hopewell Quarterback League. I turned my athletic director over two years ago to Ms. Sanford, but I stayed on to help her out, but I thought I was going to leave, but they put on the board, Ms. Wilson Commissioner, so I never left. See, I'm the commissioner. What I do is handle all the problems with the parents that … problems comes up, I go and correct all the problems with the whole field. Not the football. They have a football commissioner, but I'm the cheerleader commissioner, but I still travel with the team. Everywhere they go I go to handle problems. And I help Ms. Sanford out, because although she is the athletic director, they … not … they got to get used to her, they still, you know, look for me for personal course or help her out if I'm on the field or something.

DR. LEE: And what's her name?

MAZA WILSON: Her name is Vicki Sanford. ... She's the athletic director now.

DR. LEE: The last two years?

MAZA WILSON: The last two years I turn over to her.

DR. LEE: Did you work with Ida Cooke?

MAZA WILSON: My kids, Faye. Faye was under her. Faye did a lot of activities under Ms. Cooke.

DR. LEE: I have heard some people call her Ms. Recreation.

MAZA WILSON: Yeah. She was the Recreation Department. She stayed down there for years. And she was the Recreation Department.

DR. LEE: And it was important that you have your children involved in some kind of recreation, all your children, your grandchildren involved in some kind of recreation?

MAZA WILSON: All of them. Uh-huh. They always ... my children always been blessed because I never had a hard time of getting them into anything. They were automatic into everything, which is hard time to get in it. And then one day I was on the field, and with a bunch of white people sitting out there, and these parents are, I can't get my kids in anything. And I was saying to them, I said, why? I didn't have no problem. I got my kids into everything. They always was first in everything. And then the white lady turned around and looked, and she said, you don't know why?

I said, what you mean? She said, you are Mrs. Wilson. I said, what that got to do with it? She said, your name carried a lot. Your name carried a lot, especially at that Recreation Department. I said, it do? I didn't know that.

She said, yeah, you are Mrs. Wilson. Your kids ... if they find out that Mrs. Wilson is the mother or the grandmother, your kids can get into anything. And I didn't know that. And then the lady said, you know, a name carry you a long way.

I said, well, I didn't know that. All because by me doing karate with the Airborne.

DR. LEE: When did you start it?

MAZA WILSON: I always wanted to learn karate. Always ...

DR. LEE: How old were you when you first started?

MAZA WILSON: I went in after I had all my five kids. I was thirty-two, but my instructor didn't know my age. He thought I was eighteen, because I was small. I was only eighty-five pounds. I was small. I didn't look thirty-two. I looked like I was eighteen. And I always wanted, and one of my neighbor's sons, I saw him with his karate digs on. He said, they opened up a gym. Hu Long Willis when he went overseas …

DR. LEE: At Virginia State?

MAZA WILSON: Uh-huh. He brought karate into all tri-city area, and he brought it through Mr. Elmo into this area. He placed all his students into different areas to teach karate. And I worked under Mr. Elmore, Raymond Elmore at the time when I went in under him, and I wanted to learn it. And the rest of them learn it fast, but it took me quite a while to learn karate. But in the meantime I had my two baby girls with me, Nina and Cindy. And they was eight and nine years old when I took them with me, and they went to all my classes, and they learn it automatic by just watching because at that time you couldn't … children could not get involved in karate at that time, because they hadn't started children's class. So my two kids was the first black little kids that ever went into karate.

DR. LEE: Cindy and Nina?

MAZA WILSON: Uh-huh, as children, in an adult class. Uh-huh. And they was … Nina was so good she got her belt, her brown belt within two years because they learn it with me the whole eight years that I was going down there, they had, watching, they had learned it automatic. So one of the black belts saw them outside working, doing it. They say your little kids know everything that we're doing, and they just picked it up.

DR. LEE: Okay. When did they go to take karate, Cindy and Nina; do you remember the years?

MAZA WILSON: I think I had got my yellow belt … I think I had got my purple belt when Nina and … I went into karate in … they never … before Dana. I think I started … Dana was born in '70 and … oh, I went into karate in 1967 when I started working at Fort Lee.

DR. LEE: At the same time you started working at Fort Lee?

MAZA WILSON: Uh-huh.

DR. LEE: Okay. And was it Hu Long … I can't remember his name.

MAZA WILSON: Hu Long Willis.

DR. LEE: Willis.

MAZA WILSON: Yeah. He taught at Virginia State College, uh-huh.

DR. LEE: Okay. So 1967 you started taking karate, and you started working part-time at AAFES …

MAZA WILSON: Right, uh-huh. Right, uh-huh.

DR. LEE: And in that position you were cashier; did you start out …

MAZA WILSON: No. I mean that position part-time I was a food service helper. We all food service helper, but I didn't work … I was … like worked the floors, buffed the floors and all that stuff. I worked like that for four years before I became cashier.

DR. LEE: And you had told me previously how you had gotten to be a head cashier, but why don't you say it for the record.

MAZA WILSON: Because I just wanted to do something different, uh-huh.

DR. LEE: And at that time they didn't have any black …

MAZA WILSON: Yeah, they had black cashiers at that time, because Bernice, she was a black cashier. AAFES … AAFES, it wasn't different with race and stuff because that was government. You can get any job you want, but you had to depend on who was your manager, and if they allow … favoritism normal. They were going to get who they want in there, you know, something like that. So you really had to work to get what you want.

DR. LEE: And the way that you learned how to be cashier, would you talk a little bit about that.

MAZA WILSON: I would watch the young lady, Bernice. I would stand beside her and watch her as she ring up the register. And I told her I want to learn cashier. And she would teach me how to do it. She taught me how to do it. And I was standing … and if she had to do something, she would let me stand there and ring up the customer.

DR. LEE: On-the-job training?

MAZA WILSON: Uh-huh. Yeah. She let me ring up the customer and stuff. It was the cashier that learned me how to be one.

DR. LEE: Okay.

MAZA WILSON: And then when the new manager came in, she saw I used to stand up there all the time, so would let me be her assistant. You know, if she go off, I would take her place, or if she had something to do or go to the ladies room I would run it, and if she was off, I would run it. They call me in to run the register.

DR. LEE: And at lunch time how many people would come through?

MAZA WILSON: At that time we was in the old building so our cafeteria was only set up for 280 people at that time. So I worked over that side, the other side for around about two years, three years. Yeah, about three years. Then we transferred to the big building, Allamac had a big building, went into a school that was a 500-man cafeteria.

DR. LEE: This is still at Fort Lee?

MAZA WILSON: Huh-uh. It's the university now.

DR. LEE: Okay. All right.

MAZA WILSON: Students from all over the world come there. All right. If you work in Allamac, it's just like seeing the world coming through there because you see people from Israel, you see people from Dominions, you see people from Iraq, Italy, Rome, Mexico, Spain. It's a world thing. They coming in. And they come to learn, you know … go to school there. All over the world.

DR. LEE: How did that experience change your life working there?

MAZA WILSON: All over the world?

DR. LEE: Working there and the being around the international.

MAZA WILSON: Oh, it's a lot of fun. Lot of fun. I got to know people. In fact, I got so many awards being a cashier there because the school the one that gave me the award for being a cashier there, because first thing I (*inaudible*) and meeting the people in the morning, like if they come in, they got a bad day, or you know, some people grouchy or something, and I would go and let them in, and I would tell them if I don't see your teeth, you are not coming up in here. Who you mean … no, no … they called me Little Bit … now, Little Bit, we don't have time. I say, yes, you do. Let me see your set of teeth. I say, didn't you wake up this morning? Yeah. I say, the good Lord woke you up, right? You want to come in here? You need a cup of coffee, right? Let me see your teeth. And they had to laugh in order for to do that.

And then I remember the time the prince came in from overseas. And he had his two aides with him. And he never talk. He would point, and his aide would get everything for him. But I didn't know he was a prince, because I was just always myself joking. And this day when he came in, he went to … I said, huh-uh, we're not going to have this today. You are going to talk to me. I said, you tell me what you want. I don't want them in it. The two aides looked at me. I said, huh-uh, not until … let him talk. He said, I'll talk. I said, good. Now, what you want? And he showed me what he want. I said now, isn't this a lot better? See there. I saw your smile. Look at that. So I see … I waited on him. Then I go down the hallway, and I see this great, big picture in the hall. And I looked up,

I said, wait a minute, this is the guy that I just waited on. This man is a prince. I said, oh my goodness, I made him talk. One of the instructors came out, Little Bit, what you done did? We know you done did something. What did you do to that man? I said I made him talk. And he said, anybody could do it, it would be you to do it. I said oh, my goodness. And his wife and son was here with him. And oh, boy. So about this time every time a colonel or a general come through the line, my boss would run out front, they said, we got a general, you better get there, because Little Bit is going to say something, she has no business. So about this time a general came through the line, and this sergeant … I had it going left to right, and it was the sergeant made … so the sergeant on the right said, no, you can't wait on him. I said, why not? He's next. He said, but no. This person is next. You have to get him first. I said, I can't do that. I said it wouldn't be right. These people are in line. I got so many people to get through this line. I said, as soon as I get him, I will get this gentleman. I didn't know it was a general. I still hadn't looked up. I said, I will get this gentleman. So I said, I'll take your money, and he got … he said, but Miss, this is a general. I said, I'm sorry, sir, but he was here. He got a class to get to. He said, okay. And he said, you know what, I like what you just did. You didn't make no difference because I was a general. You put this person … they had to go first, and you was right. He was wrong. You did what you supposed to have done. I had no business being first because I was in line just like everybody else, so he told the sergeant behind, she was right, and I like … she didn't pay me any mind about my position, she just did it.

My boss came out and wiped off her face. She was so scared. She said only Little Bit can get away with all of this stuff. And then the major came down. The general was talking about you. So they did a story on me in Fort Lee. They did a story on me about why I was in karate, and they did a story on me when I drove the mobile around. They wrote … I had two stories they did on me in Fort Lee. And I was put in all of the papers from Richmond to everywhere. And I didn't know anything. And it was the colonel that did it. He put me in all the papers all over, from Richmond, all over to down Blackstone and everything. They said, you made the paper everywhere. How do you know someone can get you in the paper like that? Do you know how much money it cost to put you on the paper? I said, no. All I know, one day a newspaper reporter came in, said we need to talk to Mrs. Wilson. And they wanted to know about me and karate, because I had went into a tournament when I been into karate. I asked my instructor could I fight in the tournament. And because of my size he never wanted me to fight, you know, he … my age … looking at my age and my size. And he looking at my size so, I went … in the meantime when I put Nina, my baby, with the kids, they opened up a kids' karate, when

I was student, my instructor put them over there to teach the kids, so Nina wouldn't do it unless I went with her. That was on Saturday morning. So I had to go with Nina.

So the instructor said, Mrs. Wilson, we've been watching you. You are fast and you are good, but we want to train you so you learn how to use your power. Will you work with us? I said, okay. So they taught me. So I fought nothing but men for two years, and that's how I learned to use my strength and my power. They taught me how to do this. For two years I did that. And then I went into tournament.

And when I went into tournament, I was in Colonial Heights. I was the first black woman that ever fought in Colonial Heights. Usually it was all white. And you just don't go in there. And they saw me come in, but they didn't see me with my uniform, so when I went in, I changed uniforms, and when I walked into the gym, the gym got quiet. Said, we have a black woman fighting in the tournament today? So my original instructor, Mr. Elmore, he was shocked. He said, you fighting today? I said, yeah, I want to try it out.

I know I can do it. I can do it. He said, but you sure you want to fight over here? I said, yeah, I want to do it. I want to … I want to coumatay … I want to go into the ring. And he said, but I … so Irvin said, let her do it. She can do it. And in the meantime I had went around and I watch all my opponents and I saw how they fought and told Irvin, I have no problems. I can do it. He said, okay. So when I got into the ring, I had a heavy-set girl, and the instructor said … he said some very nasty word, and he said I want you to beat the hmmmm out of her black … you know, so and so, and I smiled. And my original instructor said, I want you to use full power, since he's so nasty, you use full power. Full power is hard. Women never been hit before with full power. He said, for him making that remark, I'm sorry he put you through that.

I said, Mr. Elmore, this doesn't bother me. We're used to this. This doesn't bother me. I want you to use full power. I said, okay, and went into the ring, I used full power. I mean, that's an open-hand technique. When you hit somebody you going to feel the pain, leave whelps and everything on her. And by me being small and fast, but I

Courtesy of the author

had power, my hands was my speed, my hand was the fastest thing they ever seen, and my hands was my speed, not my kicks, but my hands.

They did not know which way my blows was coming from. They said, she's too fast. We don't know which way she's coming. She's getting … she's hitting these women so fast out here, and I had to fight six woman that day. Six women.

In the ring, you are allowed three minutes. And fighting three minutes in the ring is like being out an hour. It takes a lot of energy to fight in the ring. You get real tired and stuff. But I had to fight because I had won all my opponents. You know, the more I fought, I had to win all my opponents, so I fought all of them, and then when I fought all of them, the guy that made the remark, he stopped coming up. He had to find out what I was doing. And then he said, I know what she's doing. He said, you have to watch her left hand. Her left hand is messing you all up. Not the right hand, but watch her left hand.

And I turned around and I smiled at him because I know he was telling them what to watch, and I smiled. So Mr. Irvin looked at me. He said, you know what to do? I said, uh-huh. I changed over.

When she came at me, instead of blocking, and like would cut there, I came across and got her this away. And the last one that I had to fight was from my class, but she was good. She was white, but she was good. She had a powerful spinning back kick, and she was my problem. That's the one that I really had to watch out for, because I hadn't quite learned yet how to duck that spinning back kick. A spinning back kick is one of the fastest, [most] powerful kicks. She could spin back so fast and she can catch you with the ball of her heel, and it come this close to your face, but she hadn't learned how to control it.

But see, when you are in karate, you are hit, you don't feel no blows of pain. My body was too well conditioned, I didn't feel pain. I didn't know I was being hit. And when she did, I had … we was tied up, and she got so anxious, she did that, she's coming up with that spinning back kick, and instead of me stepping inward, I stepped back, trying to block the spinning back kick, because I knew she was going to come up with it, and she spun around, but when she did she caught me right across here on the face, but I didn't know I was hit in the face. And I mean, about that time, the referee stepped in. He put my hand up. I thought she won. He said, no. You won. He said because she kicked in your face, and she wasn't supposed to do that. I didn't feel the blow. I knew she had kicked me, but I didn't feel the blow.

And I said, I'm sorry. Why are you apologizing? You won the thing. She the one disqualified. My instructor said, don't you ever apologize to an opponent again. I said, I didn't know that. And then the people from that class came and picked me up. And the whole gym went up in the air because I had fought six women nonstop. I was so tired. I couldn't breathe I was so tired.

DR. LEE: How old were you at that time?

MAZA WILSON: At that time I think I was about thirty-eight.

DR. LEE: Okay.

MAZA WILSON: Thirty-eight.

DR. LEE: This was like six years after you first started?

MAZA WILSON: Yeah, because I had got my purple belt. Uh-huh. I got my purple belt.

DR. LEE: What year was that?

MAZA WILSON: I started 1967, so it took me eight years to get my black belt. Took me eight years to get my black belt. And I had ... see, you had to go through the yellow ... the white belt, and the yellow belt, and the purple belt and the green belt, but I had my purple belt going at that time when I got it. They brought it into the ring. You go through all the many belts to get it. And you wear the brown belt for three years. You have to go through two or three stages in the brown belt. And I have to wear that for three years, the brown belt, but you got to earn it.

At that time, we didn't use padding. Everything had to be full contact. No pads. We never used pads at all. Fought in the ring with the blows and stuff, but you had to learn how to control your blows. You cannot contact the face at all, though you can contact the vital areas, or where you can hit. The main striking part is here where you get your points, is through here, the rib cage section.

DR. LEE: Kidney?

MAZA WILSON: Right here, the rib cage section. You come in, but you don't hit that hard, but because I was trained by men, I always hit with force. I hit my instructor one day. When he came to my retirement, he told them, he said, you know, she's small, but that is the most powerful-hitting woman I [have] ever seen. She hit me so hard I couldn't breathe. I didn't mean to, but he came into the blow, and I hit a drive punch into (*inaudible*) and got that part.

DR. LEE: Was this retirement from Fort Lee or karate?

MAZA WILSON: No. My kids gave me a great, big retirement, and invited all ... everybody that I was involved with. They surprised me. They gave me ... after I lost my husband, they gave me a great, big retirement party, and they went back from the first year that I started working, invited all my employees that worked, and all of them showed up, all of my employees, from domestic housework, they invited all of them, they invited all of my karate students, all my instructors, they all was there.

DR. LEE: Where was this held?

MAZA WILSON: At the Elks.

DR. LEE: Okay. And this was '98?

MAZA WILSON: Yes, when they gave me that, when I retired. My kids did that. They surprised me. I didn't know.

DR. LEE: Well, you certainly are deserving. That's the truth. So, now, what have you done since your retirement? You are still commissioner

MAZA WILSON: Well, when I retirement … I went into retirement because I lost my husband, and it was a sudden death. You know, I didn't know I was going to lose my husband, but he had already retired, and he got sick, he never came out of the hospital. I couldn't get over my husband's death. And then two years later I lost my daughter, a tragic death with my daughter. My daughter got killed. And that was so tragic that … between him and her, I just couldn't … I was just going down, you know, down. And my supervisor on post said, we need to bring her back to work. We need an employee that know the job, know how to work it, and she would be good. I wouldn't have to train nobody. And she called me one day, said, how would you like to come back to work? Get you out of the house. So I said, well, okay. But I was still doing my league. I never gave up the league. That's what kept me going, is the league. Being around the kids, you know, during the … because see, my daughter always on the field with me doing the league, and I never gave up the league. I still did the league the whole four years. I never gave it up. I kept doing the league.

And I went back to work, and that helped me out a whole lot. It helped me get back on my feet. Between working and doing the league, I'm never in the house. Still going.

DR. LEE: I'm sure glad you took the time today to get out of the house.

MAZA WILSON: Yeah, uh-huh.

DR. LEE: What dreams and hopes do you have for Hopewell?

MAZA WILSON: Oh, I like dealing with the kids. I want to get the kids off the street. And we just need more people to get involved in helping these kids around here, because I believe that any child can learn. No such thing that a child can't learn. You can do anything you want to do if you put your mind to it, but you have to some … parents got to have patience. They got to have patience. They need to get involved with their kids, you know, let the kids know they are loved, and they can do something. And parents need to get out of the house and get involved with their kids, and get these kids off the street, because we're not involved with these kids enough up here. All we do, degrade the kids, but if we didn't degrade the kids so much, they wouldn't be out there. We need to stop putting them down. You know, show them that they can be something, and help them out or something like that.

I watched Brad McGahey when he took over the league, and I watched how he handled the kids on the field. He is very good for this area because he has patience. If there's a problem, he's not harsh with the kids. He know how to talk to these kids and, you know, quiet them down. He is not prejudiced at all. He really get involved with all the kids and he is really a blessing to this area. …

DR. LEE: And what's his position?

MAZA WILSON: Well, he's the Athletic Director of the Hopewell Quarterback League. I hate to see him leave. He may leave this year, but he just had so much patience with the kids and the parents. He had a lot of patience. And I watch him all the time. I got a habit of watching people on the field to see who is good for the kids and who is not good for the kids. In football, he's very good for the kids. He is fair to everybody. Uh-huh.

DR. LEE: Do you feel like here in Hopewell people have the opportunity to live the American dream?

MAZA WILSON: Uh-huh. They just have to get out there and earn it, and stop thinking that someone owe them something, because no one owe you anything. You want something, you get out there and you work for it. You can achieve anything you want. Always taught my kids that nothing is given to you. You got to earn it. When you want something, you work for it and go after it. And don't never let nobody talk illiterate to you or talk down to you, or look like put you down. You stand up and hold up, you know, on your own because you can do anything you want to do. You just got to have faith, you know, and work hard for it, and get out there. I be out there all the time fussing on the field or with the kids or something.

They tell me, Ms. Wilson. I said, well, you can. You all sit up there … I tell my sponsor sometime, it's good to be soft. I told her, the athletic director, being on this field, you cannot make a difference with these parents. Parents is one of the hardest things in the world to deal with, because you do something for this parent, you better believe he's going to tell the next parent and this will cause confusion. You cannot cater to the parents and you cannot do favoritism, because if you do, it all going to come back on you.

And I tried to teach Ms. Sanford that. I said, you cannot cater to these parents because if you do, you are going to have problems.

And I said, you start that buddy-buddy system, because you know her, you can do this, you can't do that. You got to be fair to everybody.

If you have an opening, put the name down. Try to work them in. But don't because you know this person, you know, I can do this. What you do, you go let these people know in advance, you know, how to bring the kids in, and help them out to get the kids in. I don't … Brad never liked turning down no kid. I never liked turning down no kid, because I want the kids off the street, and if you can get them in there, that will keep them off the street. And right now, some of the kids we got, they are very rough kids. They come in with an attitude, you know.

And I always taught the sponsor, when you are dealing with the bigger kids, you cannot start playing with them or joking too much with them because they are going to take advantage of you. You got to let them know what they are there for, let them follow the rules and regulations, and if the rules are broke[n] the first time, correct them. Don't give them chances on top of chances. You give them one chance.

I tell them from get-go, when they call me in for a problem, I tell them, I'm Mrs. Wilson.

DR. LEE: Thank you so much, Mrs. Wilson.

MAZA WILSON: Uh-huh.

DR. LEE: Little Bit.

MAZA WILSON: Yeah, that's what they call me, Little Bit.

Conclusion

Despite hand-me-downs and daily reminders of second-class citizenship, young and old, black and white, continued to grapple with changing race relations.

Under the direction of Dr. Tomoko Hamada at the College of William and Mary, the following anthropology students conducted oral interviews with citizens of Hopewell. I am grateful for the times we had together in 2005. Their interviews provide another layer of complexity and our sense of community is deepened.

When I think of the people I have met on this project, their faces and the interviews they conducted come to mind. The words of a people are a testament to the ways in which they are making the American Dream work.

Mrs. Mattie Crockett, interviewed by Kathryn Swanson

Mrs. Crockett remembered, "We had a lot of spelling contests, we had a lot of programs for the kids. Afterschool programs at Mallonee School. We had a lot of good things here, where they would keep you out of trouble. We had school parties; we would go on different trips. Her grandmother said it doesn't matter what color people are, you always respect people, no matter what color they are. If I was prejudiced I wouldn't have a good feeling about myself. I was brought up real good because I was under elderly people more than I was people my age. I worked at Broadway Cafeteria; I was also a companion to the elderly."

Courtesy of Virginia Department of Historic Resources

Elizabeth Epps, interviewed by Rachel Estavan

Ms. Epps remembers being arrested because she and another girl were the first two blacks to go to F. W. Woolworth's to eat. Basically the churches are still segregated but they come together for the World Day of Prayer.

Ms. Lessie Judkins, interviewed by Meghan Townes

She grew up in Hopewell during the '40s and '50s.

"All of us lived in certain areas here in Hopewell. We went to Carter G. Woodson. I remember my older sisters going to a one-room school in Hopewell, over near the fire department. I remember at the school we would always get all the old furniture. I remember us going downtown to the library and they wouldn't allow us to sit. We didn't have afterschool jobs like in the bank or stores or things at that time. After school I used to go iron clothes for some families. I wanted to become a nurse, so when I finished high school I went to New York to nursing school to become a nurse. Jones Lake and Spring Lake were for blacks during that time; Moore Lake was for whites, I think."

Her family was baptized in 1947 at Jones Lake. She remembers ration coupons for shoes, sugar, etc.

Blanche Luster, interviewed by Meghan Townes

Ms. Luster talked about mac and cheese, chicken, vegetables, salad, bread, ham, fish, a variety of vegetables, and dessert. Breakfast was a true southern experience: sausage, bacon, eggs, grits, oatmeal, and bread. In the '80s and '90s a man named Carter did the catering for big events. She recalled church socials, gospel festivals, youth rallies, anniversary celebrations, senior citizen celebrations. She also remembered the recreation center near Patrick Copeland. The WPA office on First Street and Village distributed food at the end of the Depression. Tough times but a lot of things could have been better. Believes they can be better even now.

Ms. Rice, interviewed by Christine

Ms. Rice described the process of draw twisting. She performed this procedure at Allied Chemical. She later worked at Thalhimers' Department Store, where she took a 60 percent pay cut.

Violet Wright, interviewed by Melissa Anderson

Ms. Wright was graduated from Carter G. Woodson in 1956. Her recollections of school paint a vivid picture. "Our colors at Carter G. Woodson were burgundy and green and we did not have new curtains in our auditorium because the principal took the curtains from Hopewell High; their colors were blue and gold."

She spoke of the closeness between friends, "because we went to school together after we went to church together."

"In the 1960s you could really see changes especially coming into the Greyhound Bus Station. From the sign: 'colored enter here' and whatnot."

She said "big stuff" was getting on the bus going to Sea View Beach every July. "I mean that was just tops. Your mama took a picnic basket, a big picnic basket that you could eat all day. You didn't even realize. You didn't know you were being oppressed. You thought that's the way life's supposed to be."

Robert Wyche, interviewed by Meghan Townes

South B Village where he grew up was a place surrounded with businesses like "barbershops, a cabstand, a grocery store, a poolroom, a restaurant, and several bootleg houses." The family ate well, raising chickens, growing collard greens, string beans, potatoes, sweet potatoes, Irish potatoes, tomatoes. His favorite dessert was blackberry dumplings.

One of the main stores in Hopewell on Main Street was A&P. "We had three drugstores: George's no. 1, 2, and 3." Wyche attended Carter G. Woodson, an elementary school and high school combined. They won the state championship for four years in a row for basketball. Although they received the hand-me-downs from Hopewell High, they made the best of what they had at that time. He believes that experience taught him to always utilize what you have and make the best of it until you can do better.

Segregated facilities like the Carshed where blacks used a separate entrance were a part of the landscape. In addition there was the Hopewell All-Stars baseball team. The basketball team was the Hopewell Vikings basketball team.

So much remains to be uncovered and researched.

When I began this project, Herbert Bragg, public affairs coordinator of Hopewell, first informed me of Fireman First Class Robert Penn (1876–1912) of Hopewell who won a Congressional Medal of Honor for his bravery during the Spanish-American War. On July 20, 1898, a manhole gasket blew out in a boiler. Fire-room No. 2 filled with steam and the floor quickly covered with boiling water; the boiler roiled with pressurized steam. Penn and another fireman, Coppersmith P. B. Keefer, arrived on the scene in time to save a coal-passer who was already injured. The man barely escaped falling into the boiling water; Penn rescued him, carrying the man to safety. A Navy report said he then returned to create a makeshift bridge with a "board thrown across a coal bucket above a foot of boiling water." Penn rescued another sailor and he used the board to vent steam. By doing so he averted another explosion. Both he and Keefer were awarded the Congressional Medal of Honor on December 14, 1898.

Penn was one of five children living with Charles Washington and his wife, Julia Washington, all of City Point. The 1880 census record provides names of siblings, all listed as sons- and daughters-in-law of Charles Washington. A 1910 census record located Penn in Philadelphia where he lived with his wife, Hattie R. Penn. She, too, was a Virginian. Penn had previously had two sons, George and Clarence Keys. Their mother, though unnamed in the census record, was a Pennsylvanian by birth. On June 8, 1912, Penn died of pneumonia at the United States Naval Hospital in Las Animas, Colorado. He was buried in the Philadelphia area though his burial site remains a mystery. In 1987 the Naval Station in Norfolk, Virginia, dedicated the six-story residence, Penn Hall, to the Congressional Medal of Honor winner. Much of what I learned came from an editorial in the *Hopewell News*, October 15, 1987, as well as military reports and correspondence.

Another area ripe for further research is the Hopewell riot of 1918. Between 1900–1923 a series of major race riots occurred throughout America. Senator James K. Vardaman voiced his beliefs in 1914: God Almighty never intended that the Negro should share with the white man in the government of this country. He advised his listeners, "do not forget that. It matters not what I may say or others may think; it matters not what constitutions may contain or statues provide, wherever the Negro is in sufficient numbers to imperil the white man's civilization or question the white man's supremacy the white man is going to find some way around the difficulty. And that is just as true in the North as it is in the South."

Atlanta; Springfield; East St. Louis; Houston; Chicago; Elaine, Arkansas; Tulsa, Oklahoma; and Rosewood, Florida, were scenes of some of the worst riots. During the Red Summer of 1919 violence reached a frenzied peak as blacks were openly attacked. Their push for equality was frequently met with hostility and violence as whites resisted any semblance of equality with blacks. In Hopewell an altercation occurred in a plant between a black female laborer and a white male supervisor at DuPont. An October 5, 1918, article in the *Hopewell Record* entitled "Military Controls Situation" provides some of the details of a race riot in Hopewell. "The trouble broke out at two o'clock yesterday afternoon when the [steward], Gomez, discharged a negress from the mess hall and in an argument ensuing is allege to have slapped her." When she "appealed to her folks and they with friends gathered," a scuffle ensued and in a few minutes pandemonium ruled. The acting chief of police told the commander that a riot was imminent in Davisville. At that time Davisville was a suburb of Hopewell on the south side of the Norfolk and Western Railway tracks near the DuPont plant. The commander told him they needed to "keep the crowd moving on the streets." The general manager of DuPont, W. P. Allen, visited the scene and returned to his office believing the altercation had been put to rest. Later, however, a crowd of blacks, many recently off from work, gathered in front of the mess hall demanding satisfaction. The general manager attempted to calm the men with a promise that the case would be investigated. After his departure a fight broke out and guns were drawn. A crowd of white men broke a pawnshop's large plate-glass door to secure guns and ammunition. Oral history says that the men returned to the store the following day to "pay for every pistol and shell that was taken." Reinforcements from Camp Lee were summoned. At midnight the Petersburg Rifles arrived. The Hopewell Rifles and the A. P. Hill Rifles were guided by acting mayor H. J. Watkins Jr. At the time, Mayor David A. Harrison Jr. was away on business. Rumors flew; some had heard that "negroes had broken through the lines and were preparing to launch an attack on B Village." They were rounded up and bought into the police station, plant jail, and courtroom, which quickly became packed. Many of them appealed to the local police for protection while most of them proclaimed their innocence. By morning the Petersburg Guards had arrived. The Norfolk and Western Railway station was used as a guardhouse and sentinels were posted at and near the entrances to the DuPont plant. Documents in the War Commission Histories and Narratives at The Library of Virginia begin to sketch the story. Oral history gives us another layer. Some say thousands of blacks left after the riot. Some say they were killed. This historical remnant is waiting to be further developed and put into the national context of race riots.

Likewise, another historical remnant is found in the pages of the *Hopewell News*, the *Progress Index*, and the *Richmond Times-Dispatch* between October and November 1940. Theodosia Fraser was one of ten Virginia State College students enrolled in a flying program through the Civilian Training Program of the Civil Aeronautics Administration (CAA). She was also the only female in the group. All the students were seniors; Ms. Fraser hailed from Charleston, South Carolina, and rated as the leading CAA student in both adeptness and number of hours in the air. She was fatally injured while attempting to make a landing at the Hopewell Airport. As new opportunities were opening for African Americans, women, too, realized opportunities.

The following sources contextualize the social and political changes occurring in City Point and throughout the South during and after the Civil War. A. Wilson Green's *Civil War Petersburg* provides a glimpse into City Point as does Scott Nelson's study *John Henry: Steel Drivin' Man*. Once again, the area adapted to change.

Edgar Toppin's essay on Ulysses Simpson Grant lays a foundation for understanding a political leader during this tumultuous time. A collection of essays under the title *What Caused the Civil War? Reflections on the South and Southern History*, by Ed Ayers, asks readers to practice the "tradition of skepticism" when thinking about America's Civil War history. Ayers creates a braided narrative, incorporating the spectrum of human experiences, both past and present. A survey of prewar and postwar race relations provides a glimpse into the lives of people who were coming to terms with a new order. Renee Patrice Gilliam's lesson plan "Civil War to Civil Rights: A Study of Conflict and Character" helps English and writing teachers cover a span of American history through an interdisciplinary perspective. Paired with civil liberties dockets from the Meiklejohn Civil Liberties Institute Archives, one can better understand the relentless quest for equality and justice.

Courtesy of Mayor James Patterson

I was fortunate to enjoy a telephone interview with former mayor and councilman James Patterson during the late summer of 2007. His recollections of Hopewell exemplify the American Dream in action. "I grew up in Davisville, the projects. We left the projects the year I graduated [June 8, 1949] and we moved to Arlington Heights. My dad built a home there. My membership is still at Union Baptist Church." He remembers when there were two splits in the church (ages eleven and fourteen). "Dr. George Washington King was pastor; I learned a lot from him. He would teach and preach from the pulpit. It's a small church with big-hearted people." He was active in the church, particularly with public speaking, and believes it has been "a platform which helped me along greatly." He was greatly inspired by his teachers at Carter G. Woodson who were always encouraging. "They offered constructive criticism. They were like family." He spoke of Mr. Johnson, an algebra teacher, and Mr. Eppes, who was principal in 1949. While a student, Patterson had "the largest paper route in Hopewell," starting at five in the morning. He encourages "all our young people to do better. You may have done all right or OK but strive for excellence. Put your best foot forward. I don't care what your abilities are, you can always do better. It's not where you live but what's inside of you that can make you go." He currently lives "right at the edge of Hopewell" and "would like to see Hopewell with a tax base that's diversified enough that our citizens would not be overly stressed, also that we can sustain a decent tax base and a high quality of life for all citizens."

Hopewell's abundant historical sites help chronicle the evolution of America and the dreams of many. Kippax, Weston Manor, Appomattox Manor, the City Point Historic District, City Point National Cemetery, the Beacon Theatre, the Downtown Hopewell Historic District, and the Hopewell Municipal Building are all registered as Virginia and national landmarks. The memories and recollections of her people show why "Hopewell is a city that will stay upon the map."

Acknowledgments

The city council members patiently worked with me as I conducted extensive research and wrote (and rewrote) the manuscript. When Dr. Toppin became ill, former City Manager Alan Archer kept the project moving. Public Affairs Director Herbert Bragg kept the project on the city council's agenda; during the roughest times he reminded me of relevant Biblical passages. Reverend Curtis Harris gently nudged me along. When I became tired or anxious he always had a word of encouragement. Kit Weigel's research helped me tremendously.   Initially, John Porter assisted me with an oral interview and a public forum as well as administrative details. His mellow manner during my first faltering steps will always be appreciated. Carmela Hamm of Karma Communications came on board and handled the technical aspects of the interviews. George M. Halasz of Halasz Reporting and Video transcribed the interviews. The unedited interviews in the form of cassette and video tapes as well as hard copies are archived at the Appomattox Regional Library and the Curtis Harris Library at Carter G. Woodson Middle School. Marlena Brown, a graduate intern in the public history program at Virginia Commonwealth University, wrote captions for the images; in addition she wrote several of the interview summaries and bibliographic material. Her insightful commentary was thoughtful and well crafted. She also assisted me at public forums held in Hopewell; her calm and steady manner was a great help as the project moved forward. I am ever grateful for her assistance. Jeanie Lankford and the excellent staff at the Appomattox Regional Library helped tremendously as the project took shape. Because of Jeanie's long tenure at the library and her love for Hopewell, I learned a great deal about the city's history and hers was the first interview I conducted. In the early phase of this project both Micah and Joshua Justice conducted primary source research. Emily and John Salmon were invaluable during the editing phase and helped me to think through the polishing process. They came through again and helped me during the final phases with advice and an ever-present ear. Emily became my midwife. Susan, Bob, and Jennifer Sheppard stepped in at a crucial time and worked their magic on the layout and design. Bob's map not only enlivens an end paper but has practical applications as well; it serves as a guide to historical sites. Jennifer stepped in and provided emergency technical assistance as only tech-savvy young people can do. Words cannot express how grateful I am to Susan for steering the project when I floundered and flailed. How fortunate I am to meet them and learn that Bob grew up in Hopewell. Each and every one of the interviewees welcomed me into their homes and their churches. They are in my heart.

Personally, my parents and family, both immediate and extended (particularly my cousin Pauline), helped me tremendously during this project with their unflagging encouragement and delicious meals. My closest friends, Pamila Gant, Beth O'Leary, and Greg Echols, listened to my ideas, no matter how far out, and believed I could do whatever I said I wanted to do. Dr. Dorothy Cowling, "mother Dorothy," read drafts, shared her history, and preached the word. Debra Dilworth helped me create a beautiful retreat and writing space at home. Bill Gould, my computer guy, made sure I didn't have to worry about technology issues; Donna East, Tareq Elganainy, Tom Tipp, and Kwi Sang and Mihae Kim Chung addressed all my health concerns and helped me feel like a lean, mean writing machine. Jonathon Turner's calm voice and quiet demeanor helped me focus; he gave me a beautiful gift of vintage postcards of Hopewell. Thanks also to Deanna Beacham from the Virginia Council on Indians. My coworkers at the Virginia Historical Society assisted my research at every turn and listened to my ups and downs. Thank you, Frances Pollard for your help and for a great staff. Thanks also to Charlie Bryan who awarded me with a president's fellowship to attend an oral history workshop at Kenyon College in April 2004. Only months later in August I completed the oral history program at University of Berkeley and received a fellowship from the Oral History Association to attend their conference in Portland, Oregon. I returned home in early October. Since that time I have realized my calling. I love listening to people's stories.

What I have most appreciated about Hopewell is the myriad ways citizens and residents labored to make the American Dream work in their everyday lives. All of these subject areas and more are waiting to be further developed. The texture of a community history is in the voices of the people and the places they congregate. They recalled times past, both joyous and sad, as they remembered family and friends whose lives intersected with theirs. I enjoyed listening and learning and sharing our history. Hopewell, your warmth makes me smile to this day.

As I look back on this project I feel a swirl of emotions. Three years ago today, Doctor Edgar Toppin passed away. This is it. I am letting it go. The Hopewell African American oral history project has been my American Dream. Thank you.

December 8, 2007

Bibliography

Anderson, James D. *The Education of Blacks in the South, 1860–1935*. Chapel Hill: University of North Carolina Press, 1988.

Ayers, Edward L. *The Edge of the South: Life in Nineteenth-Century Virginia*. Charlottesville: University Press of Virginia, 1991.

———. *The Promise of the New South: Life after Reconstruction*. New York: Oxford University Press, 1992.

———. *What Caused The Civil War? Reflections on the South and Southern History*. New York: W. W. Norton, 2005.

Berlin, Ira. *'Generations of Captivity': The History of a Monstrous Enterprise*. Cambridge: The Belknap Press/Harvard University Press, 2003.

———.*Slaves without Masters: The Free Negro in the Antebellum South*. New York: Pantheon Books, 1974.

Blasingame, John W. *The Slave Community: Plantation Life in the Antebellum South*. New York: Oxford University Press, 1972.

Bohannan, Kirby. *The Economic Growth, Decline, and Growth of City Point, Prince George County and the City of Hopewell, Virginia*. Hopewell: Appomattox Regional Library, 1994.

Branch, Taylor. *At Canaan's Edge: America in the King Years, 1965–68*. New York: Simon & Schuster, 2006.

———. *Parting the Waters: America in the King Years, 1954–63*. New York: Simon & Schuster, 1988.

———. *Pillar of Fire: America in the King Years, 1963–65*. New York: Simon & Schuster, 1988.

Calos, Mary Mitchell, Charlotte Easterling, and Ella Sue Rayburn. *Old City Point and Hopewell: The First 370 Years*. Virginia: The Donning Company, 1983.

Carmichael, Stokely, and Charles V. Hamilton. *Black Power: The Politics of Liberation in America*. New York: Random House, 1967.

Carson, Clayborne, and Peter Holloran, eds. *A Knock at Midnight: Inspiration from the Great Sermons of Reverend Martin Luther King, Jr*. New York: IPMWarner Books, 1998.

Cell, John W. *The Highest Stage of White Supremacy: The Origins of Segregation in South Africa and the American South*. Cambridge: Cambridge University Press, 1982.

Clinton, Catherine. *The Plantation Mistress: Woman's World in the Old South.* New York: Pantheon Books, 1982.

Cohen, William. *At Freedom's Edge: Black Mobility and the Southern White Quest for Racial Control, 1861–1915.* Baton Rouge: Louisiana State University Press, 1991.

Crane, J. David, and Elaine Crane. *The Black Soldier: From the American Revolution to Vietnam.* New York: William Morrow, 1971.

Dailey, Jane. *Before Jim Crow: The Politics of Race in Post-Emancipation Virginia.* Chapel Hill: University of North Carolina Press, 2000.

Deetz, James. *Flowerdew Hundred: The Archaeology of a Virginia Plantation, 1619–1864.* Charlottesville: University Press of Virginia, 1993.

Dutton, William S. *Du Pont: One Hundred and Forty Years.* New York: Charles S. Scribner's Sons, 1951.

Faust, Drew Gilpin, ed. *The Ideology of Slavery: Proslavery Thought in the Antebellum South, 1830–1860.* Baton Rouge: Louisiana State University Press, 1981.

Foner, Eric. *Nothing but Freedom: Emancipation and its Legacy.* Baton Rouge: Louisiana State University Press, 1983.

———. *Reconstruction: America's Unfinished Revolution.* New York: Harper and Row, 1988.

Foster, Helen Bradley. *New Raiments of Self: African American Clothing in the Antebellum South.* New York: Berg Press, 1997.

Fox-Genovese, Elizabeth. *Within the Plantation Household: Black and White Women of the Old South.* Chapel Hill: University of North Carolina Press, 1988.

Franklin, John Hope. *Reconstruction after the Civil War.* Chicago: University of Chicago Press, 1994.

Giddings, Paula. *When and Where I Enter: The Impact of Black Women on Race and Sex in America.* New York: Bantam, 1984.

Glenn, Evelyn Nakamo. *Unequal Freedom: How Race and Gender Shaped American Citizenship and Labor.* Cambridge: Harvard University Press, 2002.

Greene, A. Wilson. *Civil War Petersburg: Confederate City in the Crucible of War.* Charlottesville: University of Virginia Press, 2006.

Guild, June Purcell. *Black Laws of Virginia: A Summary of the Legislative Acts of Virginia Concerning Negroes from Earliest Times to the Present.* First published in 1936 by Whittet & Shepperson. Fourth Printing: Lovettsville, Va.: Willow Bend Books, 1996.

Gutman, Herbert. *Power and Culture: Essays on the American Working Class.* New York: New Press, 1987.

Holton, Woody. *Forced Founders: Indians, Debtors, Slaves, and the Making of the American Revolution in Virginia,* Chapel Hill: University of North Carolina Press, 1999.

Isaac, Rhys. *The Transformation of Virginia, 1740–1790*. Chapel Hill: University of North Carolina Press, 1982.

Jacobson, Matthew Frye. *Whiteness of a Different Color: European Immigrants and the Alchemy of Race*. Cambridge: Harvard University Press, 1998.

Jaynes, Gerald D. *Branches without Roots: Genesis of the Black Working Class in the American South, 1862–1882*. New York: Oxford University Press, 1986.

Jordan, Ervin. *Black Confederates and Afro-Yankees in Civil War Virginia*. Charlottesville: University of Virginia Press, 1995.

Kelley, Robin D. G. *Race Rebels: Culture, Politics, and the Black Working Class*. New York; Free Press, 1996.

Kerr, Ritchie, Jeffrey R. *Freedpeople in the Tobacco South: Virginia, 1860–1890*. Chapel Hill and London: The University of North Carolina Press, 1999.

King, Martin Luther, Jr. *Stride Toward Freedom*. New York: Harper and Brothers, 1958.

King, Wilma. *Stolen Childhood: Slave Youth in Nineteenth-Century America*. Bloomington: Indiana University Press, 1995.

Kluger, Richard. *Simple Justice: The History of Brown v. Board of Education and Black America's Struggle for Equality*. New York: Vintage Books, 1975.

Langhorne, Orra. *Southern Sketches from Virginia, 1881–1901*. Edited by Charles E. Wynes. Charlottesville: University Press of Virginia, 1964.

Lerner, Gerda, ed. *Black Women in White America: A Documentary History*. New York: Vintage Books, 1972.

Levine, Lawrence. *Black Culture and Black Consciousness: Afro-American Folk Thought from Slavery to Freedom*. Oxford: Oxford University Press, 1977.

Linebaugh, Donald W. *Kippax Plantation: Traders, Merchants, and Planters: An Exhibit Celebrating the Families of Pocahontas*. The College of William and Mary Center for Archaeological Research, Williamsburg, Virginia, 1995.

Litwack, Leon. *Been in the Storm So Long: The Aftermath of Slavery*. New York: Vintage, 1979.

Lutz, Francis Earle. *The Prince George-Hopewell Story*. Richmond: The William Byrd Press, 1957.

Morgan, Edmund S. *American Slavery, American Freedom: The Ordeal of Colonial Virginia*. New York: Norton, 1975.

Morgan, Lynda. J. *Emancipation in Virginia's Tobacco Belt, 1850–1870*. Athens: University of Georgia Press, 1992.

Mullins, Gerald W. *Flight and Rebellion: Slave Resistance in Eighteenth-Century Virginia*. New York: Oxford University Press, 1972.

Nelson, Scott Reynolds. *Steel Drivin' Man: John Henry: the Untold Story of an American Legend.* New York: Oxford University Press, 2006.

Newby, I. A. *Plain Folk in the New South: Social Change and Cultural Persistence, 1880–1915.* Baton Rouge: Louisiana State University Press, 1989.

O'Leary, Elizabeth. *From Morning to Night: Domestic Service in Maymont House and the Gilded Age South.* Charlottesville: University of Virginia Press, 2003.

Purdue, Charles L., Thomas E. Barden, and Robert K, Phillips, eds. *Weevils in the Wheat: Interviews with Virginia Ex-Slaves.* Charlottesville: University Press of Virginia, 1976.

Rothman, Joshua D. *Notorious in the Neighborhood: Sex and Families across the Color Line in Virginia, 1787–1861.* Chapel Hill: University of North Carolina Press, 2003.

Schwarz, Marie Jenkins. *Born in Bondage: Growing up in the Antebellum South.* Cambridge: Harvard University Press, 2000.

Schwarz, Philip J. *Migrants against Slavery: Virginians and the Nation.* Charlottesville, University Press of Virginia, 2001.

———. *Slave Laws in Virginia.* University of Georgia Press, 1996.

———. *Twice Condemned: Slaves and the Criminal Laws of Virginia, 1705–1865.* Baton Rouge: Louisiana State University Press, 1988.

Smith, J. Douglas. *Managing White Supremacy: Race, Politics, and Citizenship in Jim Crow Virginia.* Chapel Hill: University of North Carolina Press, 2001.

Sobel, Mechal. *The World They Made Together: Black and White Values in Eighteenth Century Virginia.* Princeton: Princeton University Press, 1987.

Stampp, Kenneth M. *The Peculiar Institution: Slavery in the Antebellum South.* New York: Knopf, 1986.

Stevenson, Brenda E. *Life in Black and White: Family and Community in the Slave South.* New York: Oxford University Press, 1996.

Sullivan, Patricia. *Days of Hope: Race and Democracy In the New Deal Era.* Chapel Hill: University of North Carolina Press, 1996.

Tadman, Michael. *Speculators and Slaves: Masters, Traders, and Slaves in the Old South.* Madison: University of Wisconsin Press, 1989.

Toppin, Edgar A. *The Black American in United States History.* Boston: Allyn and Bacon, Inc., 1973.

———. *A Mark Well Made: The Negro Contribution to American Culture.* Chicago: Rand McNally, 1969.

Vlach, John Michael. *Back of the Big House, The Architecture of Plantation Slavery.* Chapel Hill: University of North Carolina Press, 1993.

———. *The Planter's Prospect: Privilege and Slavery in Plantation Paintings.* Chapel Hill:

University of North Carolina Press, 2002.

Wallenstein, Peter. *Cradle of America: Four Centuries of Virginia History.* University Press of Kansas, 2007.

Washington, James M., ed. *A Testament of Hope: The Essential Writings of Martin Luther King, Jr.* New York: Harper and Row, 1986.

Weaver, C. E., compiler. "Sketches of Hopewell – The Wonder City." Richmond: Central Publishing Co., 1915.

Williams, Heather Andrea. *Self-Taught: African American Education in Slavery and Freedom.* Chapel Hill: University of North Carolina Press, 2005.

Williams, Juan. *Eyes on the Prize: America's Civil Rights Years 1954–65.* New York: Penquin, 1967.

Willis, G. Frank. "Historical Base Maps: Petersburg, Appomattox Manor-City Point." *Report, National Park Service, Petersburg National Battlefield,* 1982.

Writers Program of the Work Projects Administration. *A Guide to Hopewell and Prince George County.* Hopewell, 1937.

Wynes, Charles E. *Race Relations in Virginia, 1870–1902.* Charlottesville: University Press of Virginia, 1961.

Articles

Crump, Nancy Carter. "Hopewell during World War I: The 'Toughest Town North of Hell.' " *Virginia Cavalcade.* (Summer 1981): ＿＿＿

Foner, Eric. "The Meaning of Freedom in the Age of Emancipation." *Journal of American History* 81 (September 1994): 435–460.

Haynes, Elizabeth Ross. "Negroes in Domestic Service." *Journal of Negro History* 8 (October 1923): 384–442.

Lehman, Forrest K. "Settled Place, Contested Past: Reconciling George Percy's 'A Trewe Relacyon' with John Smith's Generall Historie." *Early American Literature* 42, no. 2 (2007): 235–261.

Lowe, Richard. "Another Look at Reconstruction in Virginia." *Civil War History* 32, no. 1 (March 1986): 56–76.

Reid, Joseph D. "Sharecropping as an Understandable Market Response: The Postbellum South." *Journal of Economic History* 33 (March 1973): 106–130.

Robinson, Armstead. "Beyond the Realm of Social Consensus: New Meanings of Reconstruction for American History." *Journal of American History* 68, no. 3 (June–Sept. 1981): 276–297.

Russell, James S. "Rural Economic Progress of the Negro in Virginia." *Journal of Negro History* 11, no. 4 (Oct. 1926): 556–562.

Schwarz, Philip J. " 'A Sense of Their Own Power': Self Determination in Recent Writings on Black Virginians." *Virginia Magazine of History and Biography* 97, no. 3 (July 1989): 279–310.

Schweninger, Loren. "A Vanishing Breed: Black Farm Owners in the South, 1651–1982." *Agricultural History* 63, no. 3 (Summer 1989): 41–60.

Shammas, Carole. "Black Women's Work and the Evolution of Plantation Society in Virginia." *Labor History* 26, no. 1 (Winter 1985): 5–28.

Shepard, E. Lee. " 'This Being Court Day': Courthouses and Community Life in Rural Virginia." *Virginia Magazine of History and Biography* 103, no. 4 (Oct. 1995): 459–470.

Spriggs, William F. "The Virginia Colored Farmers' Alliance: A Case Study of Race and Class Identity." *Journal of Negro History* 64, no. 3 (Summer 1979): 191–204.

Toppin, Edgar A. "Ulysses Simpson Grant." In *The American Presidents*, edited by Melvin I. Urofsky. New York: Garland Publishing, 2000, p. 185.

Vaughan, Alden T. "The Origins Debate: Slavery and Racism in Seventeenth Century Virginia." *Virginia Magazine of History and Biography* 97, no. 3 (July 1989): 311–354.

Woodman, Harold D. "Class, Race, Politics, and the Modernization of the Postbellum South." *Journal of Southern History* 68, no. 1 (Feb. 1997): 3–22.

Repositories and Reference Sources

Appomattox Regional Library System, Hopewell, Virginia

The Library of Virginia, Richmond, Virginia. www.lva.lib.va.us

Virginia Center for Digital History at the University of Virginia. www.vcdh.virgina.edu

Virginia Department of Historic Resources, Richmond, Virginia. www.dhr.virginia.gov

Virginia Historical Society, Richmond, Virginia. www.vahistorical.org

Franklin, John Hope and Alfred A. Moss Jr. *From Slavery to Freedom: A History of African Americans,* vols. 1 and 2. New York: McGraw-Hill, Inc. 1994.

Gilliam, Renee Patrice. *Civil War to Civil Rights: A Study of Conflict and Character.* www.knowledge.state.va.us

Hening, William Waller. *The Statutes at Large; Being a Collection of all the Laws of Virginia, from the First Session of the Legislature in the Year 1619.* New York: R & W & G. Bartow, 1823.

Hine, Darlene Clark, William C. Hine and Stanley Harrold. *The African American Odyssey, Vol. 1 and 2.* New Jersey: Prentice Hall, 2000.

Hodges, Holly F., compiler. Revised and enlarged by Harold M. Marsh Jr. and E. Lee Shepard. *Guide to African American Manuscripts in the collection of the Virginia Historical Society.* Richmond: VHS Publications, 2002.

Lankford, Nelson, D., ed. *Guide to the Manuscript Collections of the Virginia Historical Society.* Richmond: VHS Publications, 1985.

Plunkett, Michael. *Afro-American Sources in Virginia: A Guide to Manuscripts.* Charlottesville: University Press of Virginia, 1990.

Salmon, Emily J., and Edward D. C. Campbell Jr., eds. *The Hornbook of Virginia History: A Ready-Reference Guide of the Old Dominion's People, Places and Past.* Richmond: The Library of Virginia, 1994.

Toppin, Edgar. "African Americans in the Confederacy." *Encyclopedia of the Confederacy.* New York: Simon & Schuster, 1993, pp. 4–9.

————. *Virginia History and Government: 1850 to the Present.* Morristown, NJ: Silver Burdett, 1986.

Virginia War History Commission. *Publications of the Virginia War History Commission.* Edited by Arthur Kyle Davis. Richmond: Published by order of the Executive Committee, 1924.

Weigel, Kit. Preliminary bibliography and research notes.

Oral History

Allen, Barbara, and William L. Montell. *From Memory to History: Using Oral Sources in Local Historical Research.* Nashville, TN: American Association for State and Local History, 1981.

Berlin, Ira, Marc Favreau, and Steven F. Miller, editors. *Remembering Slavery: African Americans Talk about their Personal Experiences of Slavery and Freedom.* New York: New Press, 2000.

Brecher, Jeremy. *History from Below: How to Uncover and Tell the Story of Your Community, Association, or Union.* New Haven, CT: Commonwork Pamphlets/Advocate Press, 1986.

Dunaway, David K., and Willa K Baum. *Oral History: An Interdisciplinary Anthology.* American Association for State and Local History in cooperation with the Oral History Association, 1984.

Felt, Thomas. *Researching, Writing and Publishing Local History.* Nashville, TN: American Association for State and Local History, 1976.

Frisch, Michael. *A Shared Authority: Essays on the Craft and Meaning of Oral and Public History.* New York: State University of New York Press, 1990.

Hampton, Henry, and Steve Fayer. *Voices of Freedom: An Oral History of the Civil Rights Movement from the 1950s through the 1980s.* New York: Bantam Book, 1990.

Honey, Michael Keith. *Black Workers Remember: An Oral History of Segregation, Unionism, and the Freedom Struggle.* Berkeley: University of California Press, 1999.

Kammen, Carol, ed. *The Pursuit of Local History: Readings on Theory and Practice.* Walnut Creek: AltaMira Press, 1996.

King, Mary. *Freedom Song: A Personal Story of the 1960s Civil Rights Movement.* New York: William Morrow, 1987.

Lewis, Catherine. *The Changing Face of Public History: The Chicago Historical Society and the Transformation of an American History Museum.* Illinois: Northern Illinois University Press, 2005.

Mercier, Laurie, and Madeline Buckendorf. *Using Oral History in Community History Projects.* Oral History Association, 1992.

Moon, Elaine Latzman. *Untold Tales, Unsung Heroes, An Oral History of Detroit's African American Community, 1918–1967.* Detroit: Wayne State University Press, 1994.

Mundell, Kathleen, and H. A. Frost-Kumpf. *Sensing Place: A Guide to Community Culture.* Maine: Maine Arts Commission, 1997.

Perdue, Charles L., and Nancy J. Martin-Perdue, eds. *Talk about Trouble: A New Deal Portrait of Virginians in the Great Depression.* Chapel Hill: The University of North Carolina Press, 1996.

Perks, Robert, and Alistari Thomson. *The Oral History Reader.* New York: Routledge, 1998.

Slim, Hugo, and Paul Thompson. *Listening for a Change: Oral Testimony and Community Development.* Philadelphia: New Society Publishers, 1995.

Terkel, Studs. *American Dreams: Lost and Found.* New York: Pantheon, 1980.

———. *Hope Dies Last: Keeping the Faith in Troubled Times.* New York: New Press, 2004.

———. *Race: How Blacks and Whites Think and Feel about the American Obsession.* New York: The New Press, 1992.

———. *Working: People Talk about What They Do All Day and How They Feel About What They Do.* New York: Pantheon, 1974.

Papers

City Point and Hopewell Collection, Virginia Historical Society, Richmond, VA.

Eppes Family Papers, National Park Service and Virginia Historical Society, Richmond, VA.

Gilliam Family Papers, vertical file, Appomattox Regional Library Headquarters, Hopewell, VA.

Du Pont Company. Hopewell *Splinters*. Appomattox Regional Library System, Hopewell, VA.

Tubize Artificial Silk Company. *Tubize Spinnerette*. Appomattox Regional Library System, Hopewell, VA.

Book Blurb

Lauranett Lorraine Lee is a native of Chesterfield County. She has earned a B.A. in communications from Mundelein College (now a part of Loyola University-Chicago), an M.A. in history from Virginia State University and a Ph.D. in American history from the University of Virginia. In 2001 she became the founding curator of African American history at the Virginia Historical Society. She received a staff fellowship from the VHS to attend the Oral History Institute at Kenyon College in 2004. She then participated in an advanced workshop at the University of California, Berkeley. With a fellowship from the Oral History Association she attended her first oral history conference. Upon her return Hopewell officials asked her to write a history of African Americans in Hopewell.

Author interviewing the Reverend Curtis Harris (Right).

INDEX

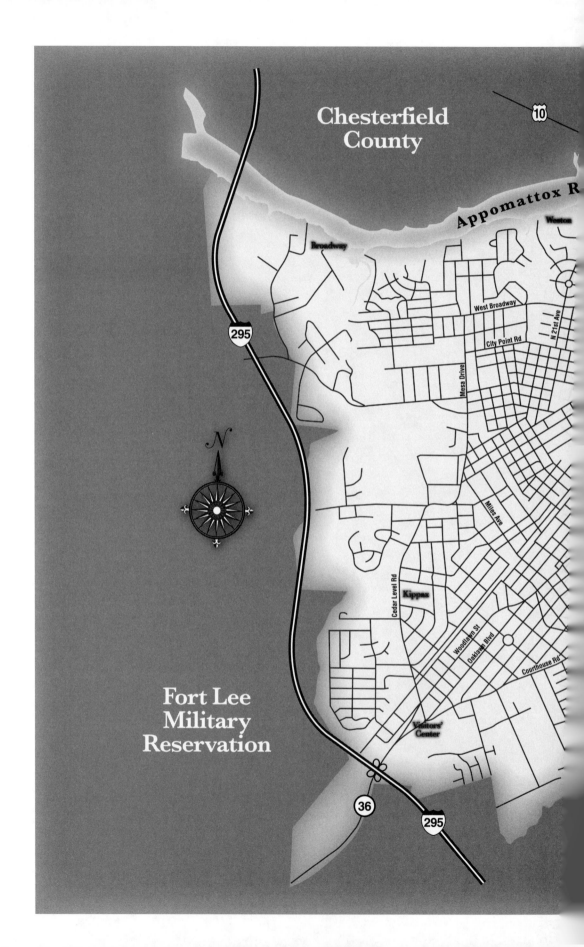

James River

Appomattox Manor

Pecan Ave

Water St

Cedar Lane

Brown Ave

John Randolph Hospital

Patrick Copeland School Site

Appomattox St

West Broadway

6th St

Municipal Building

Beacon Theatre

Station St

Main St

West Broadway

City Point Rd

Dupont & Tubize Site

6th St

Randolph Road

10

Winston Churchill Drive

Carter G. Woodson School

Prince George County